About Island Press

AN INTRODUCTION TO

Coastal Zone Management

SECOND EDITION

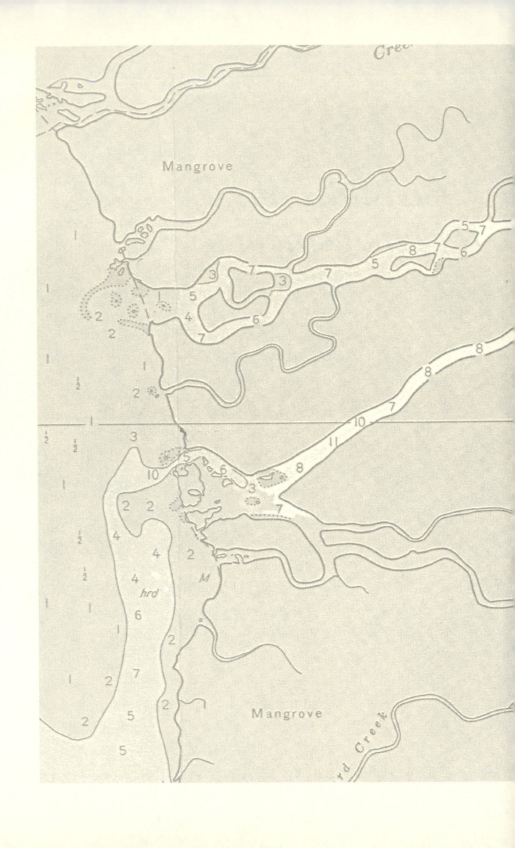

AN INTRODUCTION TO

Coastal Zone Management

SECOND EDITION

TIMOTHY BEATLEY

DAVID J. BROWER

ANNA K. SCHWAB

ISLAND PRESS

Washington • Covelo • London

Library of Congress Cataloging-in-Publication Data
Beatley, Timothy, 1957–
   An introduction to coastal zone management / Timothy Beatley, David J. Brower, Anna K. Schwab.—2nd ed.
       p. cm.
Includes bibliographical references and index.
   ISBN 1–55963–915–6 (pbk. : alk. paper)
   1. Coastal zone management—United States. I. Brower, David J.
II. Schwab, Anna K. III. Title.
   HT392 .B43   2002
   333.91'7'0973—dc21   2002001462

British Cataloguing-in-Publication Data available.

Printed on recycled, acid-free paper

Manufactured in the United States of America
09 08 07 06 05 04 03 02   8 7 6 5 4 3 2 1

Contents

Chapter 3. Coastal Pressures and Critical Management Issues   53

Chapter 4. The Coastal Management Framework   91

Chapter 5. Federal Coastal Policy 101

Chapter 6. State Coastal Management Programs 135

Chapter 7. Regional Management of Coastal Resources   173

Chapter 8. Local Coastal Management   197

Chapter 9. Creative Coastal Development: Building Sustainably along the Coast   249

Chapter 10: Conclusions: Future Directions in U.S. Coastal Management   283

List of Acronyms and Abbreviations

Area of Environmental Concern	AEC
Arcata Marsh and Wildlife Sanctuary	AMWS
Action Plan Demonstration Projects	APDP
San Francisco Bay Conservation and Development Commission	BCDC
Base flood elevation	BFE
South Carolina Beachfront Management Act	BMA
Best management practices	BMP
Clean Air Act	CAA
Coastal Area Management Act	CAMA
Florida's Conservation and Recreation Lands	CARL
Chesapeake Bay Foundation	CBF
Coastal Barrier Resources Act	CBRA
Coastal Barrier Resources System	CBRS
Comprehensive Conservation and Management Plan	CCMP
Community Development Block Grant	CDBG
Comprehensive Environmental Response, Compensation, and Liability Act	CERCLA
Capital improvement program	CIP
Coastal management program	CMP
Congress of New Urbanism	CNU
U.S. Army Corps of Engineers	COE
North Carolina's Coastal Resources Advisory Council	CRAC
Coastal Resources Commission	CRC
Community Rating System	CRS
Coastal States Organization	CSO
Clean Water Act	CWA

Coastal Wetlands Planning, Protection, and Restoration Act	CWPPRA
Coastal Zone Management Act	CZMA
North Carolina Division of Coastal Management	DCM
Maine's Department of Environmental Protection	DEP
Oregon's Department of Environmental Quality	DEQ
Metro Dade Department of Environmental Resources Management	DERM
Oregon's Department of Fish and Wildlife	DFW
Oregon's Department of Land Conservation and Development	DLCD
Maine's Department of Marine Resources	DMR
Department of Energy	DOE
Oregon's Department of Geology and Mineral Industries	DOGAMI
Department of the Interior	DOI
Department of Transportation	DOT
Oregon's Division of State Lands	DSL
Exclusive economic zone	EEZ
Erosion hazard area	EHA
Environmental Protection Agency	EPA
Endangered Species Act	ESA
Federal Emergency Management Agency	FEMA
Federal Housing Administration	FHA
Federal Insurance Administration	FIA
Finding of no significant impact	FONSI
Florida Power and Light	FPL
Forest Stewardship Council	FSC
U.S. Fish & Wildlife Service	FWS
General Accounting Office	GAO
Geographic information system	GIS
Great Lakes Program	GLP
Great Lakes Water Quality Agreements	GLWQA
Habitat conservation plan	HCP
Hazard Mitigation Grant Program	HMGP
Department of Housing and Urban Development	HUD
International Building Code	IBC
Institute for Business and Home Safety	IBHS
Individual and Family Grants	IFG
International Joint Commission	IJC
Intergovernmental Panel on Climate Change	IPCC

Integrated pest management	IPM
Internal Revenue Service	IRS
Intermodal Surface Transportation Efficiency Act	ISTEA
Oregon's Land Conservation and Development Commission	LCDC
Leadership in Energy and Environmental Design	LEED
Maximum available control technology	MACT
Mean high water	MHW
Marine Protected Areas	MPA
Marine Protection, Reserve and Sanctuary Act	MPRSA
National Ambient Air Quality Standards	NAAQS
Nonpoint Education for Municipal Officials	NEMO
National Estuary Program	NEP
National Environmental Policy Act	NEPA
National Estuarine Research Reserve System	NERRS
National Flood Insurance Program	NFIP
Nongovernment organization	NGO
National Marine Fisheries Service	NMFS
National Marine Sanctuary Program	NMSP
National Oceanic and Atmospheric Administration	NOAA
National Pollutant Discharge Elimination System	NPDES
Nonpoint source	NPS
National Park Service	NPS
National Research Council	NRC
Nuclear Regulatory Commission	NRC
Natural Resources Protection Act	NRPA
Office of Ocean and Coastal Resource Management	OCRM
Office of Wetlands, Oceans and Watersheds	OWOW
Purchase of development rights	PDR
Puget Sound's Public Involvement and Education program	PIE
Oregon's Park and Recreation Department	PRD
Planned unit development	PUD
Photovoltaic	PV
Special Area Management Plan	SAMP
Shore Erosion Control Program	SECP
Structural insulated panels	SIPs
Systemwide monitoring program	SWMP
Transfer of development credits	TDC

Transfer of development rights   TDR
The Nature Conservancy   TNC
Traditional neighborhood development   TND
Urban growth boundary   UGB
Urban Land Institute   ULI
United Nations Convention on the Law of the Sea   UNCLOS
U.S. Department of Agriculture   USDA
Department of Veterans' Affairs   VA
Volatile organic compounds   VOCs
Velocity zones   V-Zones
Stillaguamish Watershed Management Committee   WMC

Preface

As we finish writing this second edition, conflicts over the use of the coastal resources continue to intensify and demonstrate the increasing importance of studying coastal zone management. Bush administration plans for increased energy production through offshore oil and gas development are at odds with desires to protect and preserve the beaches and coastlines in states such as California and Florida. These issues demonstrate the tough challenges of balancing competing demands placed on coastal resources and the growing sense of popular and political support for coastal conservation.

These conflicts and competing demands will heighten as coastal communities and regions in the United States continue to attract population and development at an alarming rate. Now more than half the nation's population lives along the coast, an area representing only about 17% of the nation's land base. This concentration of population along our coasts probably will increase, with some estimates putting three-quarters of our nation's population in coastal areas by 2025.

As development and population growth continue, so will the pressures on the coastal resource base, both natural and human-made. Nearly a half million single-family dwellings are constructed each year in coastal areas, according to National Oceanic and Atmospheric Administration estimates, straining the carrying capacities of coastal land and water. The states and regions growing the fastest—states such as California and Florida, which together are expected to add another 13 million in coastal population between 1998 and 2015—harbor tremendous ecological resources. Protecting the coastal environment while accommodating such growth pressures will be a major challenge for coastal planners.

Sustaining the ecological health and productivity of our coastal and

marine environments is one of our most daunting tasks. Fishery depletion, coastal wetland loss, and destruction of critical coastal and marine
habitats, from coral reefs to seagrass beds, are pressing issues. At the
same time, new demands are being placed on coastal environments.
Pressures for offshore oil and gas development compete with the need
to protect the recreation and tourism values of the coast. Efforts to
establish new marine protected areas are at odds with desired access
to these areas by commercial fishers. Resort and second home development is increasingly in conflict with the need to expand coastal parks
and provide public access to coastal resources. As population and
development pressures accelerate, these conflicts will become more
difficult to resolve.

Furthermore, coastal areas are extremely vulnerable to hurricanes
and other natural hazards. Therefore, growing population and development mean increasing damage from natural hazards and more difficulty in evacuating and otherwise protecting coastal residents. New
visions, and new ideas and tools for realizing them, will be essential.
The expanded and revised chapters that follow emphasize successful
and innovative management and planning.

Although the growing numbers of people who are drawn to the
coast place increasing burdens on the natural environment and infrastructure, these trends also affirm the attraction of these special areas.
This is a profound paradox for coastal places. It is the both the best of
times and the worst of times for coastal management.

Indeed, these ominous trends and conditions suggest that we are at
a critical juncture in coastal management. The actions we take and the
plans and policies we put in place today have the potential to ensure
that the nation's coast will be cherished and enjoyed by many future
generations.

We are more convinced than ever that a primer in coastal management is needed, both for use in coastal management classes and as an
important resource for coastal managers, public officials, and citizens
involved in coastal planning and development issues. This second edition, in its basic content and structure, is quite similar to the first edition. However, in many ways and in many places the specific information about coastal management programs and laws has been updated
and expanded. Over the last 5 years, there have been substantial
changes in important programs such as the National Flood Insurance
Program and the Federal Disaster Assistance Act, which exert great
influence on the coastal zone. Additional research on many important

coastal issues and topics has also occurred in this time, and newer insights and information are included throughout. New research on the impacts and effectiveness of coastal management programs and new information on the nature of coastal threats and pressures are included in this edition.

Several other important changes are reflected in this second edition. Most significantly, a new chapter on creative coastal design and development has been included, which reviews a variety of new green building ideas and sustainable coastal development projects. This chapter reflects an increasing recognition that sustainable development in the coastal zone relies on the enthusiasm, sense of responsibility, and good practice of the private development community as well as the public sector. Development will continue to occur in coastal areas, and we believe it is important to examine how the ecological footprint of this development and growth can be creatively kept to a minimum. In Chapter 9 we present a number of tangible examples of more responsible coastal development, including projects such as Dewees Island (South Carolina) and the Philip Merrill Environmental Center (the new headquarters building of the Chesapeake Bay Foundation). The ways in which we design and build do make a significant difference.

The second edition also reflects greater attention to the broader ways in which government, especially local coastal jurisdictions, can promote sustainability. Chapter 8, which discusses local coastal management, now addresses a variety of additional strategies that coastal jurisdictions can use to promote a broader agenda of sustainability, including more sustainable mobility patterns and policies to promote renewable energy. These are topics largely absent in the earlier edition.

In preparing the second edition, we received assistance from many people. Timothy Beatley wants to acknowledge the work of Elizabeth Lahey, a graduate planning student, who did considerable work researching examples of creative design and development in the coastal zone. He also wants to thank the students in his Coastal Planning Workshop, who also helped unearth good practice and served as a constructive sounding board for many of the ideas and projects contained here.

David Brower wants to acknowledge the tremendous contributions and the unfailing energy and good cheer of Margaret Anders Limbert and Frank M. Lopez, both of whom had many other things on their minds (during publication, Marge added Limbert to her name and Frank moved to a new job the day the manuscript went in the mail.)

We all want to thank Patrick Jefferson Tate, born to Anna K. Schwab and Jeff DeWayne Tate on June 27, for his enthusiastic and vocal support.

We also want to thank Heather Boyer of Island Press for her continued strong support and encouragement during this project.

As always, the authors take full responsibility for the opinions and information contained herein.

AN INTRODUCTION TO

Coastal Zone
Management

SECOND EDITION

"The edge of the sea is a strange and beautiful place. All through the long history of earth it has been an area of unrest where waves have long broken heavily against the land, where the tides have pressed forward over the continents, receded, and then returned. For no two successive days is the shoreline precisely the same. Not only do the tides advance and retreat in their eternal rhythms, but the level of the sea itself is never at rest. . . .

"On all these shores there are echoes of past and future: of the flow of time, obliterating yet containing all that has gone before; of the sea's eternal rhythms—the tides, the beat of surf, the pressing rivers of the currents—shaping, changing, dominating; of the stream of life, flowing as inexorably as any ocean current, from past to unknown future.

"Contemplating the teeming life of the shore, we have an uneasy sense of the communication of some universal truth that lies just below our grasp. . . . The meaning haunts and even eludes us, and in its very pursuit we approach the ultimate mystery of life itself."

—Rachel Carson, *The Edge of the Sea*

"I take joy and wonder from the heron for many reasons, but most of all, I envy its perspective on the edge. It spends its days wriggling long toes in the warm, rich muck of the shallows, golden gimlet eyes spying out the camouflaged minnows and crabs. But in a few flaps of its wings, it can soar to immense heights, and from here the margins of coiled land and water present a fundamental beauty."

—Tom Horton, *Water's Way: Life Along the Chesapeake*

"We humans may have evolved in grasslands, but of late we have spun out from the prairie center and landed on the periphery. People move to the littoral like moths to a porchlight. . . . What is the draw of the edge? When I come to face the sea, the great bulk of the land at my back falls away. It is the measurable and the known; before me is all unfathomed magnitude and mystery. If there is magic on this planet, it lies beneath that azure surface."

—Jennifer Ackerman, *Notes From the Shore*

"I really don't know why it is that all of us are so committed to the sea, except I think it's because in addition to the fact that the sea changes, and the light changes, and ships change, it's because we all came from the sea. And it is an interesting biological fact that all of us have, in our veins the exact same percentage of salt in our blood that exists in the ocean, and therefore, we have salt in our blood, in our sweat, in our tears. We are tied to the ocean. And when we go back to the sea—whether it is to sail or to watch it—we are going back from whence we came."

—John F. Kennedy

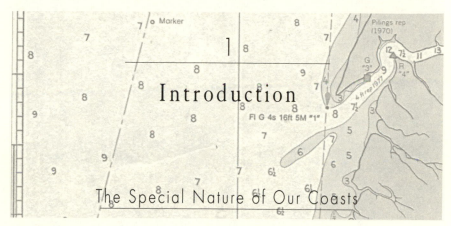

Introduction

FI G 4s 16ft 5M "1"

The Special Nature of Our Coasts

In eloquent fashion, Rachel Carson expresses what is so difficult for many of us to articulate about the pull and attraction of the coast. It is a dynamic, ever-changing zone, an environment of mystery, a timeless, eternal place where at the same moment the rhythms of nature are so incredibly visceral and immediate. Wonder and beauty are common feelings, and the American coastline is unusually blessed with these qualities.

The coastal regions of planet Earth are amazing areas. The interface between land and sea, the coast is a unique geologic, ecological, and biological domain of vital importance to an astounding array of terrestrial and aquatic life forms, including humankind.

The importance and value of the coastal zone cannot be overstated. It is one of the most productive areas accessible to people. Fish and other seafood meet a significant portion of the dietary needs for millions of people around the world, and the fishery and aquaculture industries are commercial mainstays for thousands of coastal communities.

The coast also is an important safety feature for people living near the ocean. Many types of coasts provide a barrier from natural hazards emanating from the turbulent seas. Beaches, dunes, cliffs, and barrier islands all act as buffers against the high winds and waves associated with coastal storms.

The recreational aspect of the coastal zone is another reason we value the region. Stretches of beach and rocky cliffs along the Pacific and Atlantic Oceans and along the Gulf coast provide numerous recre-

Photo 1.1. Much coastal development in the United States is occurring in very dynamic and sensitive locations, such as along barrier islands. Barrier island communities such as Wrightsville Beach, North Carolina, shown here, face a host of serious management issues, including coastal erosion, hurricanes, and coastal storms. (Photo by Tim Beatley.)

ational opportunities for thousands of Americans. Boating, fishing, swimming, walking, beachcombing, and sunbathing are among the numerous leisure activities our society enjoys. More than 180 million Americans visit the coast each year, more than visit any other recreational destination.

Many of us go to the coast for the sheer beauty of it. There is something restorative and regenerative about the waves crashing and wind whistling. The aesthetic and scenic elements of the coastal zone make it invaluable as a source of inspiration and peace.

The coastal zone also provides a unique habitat for thousands of plant and animal species. The coastal ecosystem is made up of myriad interconnected subsystems whose functions cannot be duplicated elsewhere. For instance, estuaries, with their unique mix of freshwater and saltwater, provide a nursery area for numerous species of fish. Likewise, coastal wetlands are home to a variety of birds, plants, and other biota and also serve the important role of filtering impurities in the water coursing through them. These and other segments of the coastal ecosystem are precisely balanced, fragile areas susceptible to a variety of threats, including those posed by human interference in the natural system.

Photo 1.2. Coastal areas are increasingly important for recreation and tourism. Americans are attracted to the special qualities of beaches and coastlines. (Photo by Tim Beatley.)

Despite its fragility, the coastal zone is amazingly resilient. The ecosystem as a whole is a dynamic and regenerative force; if left alone, natural mechanisms maintain an equilibrium between living things and the natural environment. However, there are limits to the extent to which the coastal ecosystem can withstand external assaults to its integrity. Pressures emanating from human activities are particularly threatening.

The Pressures on the Coastal Zone

Many pressures are exerted on the coastal zone every day. Some of these are part of the natural operation of coastal processes. Every day, winds and waves move material and affect the landscape. More dramatic action occurs with coastal storms, including hurricanes and nor'easters, which can bring high winds and wave surge forceful enough to change coastal topography overnight. For instance, barrier islands are very unstable areas. Over time, in reaction to storms and the accumulative daily buffeting of winds and waves, the islands move; they are constantly migrating, usually landward. Inlets are another example of a migratory coastal feature. Inlets can shift laterally or be closed entirely, and new inlets can be created during a particularly forceful storm.

Such alterations in the landscape are part of the natural processes in motion in the coastal region. Coastal areas are dynamic yet adaptable. Changes in the natural environment are to be expected, and the region can recuperate when allowed to continue its evolutionary process. It is when additional external pressures are exerted on the coastal zone that the area cannot recuperate fully. Human interference with natural processes can alter natural dynamics. For instance, hard structures built up along the beach to prevent erosion (e.g., groins, jetties) can exacerbate erosion by trapping sand in one area and preventing its natural lateral drift to areas downstream.

The Pressures Exerted by Humans

Just the fact that people live in the coastal area is a form of pressure itself. The coastal regions of the United States are some of our most attractive places to live, both economically and aesthetically. The resources of the coastal zone provide numerous job opportunities, and many people come to the coast for recreation. Population density is another measure of the stresses placed on coastal areas; when more people are using a limited resource, the carrying capacity of the region can be exceeded.

Both the numbers and the density of population can increase dramatically during the vacation season. In summer the population of many coastal communities can double, triple, or increase even more. Increased leisure time, a rise in disposable incomes, and a penchant for travel mean that more Americans are spending more time at the shore.

Of course, people at the shore, both residents and visitors, need to be housed, fed, and entertained. The pressures exerted by the presence of human beings at the coast emanate from these needs. Houses, hotels, condominiums, restaurants, gas stations, shopping malls, golf courses, piers, and amusement parks are spreading along all reaches of America's coastline. All these development projects necessitate infrastructure—roads, bridges, parking lots, sewers—which can exert pressure on the environment or lead to various negative impacts. For instance, the increased area surfaced by impervious materials for development projects and the infrastructure supporting them can increase runoff into surrounding coastal waters. The amount of new develop-

Photo 1.3. Hurricanes and coastal storms are a serious threat and major challenge for coastal communities. Damage from Hurricane Hugo, shown here, amounted to about $7 billion. (Photo by Tim Beatley.)

ment along the American coast is staggering: More than 800,000 new housing units are built each year. Much of this is happening in scattered, wasteful patterns of sprawl, with loss of forests, wetlands, and other natural lands.

People also need potable water, and many coastal communities are largely dependent on groundwater for their supply. However, there is a limit to the quantity of groundwater that can be withdrawn at a certain location within a certain time without adverse impacts. The water needed to serve projected population growth cannot exceed the gap between current withdrawals and this limit. The cumulative impact of groundwater usage can lead to changes to the water table, resulting in saltwater intrusion. Groundwater can also become polluted through the introduction of organic and inorganic contaminants associated with human settlement.

Human pressure exerted on the coastal region also involves waste disposal. We have been using the oceans and the coastal zone as dumping grounds for years, hoping the assimilative capacity of the ecosystem would take care of the problem. For instance, medical waste washed up on the shores of the East coast has been known to close beaches for weeks. Barges filled with garbage have been unloading their cargo at sea for years, and not too far from the shoreline. Although the recuperative abilities of the coastal region are high, over time the natural environment will not be able to withstand the pressures without serious alteration or degradation. In other words, we are using the oceans and coasts as sinks for our wastes, and the sinks are filling rapidly to overflow levels.

The Effects of Human Pressure

The effects of human-induced pressures on the coastal zone can be far-reaching and long-lasting. As noted earlier, human activity can interfere with the natural processes of the coast and prevent the ecosystem from maintaining the equilibrium so necessary to its continued vitality. Both the marine and the terrestrial environments are tightly integrated systems in which all parts are interrelated and dependent on one another. Destruction or degradation of one component can damage other parts or the ecosystem as a whole.

The cumulative impacts of human-induced pressures can be severe in coastal regions. Until recently, cumulative impacts of development on the coastal ecosystem have not been regarded as a serious problem because human and development pressures generally have not over-taxed the assimilative capacities of natural systems. As the coastal population continues to grow, however, long-term cumulative impacts will become more evident. The adverse impact of a single project can sometimes be limited to a certain extent. Together with other development projects, however, the single project becomes part of a much larger ecological problem. As more projects are permitted in the coastal region and more are concentrated in popular and economically profitable locations, the cumulative impacts will undoubtedly grow.

Areas with sensitive coastal resources (e.g., wetlands, water bodies, fish and wildlife habitats) are particularly vulnerable to cumulative impacts. Areas of the coast experiencing rapid population growth are also especially prone to cumulative impacts. Population is an important gauge because changes in size and composition of the population directly affect the amount and character of development in an area. Changes in population and development patterns impose new impacts and demands on natural and built systems in the area. In addition, population change increases the significance of natural processes such as barrier island migration, sea level rise, or coastal storms.

Many of the threats faced today as a result of human pressures are unprecedented in magnitude and scope. Overharvesting of the world's fisheries threatens both the sustainability of marine ecosystems and our ability to feed ourselves. Some two-thirds of the world's fisheries are considered overfished, and species such as tuna and Atlantic cod are threatened with extinction. Global climate change is producing monumental threats to coral reefs, coastal wetlands, and other coastal and marine ecosystems.

As more people and activities are focused on the coast, conflicts over how to use these finite resources heighten. Plans to expand energy production clash with desires to preserve the recreational and aesthetic qualities of beaches and coasts. Desires to build second homes or resorts clash with the need to preserve the ecosystem functions—healthy bays, estuaries, and beaches—on which all coastal residents (and many living outside of coastal areas) depend. Reconciling these competing demands becomes a challenge for coastal planners.

The coastal zone is also a very hazardous area. Hurricanes and other coastal storms have been known to destroy entire communities in a matter of hours. People are displaced, homes and businesses are destroyed, infrastructure can be uprooted, and human lives can be lost. But why do these disasters occur? Because people have put themselves in the way of a natural force that cannot be diverted or stopped. The coastal zone is hazardous because humans have made it so. Coastal storms have no power to create thousands or even millions of dollars in damage to property if no property is within the storm's reach, nor can a storm kill people if no people are in its path.

Of course, there are hazard mitigation practices that can lessen the impact of a storm on a coastal community. For instance, buildings can be designed and constructed to withstand all but the most forceful winds and wave surge. Well-planned and executed evacuation measures can reduce the risk to humans by getting them out of the way before a storm hits land. But the fact remains that coastal areas are hazardous only when there is something at risk in the area, something put there by people.

Public Policy
Exacerbates the Pressures

Many of our current public policies can exacerbate the pressures placed on the coastal zone. Without the intention to inflict harm, our regulatory and political structure nevertheless tends to encourage the exact type of behavior that endangers the fragile natural resources of the coastal area. The most obvious of these policies are those that encourage development in coastal communities. Such growth, which can increase the dangers to the environment, also places more people and property at risk from coastal hazards.

For instance, infrastructure, a necessity for growth and development, usually is provided by various levels of government. While ensuring safe transportation routes for local residents, paved roads and highways also allow more people access to more coastal areas. Similarly, bridges can open formerly isolated areas (such as barrier islands) to numbers of people that may exceed the carrying capacity of that particular locale. Sewer systems and municipal wastewater treatment plants allow the density of coastal populations to increase dramatically. And the provision of public water supplies can deplete aquifer reservoirs at a faster rate than they can be replenished.

The availability of various types of hazard insurance also encourages development in coastal areas. The availability of federal flood insurance in particular often is cited as a primary example of how hazardous coastal development is subsidized and how the wrong kind of incentives are created. Owners of property damaged by coastal storms and flooding often are allowed to rebuild in the same or equally hazardous locations. The damage–rebuild–damage cycle accounts for many damage claims, and there are few incentives for avoiding development in hazard-prone areas.

Coastal development subsidies are also provided in the form of tax expenditures, deductions, or other subsidies contained in federal and state tax codes. For instance, casualty loss deductions reimburse owners for damage to property that is not covered by insurance. Deductions also are allowed for interest and property taxes on second homes, typical of coastal development.

Sustaining the Coast: The Overarching Challenge

As discussed in the previous paragraphs, human activities are placing burdens on the natural resources of the coastal zone beyond their capacity to absorb the impact. Human society is using resources and producing wastes at rates that are not sustainable. Our nation's penchant for growth and our consumption habits threaten the vitality, even the very existence, of a healthy, aesthetically pleasing, and productive coastal zone.

Although the presence of human beings has been the major causal factor in most of the environmental problems now experienced in the coastal zone, *not* living there is not a realistic solution. We are not suggesting that all built structures be razed, all roads be removed, and all people leave the coast. Instead, we as a nation must change our attitude as well as our behavior. What is needed is a new way of thinking: humankind as a part of the system, not its master.

This new attitude could result in many innovative and complex solutions to the world's environmental problems; one key concept for changing human behavior and breaking out of the destructive growth cycle is sustainability or sustainable development. Today, sustainability is a foreign concept to our growth-acclimated culture. We do not view the earth and its resources as finite, but even renewable resources can become finite if used and managed improperly.

Sustainable development became a catch phrase in the environmentally conscious 1990s. Many different definitions are in current usage, none of them accurately or fully embodying the two components—"sustainable" and "development"—and the relationship between these often dichotomous concepts. However, one generally accepted definition has emerged from the report *Our Common Future,* published by the World Commission on Environment and Development (commonly called the Brundtland Report): Sustainable development is "development that meets the needs of the present without compromising the ability of future generations to meet their own needs." The Brundtland Report elaborates on its definition by stating that sustainable development is "not a fixed state of harmony, but rather a process of change in which the exploitation of resources, the direction of investments, the orientation of technological development and institutional change are made consistent with future as well as present needs."

Sustainable development does not mean *no* growth. It does mean not wasting resources, but most proponents of sustainable development realize that without some growth, communities would not be in a position to provide for their citizens a decent standard of living and work to improve the environment. However, sustainable development does entail a change in the content of growth to make it less material- and energy-intensive.

Although not every approach to sustainable development necessarily encompasses the same set of assumptions, some basic principles emerge to guide our endeavor to reach development that is truly sustainable. All proponents of sustainable development emphasize that greater knowledge and appreciation of and respect for the natural world are essential. To this end, education and consciousness-raising about our environment must be first and foremost. Furthermore, the active and full participation of all the citizens in the community is crucial. This includes an awareness of the destructiveness of current overconsumptive lifestyles. Participation in grassroots organizations can make a big difference in our lifestyles and habits. We must then go further and become involved in the political structure that shapes much of the policy regarding growth and development at the state, national, and international levels.

We must engage in efficient resource use, reversing the degradation of renewable resources and implementing strategies for the sustainable use of land, water, biological and genetic resources, and energy. Reducing waste generation, recycling wastes into productive activities, and finding safe ways to dispose of wastes that remain are essential elements in creating a healthy and habitable world. Polluters should pay for the costs of remediation, but it is even more important to prevent pollution and resource waste in the first place.

And finally, and perhaps most importantly, all human activity should be judged from its long-term environmental impact, not just from its short-term gain. The philosophical principle guiding sustainable development lies in its future orientation, without ignoring the needs of living people. An appropriate formula for determining whether an action lends itself to sustainable development may well be, "Will children be able to enjoy equivalent or better opportunities than their parents did?" (Beller et al., 1990).

The Rationale for Government Intervention

Each person in our overconsumptive society must participate in the change of attitude necessary to achieve development that is truly sustainable. But in addition to the changes we must make in our daily habits and patterns of behavior, society as a collective body of individuals must change its attitude and actions as a whole. We can speculate about a number of different methods of achieving this universal behavior modification, but one method for which the institutional mechanisms are already in place is government directive.

However, to achieve such an approach, we must overcome the strong aversion in our country to what is often viewed as overly intrusive government action, especially in the area of land use. Private property rights are deemed almost inviolate in the United States. However, much of the abuse we have inflicted on the natural environment has as its source the way we use and manage our land and the attendant natural resources. This is especially true in the coastal zone, where development is taking place in inappropriate areas at an accelerating pace.

What land use regulation does take place in the United States falls mostly within the domain of local governments. This traditional view of land use regulation as a local prerogative is in many cases appropriate because the function of regulator is necessarily site-specific. However, because of the nature of the coast and the coastal ecosystem, local governments may not have the financial resources, technical ability, or political willpower to fulfill the role of official protector and conservator of the coastal zone. Natural resources do not necessarily conform to humanity's artificial political boundary systems, and ecosystem limits often transcend local jurisdictions. Many coastal environmental problems are regional in scope, and local governments may not have the authority to deal with such wide-ranging issues. Furthermore, local governments may have too parochial an outlook to be effective at implementing the principles of sustainable development community-wide.

Recognizing that local powers generally are insufficient to manage the coastal region effectively, state and federal governments have to some degree stepped in to fill the gap. This book describes several measures being undertaken to control land use patterns, use of natural resources, and human activities that affect the coastal zone. However, though well-intentioned, these federal and state programs are also found to be lacking. The traditional processes of government control and regulation have limited effectiveness, especially in promoting the long-term health and vitality of the coastal ecosystem.

What is needed now is a new and different set of values on which to base our government actions. Coastal zone management for the last two or three decades has focused on the catchword *balancing*—a balancing of economic development and preservation of the environment. This is all well and good, but we must go beyond balancing and operate under the principles of sustainability if we are to ensure that humankind's presence in the coastal region will not produce its demise.

This new approach to government intervention based on the principles of sustainable development calls for an integrated program of
coastal zone management. The system must operate at all levels of
government and involve all participants in the coastal region. Many of
the tools are in place; the regulatory authority and financial resources
already exist, should we choose to direct them to the appropriate
needs. What is missing is the wisdom, the will, and the political fore-
sight to create a management system that will protect, enhance, and
preserve our coastal zone for us and for future generations.

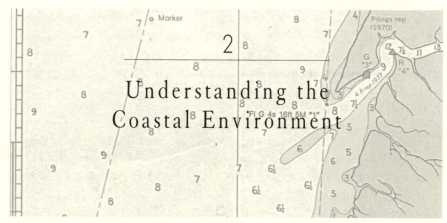

2
Understanding the Coastal Environment

A solid understanding of the workings of coastal ecological and geomorphologic systems is essential to managing the complex and dynamic environments of the coastal zone. This is not to discount the effects of human intervention, which is essentially what management is all about; we do not manage the natural systems themselves, but rather, we seek to manage the human behavior that affects and is affected by those systems. The diversity of the coastal zone mandates that the manager of these resources understand the qualities of the environment; there is no one-size-fits-all approach for all coastal regions. The goal of this chapter is to give a brief overview of the natural systems and processes that make up the coastal zone. The reader is encouraged to constantly ask how these natural phenomena will affect the management approach needed so that humans can coexist with nature in an unpredictable, evolving, and often hazardous environment.

Defining the Coastal Zone

Coastal zone management involves managing human activity to protect the natural resources of the coastal zone and to protect humans from coastal hazards. To do this effectively, the boundary of the management program should correspond with the boundaries of the resource. However, natural systems have transient and often fuzzy boundaries that rarely, if ever, correspond to political boundaries. This makes delineating the extent of the management area difficult.

Coastal regions are dynamic interface zones where land, water, and atmosphere interact in a fragile balance that is constantly being altered by natural and human influence. When establishing physical boundaries for the coastal zone, it is important to remember that critical physical and ecological interconnections extend beyond these areas and that coastal zones can be affected significantly by human and other activities that happen at great distances from the coast itself. Where influences are generated farther inland, a definition of the coastal zone should encompass the entire watershed or river basin, which drains into coastal waters. The condition of coastal waters is clearly influenced by actions remote from the shoreline, such as activities within the larger river catchment. The watershed for the Chesapeake Bay, for instance, includes portions of six states, extending well beyond any usual definition of the coastal zone. Yet activities happening many hundreds of miles upriver, such as acid deposition from coal-fired power plants, soil erosion, and nonpoint source pollution, have a major influence on the water quality of the bay.

Figure 2.1 illustrates the physical components of the shore zone,

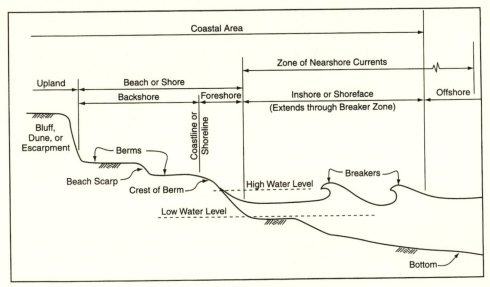

Figure 2.1. The shore zone. (From FEMA, 2000b.)

which lies between the marine and terrestrial environments. The dry side (backshore) of the shore zone includes land formations such as dunes and ridges and, for management purposes, can extend upland to include watersheds and river basins that drain into the ocean. The wet side of the shore zone includes the edge zone or transitional area, which involves shallow water and intertidal areas (foreshore). The wet side can also be extended to include deeper ocean waters and their resources (offshore) (Viles and Spencer, 1995). The shore zone includes barrier islands, beaches, dunes, cliffs, tidal and brackish water wetlands and marshes, coral reefs, mangrove swamps, and other larger-scale coastal ecosystems such as estuaries and bays.

Types of Coastal Landforms

Coastlines around the world exhibit a variety of physical types and characteristics, the result of major differences in geology and natural processes. Such differences establish a basis for coastline classification systems that scholars have devised. One common system is based on the theory of plate tectonics, which explains why coastlines have evolved in such dramatically different ways. Some coasts have also been classified according to the types of wave forces to which they are subject, whereas other coasts are considered to be tide dominated or wind dominated (French, 1997). Additionally, coasts can be referred to as erosional or depositional, or can be differentiated by sediment type.

In the United States, major differences exist in land formations from coast to coast (Figure 2.2). For instance, the Atlantic coast is characterized by a system of barrier beaches and a wide continental shelf. The Pacific coast, on the other hand, is characterized by a narrow continental shelf, limited barrier beaches, a mountainous coastal region, and a tectonically active geological system. The broad, flat coastal plain found along much of the eastern United States has allowed the formation of extensive coastal marshes, whereas few such marshes exist along the Pacific coast. Some coastal areas are heavily influenced by river systems, such as the Mississippi delta, and the extensive flows of sediments injected into the coastal system.

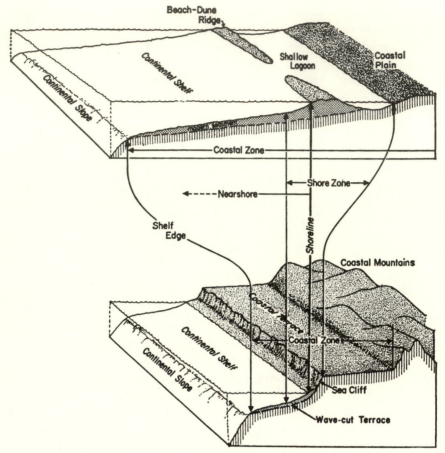

Figure 2.2. Wide-shelf plains coast (upper), characteristic of the U.S. East coast (trailing edge), and narrow-shelf mountainous coast (lower), characteristic of the U.S. West coast. (From Clark, 1977.)

Time Scales of Change

Coastal areas are dynamic, transient environments where landforms are created and destroyed, coastal processes shift and fluctuate, and ecosystems are modified and reformed over time in response to both human-made and natural influences. This coastal dynamism occurs over a range of time scales, from geologic periods of change measured in millennia to short-term fluctuations over a few weeks or months, or even minutes or seconds. Table 2.1 presents some examples of how the

Table 2.1. Time Scales of Coastal Change in Relation to Absolute
Time Scales, Human Processes, and Coastal Processes

Absolute time scale	Human processes	Coastal processes
Millennia		Response of sea level to cycles of glaciation and global warming
Centuries	Establishment of coastal settlement and industry patterns	Formation and erosion of primary capes; rotation of barrier islands
Decades	Impacts of rapid population growth and development; pollution	Formation and loss of habitats (e.g., marshes, dunes)
Years	Impacts of coastal engineering and management plans; pollution	Longshore drift; erosion and accretion of barrier beaches
Months	Impacts of tourism; pollution	Seasonal variation; shore profiles
Weeks	Impacts of tourism; emergency coastal protection works; pollution	Shore profiles; spring–neap tidal cycles
Days	Emergency flood protection works; pollution	Hurricane and coastal storm surge; inlet formation or closure
Hours	Sewage and other waste disposal; evacuation	Tidal cycles; hurricane and coastal storm surge and winds
Minutes	Litter	Waves and currents
Seconds		Sediment grain movement (wind and water)

Sources: Adapted from French (1997), Viles and Spencer (1995), Platt et al. (1992b).

changes in coastal processes relate to the timeframe of human activity in the coastal zone.

Coastal Ecosystems

There are a number of distinctly different habitat or ecosystem types within the coastal zone as we have defined it, each suggesting unique management and planning needs. The introductory discussion here is oriented toward several of the more common of these ecosystem types, including barrier islands (which include beaches, dunes, and inlets), estuaries, coastal marshes, coral reefs, and rocky shores and bluffs.

A full cataloging of coastal ecosystems is beyond the scope of this text. For a fuller and more comprehensive presentation the reader is referred to more detailed coastal ecology texts (e.g., Clark, 1996).

Barrier Islands

The Gulf and Atlantic coasts of the United States are characterized by a system of barrier islands, generally running from Maine to Texas. This system comprises about 300 different islands and a combined ocean-front distance of 2,700 miles (Figure 2.3). The system extends over 18 coastal states and comprises some 1.6 million acres (Dolan and Lins,

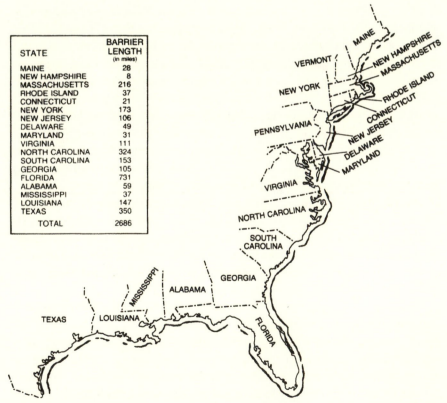

STATE	BARRIER LENGTH (in miles)
MAINE	28
NEW HAMPSHIRE	8
MASSACHUSETTS	216
RHODE ISLAND	37
CONNECTICUT	21
NEW YORK	173
NEW JERSEY	106
DELAWARE	49
MARYLAND	31
VIRGINIA	111
NORTH CAROLINA	324
SOUTH CAROLINA	153
GEORGIA	105
FLORIDA	731
ALABAMA	59
MISSISSIPPI	37
LOUISIANA	147
TEXAS	350
TOTAL	2686

Figure 2.3. Hundreds of coastal barriers (shaded line) protect the Atlantic and Gulf coasts. (From Wells and Peterson, undated.)

1987; Wells and Peterson, undated). Such a system of barriers does not occur on the Pacific coast.

The explanation for the formation of the barrier island system has long been the subject of speculation. Most coastal geologists believe that their formation results from the natural process of sea level rise. This may also account for the gradual landward movement (or "migration") that is characteristic of barrier islands. When the last period of major sea level rise began to occur approximately 18,000 years ago, wind-formed dunes were breached. As sea level rise continued, it is hypothesized that the islands gradually moved landward. Although some barrier islands are experiencing accretion in the short term, the barrier island system as a whole is continuing to retreat (Kaufman and Pilkey, 1979; Pilkey et al., 1980).

Barrier islands are formed of loosely consolidated materials, primarily sand, and generally include a sandy beach, frontal and secondary dunes, interior wetlands and maritime forest, a backshore zone (often marsh), and the lagoon or sound that separates the island from the mainland (Figure 2.4). They are highly vulnerable to the forces of wind, waves, and sediment transport and the effects of hurricanes and sea level rise. As a result, their size, shape, and location are constantly changing.

Dunes: Dunes are a particularly fragile component of the barrier island ecosystem. Despite their fragility, they play a critical role in maintaining the integrity of the island and protecting development that occurs behind the dune line. From a process point of view, dunes represent the temporary store of beach sediment in the supratidal zone. Sediment that is regularly moved and reworked onto the beach tends to be highly mobile, whereas that which has been in the dune system for greater periods of time tends to become vegetated, which provides increased stability. Although it can withstand wind, the vegetation is rarely sufficient to withstand the impacts of trampling, off-road vehicles, horses, or trail bikes (French, 1997).

Beaches: The beaches of barrier islands tend to be low-lying and sloping and serve as the first line of defense against the forces of wind, waves, currents, and coastal storms. There is an intricate relationship between the dune and beach systems, with a complex and ever-changing transfer of sediment back and forth. The width of barrier island beaches is in a normal state of flux from season to season. The shape and profile of the beach can also change dramatically after hurricanes and coastal storms. It is generally the beach area of barrier islands that

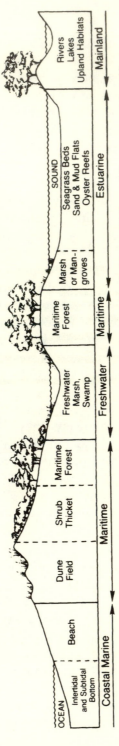

Figure 2.4. A cross-section of a well-developed barrier island and nearby mainland. (From Wells and Peterson, undated.)

makes them so attractive to development. They provide abundant recreational opportunities, and their existence is the economic mainstay of many barrier island communities. Unfortunately, the very aspect of the beach that attracts visitors—its proximity to the ocean—is what makes the area so unsuitable for human exploitation.

Inlets: Inlets are another important feature of the barrier island system. Although the complexity of their existence and the degree of hazard they present often are poorly understood or grossly underestimated, the complicated dynamics of inlets and their importance to barrier island geomorphology have profound ramifications for management of barrier islands. Inlets connect lagoons and sounds behind islands with the ocean and are constantly fluctuating. Each inlet is unique, and when left to follow their own natural mechanics, inlets open and close, narrow and widen, and migrate and reform in complex patterns.

Inlets are formed during storms, usually when storm-driven water is pushed into the lagoon and then forced back out to sea again, carving the path of least resistance as it moves. Once formed, an inlet may remain in place for several years, although some inlets close much more rapidly. Tidal range and the amount of sediment traveling

Photo 2.1. Inlets such as Tubb's Inlet in North Carolina, shown here, are a highly dynamic aspect of barrier island systems. They move and migrate dramatically over time, especially in response to storm events, and therefore are best avoided as places to develop. (Photo by Tim Beatley.)

through the longshore drift are major factors in determining the life of an inlet. For instance, in the Outer Banks of North Carolina, where tidal currents are weak and there is abundant sand supply, inlets change rapidly.

There is a range of inlet types. Relict and historical inlets are now closed but have the potential to reopen in the same or a nearby location. Both natural and human-made modern inlets can migrate significantly, and they erode the adjacent shoreline as they do so. They also erase the entire downdrift island as a new updrift island forms. Even so-called stable inlets are potential hazard areas because they can widen, narrow, or migrate without warning (Bush et al., 1996).

When left alone, inlets and their transitory nature are part of the nat-

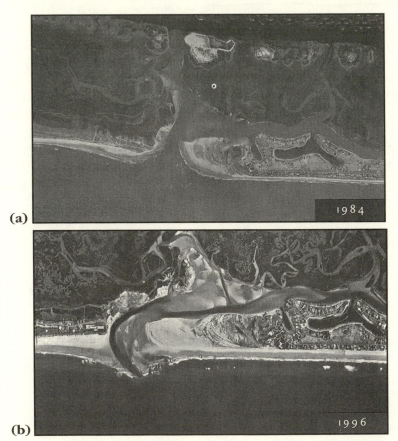

(a) 1984

(b) 1996

Photo 2.2. Mason Inlet, near Wrightsville Beach, North Carolina. These two photographs show the inlet's change from 1984 to 1996. (North Carolina Sea Grant from Cleary and Marden, 1999.)

Photo 2.3. Shell Island Resort stands on the south side of Mason Inlet and has been the center of a lawsuit concerning the construction of a permanent structure to protect the property. The resort is visible in Photo 2.2b on the shore of the inlet. (Photo by North Carolina Department of Environment and Natural Resources.)

ural system (Photo 2.2). However, when development is located unadvisedly within the active inlet zone, especially in the path of the migratory direction, extremely hazardous conditions arise. Barrier island communities that have halted the migratory process of their inlets by constructing sand-trapping jetties (as is quite common along the coast of Florida) have replaced the inlet hazard with extensive erosion problems (Bush et al., 1996; Dean, 1999).

Estuaries

Estuaries are some of the most ecologically productive elements of the coastal environment, rivaling tropical rainforests in their primary productivity. Estuaries are coastal aquatic systems formed by the mixing of freshwater from riverine systems and saltwater from the ocean. Prichard (1967) presents one of the more commonly cited definitions of an estuary: a "semi-enclosed coastal body of water which has a free connection with the sea and within which sea water is measurably diluted with freshwater derived from land drainage" (p. 3). The defining feature of an estuary, then, is its fluctuating salinity, and estuaries vary depending on the relative dominance of freshwater or saltwater. In turn this is heavily influenced by the tidal range. Some estuaries, known as salt-wedge estuaries, are dominated by freshwater and have small tidal ranges and therefore small marine inputs (Hansom, 1988); the Mississippi River is a major example of this type of estuary. Partially mixed estuaries have a larger tidal effect and smaller river flow, resulting in more pronounced mixing of saltwater and freshwater (with the freshwater usually on top and the saltier waters on the lower layers); the James River in Virginia is an example of this form of estuary. Fully mixed estuaries have even stronger tidal flows and weaker river inputs.

Estuaries often are classified by their geologic origin and geomorphology. Most estuaries have formed as the tidal mouths of rivers. Consequently, they are often called drowned river valley estuaries and were formed as recently as 6,000 years ago in response to sea level rise. The Chesapeake Bay estuary was formed from and largely comprises the ancient Susquehanna River valley (Lippson and Lippson, 1984). Bar-built estuaries represent a different type of formation. They lack the deep river indentation, usually are much shallower, and are separated from the ocean by barrier islands and sand spits, with intermittent inlets (Knox, 1986). The Texas estuarine system is perhaps the best example of this type in the United States (Figure 2.5). Some estuaries have been formed through tectonic processes (e.g., land subsidence and faulting, as illustrated by the formation of the San Francisco Bay).

Estuaries exhibit plant life specially adapted to these saline conditions, including extensive salt marshes, mangroves, and eel grass beds. (Coastal marshes are described in more detail later.) Estuaries exhibit a tremendous level of primary productivity and in turn serve as important nursery grounds for a variety of fish and shellfish. They are also characterized by high biotic diversity (Hobbie, 2000).

Estuarine systems feature a complex food chain (e.g., see the diagram of food web and energy flows in Clark, 1996). Estuarine plants serve as direct food for certain animals (fish and shellfish) but more importantly provide small particles of decay (detritus), which are consumed by microscopic life forms (zooplankton), which in turn are consumed by fish and then by other animals higher on the trophic scale, including humans. This food web often is characterized in terms of producers (plants), consumers (plant-eating animals such as zooplankton and oysters), foragers (those who prey on consumers), and predators (those who prey on foragers). (See Clark, 1996, for a more detailed explanation of the estuarine food chain.)

The ecology of the estuary depends heavily on the salinity gradient.

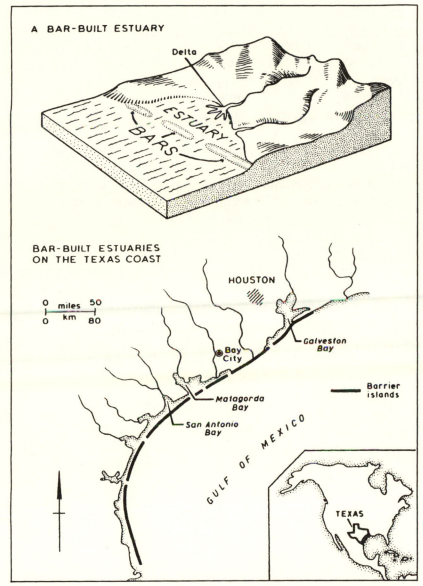

Figure 2.5. Bar-built estuaries on the Texas coast. (From Petrick, 1984.)

Different plant and animal species are able to tolerate different levels of salinity. Interestingly, although the primary productivity (amount of organic matter produced) is greater in more saline or brackish portions of the estuary, species diversity tends to be lower (Thorne-Miller and

Catena, 1991; Chabreck, 1988). However, the species that can flourish in saline or brackish conditions tend to reproduce in abundance. It has been estimated that 75% of the U.S. commercial fish catch and almost 90% of its recreational fish depend on the estuary for a portion of their life cycle.   ← mangroves ⟶

Because of their sensitivity and complexity, estuaries are highly susceptible to human influence. "The rise in population and changing land use in coastal regions is inevitably affecting the flow of water, sediments, organic matter, and inorganic nutrients into the estuaries of the world. Successful management of estuaries and their watersheds for sustainable use in the future requires us to bring all applicable knowledge to bear on the development of practical models that predict the results of various strategies" (Hobbie, 2000, p. 1).

Coastal Marshes

Coastal marshes are an ecological subunit of estuaries and are a class of wetlands found, to some extent, along all U.S. coastlines. These are extremely productive habitats, formed primarily from river sediment and home to saline-adapted plant life. Most are located along the Gulf and Atlantic coasts (Alexander et al., 1986; Chabreck, 1988). Especially large areas of marshes are found in the southern Atlantic states (North Carolina, South Carolina, and Georgia in particular) and the Gulf (Louisiana and Texas). Few coastal marshes are found in New England or along the Pacific coast because of the rockier nature of these shorelines, although some are found in protected bays and river mouths. Of the limited coastal marshes on the Pacific coast, the majority are associated with the San Francisco Bay (Chabreck, 1988).

Coastal marshes generally are classified according to their salinity regimes, with four types commonly identified: salt marshes, brackish marshes, intermediate marshes, and freshwater marshes. The majority of coastal marshes (some 70%) are salt marshes. Salinity levels in turn influence the types of vegetation found in marshes, with some plant species, such as mangroves and cordgrass, very resistant to high saline levels and other species, such as sawgrass and water hyacinth, not very suited to saline water conditions.

Coastal marshes have been heavily modified by humans. The rate of marsh loss has slowed in recent years (from an all-time high of 40 square miles per year in Louisiana in the 1980s), but marshes continue to be destroyed or damaged by a variety of activities, including con-

Photo 2.4. Lotus plants in a Mississippi delta marsh. (Photo by NOAA.)

version of land to agricultural production, filling for coastal homesites and development, and construction of canal dredging. In coastal Louisiana, marshes have been disappearing largely as a result of extensive river diversion and flood control levee building. Because the marshlands of the Mississippi delta naturally subside, these flood control projects have deprived the marshes of the needed replacement sediment, so the wetlands are drowning. Because of the extensive levee and channelization project, the Mississippi River now deposits its sediments right off the edge of the continental shelf, losing the material from the coastal system (Chabreck, 1988). Extensive canal dredging along the gulf for navigation and oil and gas production activities has also been a major cause of marsh degradation and gradual saltwater intrusion.

Sea level rise in many ways is the most serious current threat to marshes. Increases in sea level threaten to inundate these productive areas faster than they can migrate landward (see Titus, 1991; Reid and Trexler, 1991).

Coastal marshlands are extremely productive and serve a number of functions beneficial to the environment and to humans. They are an important food source for fish and shellfish, are home to a variety of wildlife, are important recreational areas, and help reduce shoreline erosion. They also act as natural sponges to absorb floodwaters and can filter high volumes of wastewater and other pollutants.

ecosystem services

Coral Reefs

Coral reefs are one of the earth's most ecologically productive habitats. Globally, coral reefs comprise about 600,000 square miles and support at least half a million species. The net productivity of coral systems is higher than that of many tropical forests. Though extremely productive, living coral systems are limited in the United States, with the most extensive system along the Florida Keys. Threats to coral reef systems are numerous and include coral harvesting, blast fishing, damage from overuse by snorkelers and divers, damage from ships, and sedimentation and water pollution. In the Caribbean, coral bleaching has been a concern in recent years and is seen by many as indicative of the level of stress placed on these living systems. Global climate change and the resultant sea level rise and rises in seawater temperatures could have a major damaging effect on the world's coral reef systems. Sunlight does not penetrate the ocean very far. Therefore, the symbiotic algae that make up coral reef systems may be threatened if the reef cannot grow as fast as the sea is rising. *Interesting point ↑*

Rocky Shores and Bluffs

Rocky shores form on high-energy coasts where mountains meet the sea and at the base of sea cliffs. Active tectonic environments, such as those in California, produce rocky coasts as a result of mountain-building processes, faulting, and earthquakes. Rocky coasts also form where ice and strong waves have removed fine-grained sediment. In Maine and parts of Alaska, glaciers have scoured most of the sediment cover from the shore. In the Arctic, ice gouging and rafting have removed sand-sized particles from some beaches, leaving cobbles and boulders.

The precipitous cliffs, steep-walled bluffs, and rocky headlands that characterize much of the Pacific Northwest coastline have been created by the geologic processes that shaped the western margin of the North American continent. In contrast to the sloped shores of the Atlantic and Gulf coasts, formed by the gradual submergence of the continental shelf, the sheer walls and elevated terraces of the Pacific coast were created by abrupt faulting and uplift. Headlands have withstood weathering and erosion, whereas bluffs and sea cliffs have been continuously eroded by waves, storms, and wind (California Coastal Commission, 1987).

Coastal bluffs actually are the seaward edges of marine terraces, shaped by ocean waves and currents and uplifted from the ocean floor. Bluffs are composed mainly of sedimentary rocks such as sandstone

Photo 2.5. Near Shore Acres State Park, west of Coos Bay, Oregon. (Photo by NOAA.)

and shale that are highly susceptible to erosion. These loosely consolidated deposits crumble easily; when wet, shales and siltstones disintegrate, and clays and mudstones soften and liquefy. Rocky headlands, composed of igneous rocks such as granite and basalt, are much more resilient and less prone to erosion.

Landslides and cliff retreat are part of the natural process of coastal erosion along rocky shorelines. Waves that undercut bluffs often initiate landslides. The majority of cliff erosion occurs during severe storms, when heavy surf transports sand offshore, denuding the beach in front of the cliff and exposing the cliff base to direct wave attack. Coastal bluffs are also slowly degraded by winter rains that penetrate fissures in the rock face. Fractured shales, sandstones, and siltstones slip and cause landslides, especially where the terrain is sloped toward the beach. A coastal landslide can be extremely hazardous, sweeping away buildings, cars, roads—anything in its path—as it plunges seaward. Areas well known for landslides are Devil's Slide in San Mateo County and Pacific Palisades in Los Angeles County, California (California Coastal Commission, 1987).

Human activity along some areas of the Pacific coast has increased the rate of erosion, endangering lives and damaging property. Drainage pipes and septic tanks that accompany development along coastal bluffs can saturate soils with runoff, exacerbating erosion. The irrigation of lawns and gardens can cause even the most stable sedimentary bluffs to collapse and slide into the sea (California Coastal Commission, 1987).

The flora and fauna that live in the windy and dry environment of Pacific cliffs have adapted to the harsh conditions and shallow, salty soil in numerous ways. Ledges, gullies, slopes, and cracks provide spaces where soil can collect and seeds can germinate. Sea figs, ice plants, and coyote bush grow on steep bluffs. Wildflowers such as poppies, iris, and lupines bloom, and introduced grasses and native fescue flourish in these harsh conditions. Seabirds such as the common murre can survive on protected ledges of the bluff face and are attracted to cliffs and bluffs as safe nesting areas away from humans and other predators.

Coastal Forces and Processes

The coastal environment is one of constant change. Complex coastal processes interact to create a dynamic equilibrium and provide the energy necessary to create the landforms and coastal ecosystems discussed in this chapter. This section introduces some of the basic characteristics of these important coastal forces and processes, including wind, waves, currents, tides, hurricanes and other coastal storms, and sea level rise. The net result of these energy sources—erosion and accretion—is also discussed in this section.

Wind

Wind plays several critical roles in shaping and changing the coastal environment: It serves as an important mover of sediment and a major generating and sustaining force of waves. Wind can also be a devastating element of coastal storms.

As a mechanism of sediment transport, onshore winds traveling with sufficient velocity deliver sand and other coastal sediments to feed beach and dune systems. Low wind speeds can move dry sand, but higher wind speeds are necessary for rapid sand transport or for movement of wet sand because wet sand has more cohesive strength. This, in turn, depends on the tidal range in a particular coastal region because the sediment must be exposed above water to dry sufficiently to become airborne. Therefore, dunes occur in coastal areas with a large tidal range where the foreshore is wide and shallow, allowing a longer and broader low tide during which dry sand can be blown into the dunes. The sand accumulates when the wind velocity decreases or when the grains of sediment are trapped by an intervening obstacle (French, 1997), which is the principle behind sand fencing.

In addition to serving as a daily transporter of sediment, wind has a severe impact in the coastal zone during storms. The winds associated with hurricanes and other coastal storms have tremendous force; hurricane winds can exceed 200 miles (320 kilometers) per hour. The maximum wind speeds of super coastal storms are largely unknown because instruments of wind measurement have not survived such winds (Bush et al., 1996).

Hurricane-force winds can cause severe damage to the natural and built environments. The direct impact of wind on buildings during storms is highly destructive, including the phenomenon of missiling (flying debris). Vegetation in the coastal zone, including trees, shrubs, and grasses, can be uprooted, knocked over, and defoliated by the force of wind and blasts of airborne sand. Ocean spray carried inland by storm-force winds can destroy vegetation that is not salt tolerant (Bush et al., 1996).

Waves

Waves are generated when the surface of the sea is disturbed by wind, tides, or seismic activity. Wave movement and energy transfer have significant implications for coastal management. Wave conditions greatly influence sand transport, are a major factor in erosion and accretion processes, and interact with currents along the coast.

Broadly speaking, waves can be classified as either constructive or destructive. Constructive waves typically input more sediment than they remove, resulting in net sediment accretion. Destructive waves remove more sediment than they deliver, resulting in net sediment removal. Coasts often experience both wave types, often on a seasonal basis (French, 1997).

Wind waves, also called gravity waves (because gravity is the main force acting to return seawater to its equilibrium position), are perhaps the most important type of wave for coastal management purposes (French, 1997). The wave height is determined by the extent to which atmospheric energy is transferred by friction to the surface of the ocean and is therefore controlled by three factors: how fast the wind blows (wind velocity), how long the wind blows (wind duration), and how far the wind blows (wind fetch).

Wave steepness, technically defined as the ratio of wave height to

wave length, is an influential wave characteristic. Steeper waves—
waves with large height and short duration—generally are associated
with hurricanes and winter storms and tend to cause beach erosion,
which is reversed during summer when the waves are milder and of a
larger period. These seasonal changes in wave characteristics in turn
result in seasonal changes in the width of beaches (i.e., beaches tend
to be wider in the summer and narrower and flatter in winter).

A *fully developed sea* arises when the long fetch of a storm (e.g., up
to a thousand miles) and long duration (up to several days) combine to
create maximum wave heights (Viles and Spencer, 1995; Bush et al.,
1996). As waves move out of the area of generation, swell waves of
more regular height, length, and period evolve. "Swell waves may travel
over huge ocean distances with little energy loss before making landfall;
thus waves breaking on the Alaskan coastline may have been generated
by the great storms that characterize the southern oceans around Antarc-
tica" (Viles and Spencer, 1995, citing Snodgrass et al., 1966, p. 26).

The degree to which waves affect sediment transport depends
largely on the depth of the waves and the profile of the shoreline. In
deep water, the wave does not reach the bottom, and sediment remains
undisturbed. As the wave moves closer to shore, the water shallows,
allowing the wave to move the sediment. In protected coastal areas,
less wave energy is available to cause this disturbance of sediment,
whereas in areas open to the ocean, more sediment transfer occurs.
From a management point of view, we can see that the steeper the
beach profile, the more wave energy increases. Activities that cause
steepening (such as some forms of shoreline defense engineering)
result in increased wave energy and greater sediment disturbance.

Currents

The coastal wave system gives rise to two types of currents: shore-
normal and shore-parallel (longshore) currents. The latter is sometimes
called *littoral drift*. These two forms of current are largely responsible
for most coastal sediment movement, which results in changing coastal
landforms. Shore-normal currents move sediment onshore and offshore. These currents fluctuate according to the tides and also vary seasonally. The longshore current is a surf zone phenomenon and can
move sediment and other objects (including trees, stairways, decks, and
other storm debris) along the coast, removing sand from one area and
adding it to another (Bush et al., 1996). These currents are determined
by wave height or by the oblique approach of waves to the shore.

longshore = littoral drift

Bottom currents occur during major storms, when a fully developed sea approaches land. These currents move at high angles, even perpendicular to the shoreline. Although bottom currents are weak, in concert with large storm waves they can transfer large amounts of sand from the beach many miles offshore, where it may be permanently lost to the local sediment exchange system (Bush et al., 1996).

Tides

Coastal dynamics are integrally connected with tidal processes. Tides produce critical currents, affect the movement of sediment, and influence the zonation of coastal organisms, landforms, and weathering processes. Although all coastal areas are affected by tidal influences to some degree, not every coastal area experiences the same tidal heights; tides most significantly influence coastal areas with low wave energy, including lagoons, tidal bays, and estuaries (Viles and Spencer, 1995).

Tidal range—that is, the difference in elevation between high and low water marks—can be divided into three classes (French, 1997):

- Microtidal: <2 m
- Mesotidal: 2–4 m
- Macrotidal: >4 m

Open coastal areas and inland seas experience microtidal ranges, whereas macrotidal regimes are found where the tidal wave is dissipated across wide continental shelf slopes or confined in estuaries and gulfs. Around the globe, the majority of coastal environments are either macrotidal or mesotidal (Viles and Spencer, 1995). Tidal range is an important concept for managers to understand because, by controlling the width of the coast subjected to alternate periods of wet and dry, it is a major determinant of coastal ecology. For instance, intertidal habitats such as salt marshes exist only in areas where the tidal pulses can reach. Coastal geomorphology is also affected by tidal range as it affects the impact of waves on a particular shoreline and the formation of deltas (Viles and Spencer, 1995; French, 1997).

Tides are cyclical, influenced by the gravitational forces of the sun and the moon. The most obvious tidal event is the twice-daily (semidiurnal) rise and fall of the sea. Other astronomical tidal cycles also occur. Every 29 days the tides fluctuate between increased height, known as the spring tide (with no inference of season), and decreased height, or the neap tide. Spring tides occur when the earth, moon, and sun are aligned; neap tides occur when the earth–moon and earth–sun axes are at right angles to each other (Viles and Spencer, 1995; French, 1997). In addition to these cycles, seasonal fluctuations in tides occur. In the spring and autumn, the fortnightly spring tides reach their maximum, whereas the lowest tides occur in the summer and winter. Finally, there is tidal variation on even longer time spans such as annual cycles and the maximum 18.6-year nodal cycle, controlled by variations in the lunar orbit, when the highest tides of all occur. In sum, tidal heights fluctuate on several scales:

- twice a day (high and low tide)
- fortnightly (spring and neaps)
- seasonally (equinox tides)
- annual cycles
- every 18.6 years (nodal cycle) (French, 1997)

The physics of these tidal dynamics is a complex relationship between the influence of lunar processes and wave motion. The ramifications for coastal management become most obvious when regulatory requirements are imposed based on tidal boundaries (e.g., construction setbacks for oceanfront property) or when the tidal influence defines the jurisdictional boundaries of management authority or property ownership.

Hurricanes and Extratropical Storms

Hurricanes and extratropical storms are a normal part of the coastal environment and major actors in modifying coastal landforms and ecosystems. As population and development pressures along coastlines continue to rise, these large storm events pose an increasing threat to people and property. As coastal communities continue to grow, we can only expect that both direct and indirect costs associated with natural hazards will rise. Not only will property loss and disaster relief expenses continue to increase, but long-term impacts of disasters will also rise, including more business interruptions and failures, increased social and family disruption and dislocation, and damage to natural resources and ecosystems (Heinz Center for Science, Economics, and the Environment, 2000b). Managing coastal areas to mitigate the impacts of natural hazards will only become more imperative as development continues to boom along shorelines. (The topic of hazard mitigation is developed further in Chapter 3.)

On average, three hurricanes strike the Atlantic and Gulf coasts every 3 years. The probability of being hit by a hurricane or an extra-

Photo 2.6. In 1996 Hurricane Fran destroyed this home in North Topsall Beach, North Carolina. (Photo by Federal Emergency Management Agency.)

Photo 2.7. Hurricanes have social and economic effects that are felt by residents and businesses alike. Here, a commercial district in Kinston, North Carolina is flooded following Hurricane Floyd in 1999. (Photo by North Carolina Division of Emergency Management.)

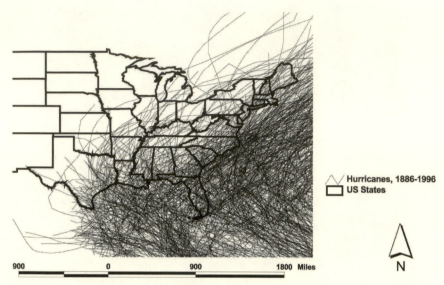

Figure 2.6. Hurricanes pose significant risk to the East and Gulf coasts of the United States. This figure depicts the paths of all Atlantic Basin hurricanes from 1886 to 1996. (From Coastal Service Center, NOAA: Alabama Coastal Hazards Assessment.)

tropical storm is not uniform but varies geographically. As might be expected, certain states are more exposed and have received a greater number of hits. Florida has received the greatest number of hurricane landfalls, followed by Texas, Louisiana, and North Carolina. The hurricane track map depicted in Figure 2.6 clearly illustrates the frequency of hurricanes along the Eastern seaboard.

Hurricanes are cyclonic storms that originate in tropical ocean waters poleward of about 5 degrees latitude. Basically, hurricanes are heat engines, fueled by the release of latent heat from the condensation of warm water. Their formation requires a low pressure disturbance, sufficiently warm sea surface temperature, rotational force from the spinning of the earth, and the absence of wind shear in the lowest 50,000 feet of the atmosphere.

Hurricanes that strike the Atlantic coast form in the Atlantic Basin, from the west coast of Africa westward into the Caribbean Sea and Gulf of Mexico. Hurricanes in this basin generally form between June 1 and November 30, with a peak around mid-September. As an incipient hurricane develops, barometric pressure at its center (or eye) falls and

Photo 2.8. Satellite photograph of Hurricane Fran making landfall in 1996. (Photo by NOAA.)

winds increase. Winds at or exceeding 39 mph result in the formation of a tropical storm, which is given a name and closely monitored by the National Oceanic and Atmospheric Administration (NOAA) National Hurricane Center in Miami, Florida. When winds are at 74 mph or more, the tropical storm is deemed a hurricane.

Hurricanes have the greatest potential to inflict damage as they cross the coastline from the sea, which is called landfall. Because hurricanes derive their strength from warm ocean waters, they are generally subject to deterioration once they make landfall. The forward momentum of a hurricane can vary from just a few miles per hour to up to 40 mph. This forward motion, combined with a counterclockwise surface flow, makes the right front quadrant of the hurricane the location of the most potentially damaging winds (see Photo 2.8).

Hurricane intensity is measured using the Saffir–Simpson scale, ranging from category 1, the weakest, least damaging hurricane, to category 5, a catastrophic hurricane (Table 2.2). The scale categorizes hurricane intensity linearly based on maximum sustained winds, minimum barometric pressure, and storm surge potential, which are combined to estimate the potential flooding and damage to property given a hurricane's estimated intensity (Table 2.3).

In addition to hurricanes and tropical storms, all U.S. coastlines are

Table 2.2 Saffir–Simpson Hurricane Scale

Saffir–Simpson category	Maximum sustained wind speed			Minimum surface pressure	Storm surge	
	mph	meters/ second	knots	millibars	feet	meters
1	74–96	33–42	64–83	Greater than 980	3–5	1.0–1.7
2	97–111	43–49	84–96	965–980	6–8	1.8–2.6
3	112–131	50–58	97–113	945–964	9–12	2.7–3.8
4	132–155	59–69	114–135	920–944	13–18	3.9–5.6
5	156+	70+	136+	Less than 920	19+	5.7+

Table 2.3. Hurricane Damage by Category

Category	Level	Description	Example
1	Minimal	Damage primarily to shrubbery, trees, foliage, and unanchored homes. No real damage to other structures. Some damage to poorly constructed signs. Low-lying coastal roads inundated. Minor pier damage. Some small craft in exposed anchorage torn from moorings.	Hurricane Jerry (1989)
2	Moderate	Considerable damage to shrubbery and tree foliage; some trees blown down. Major damage to exposed mobile homes. Extensive damage to poorly constructed signs. Some damage to roofing materials of buildings; some window and door damage. No major damage to buildings. Coast roads and low-lying escape routes inland cut by rising water 2 to 4 hours before arrival of hurricane center. Considerable damage to piers. Marinas flooded. Small craft in unprotected anchorages torn from moorings. Evacuation of some shoreline residences and low-lying areas needed.	Hurricane Bob (1991)
3	Extensive	Foliage torn from trees; large trees blown down. Practically all poorly constructed signs blown down. Some damage to roofing materials of buildings; some wind and door damage. Some structural damage to small buildings. Mobile homes destroyed. Serious flooding at coast and many smaller structures near coast destroyed; larger structures near coast damaged by battering waves and floating debris. Low-lying escape routes inland cut by rising water 3 to 5 hours before hurricane center arrives. Flat terrain	Hurricane Gloria (1985), Hurricane Fran (1996)

Category	Level	Description	Example
		5 feet or less above sea level flooded inland 8 miles or more. Evacuation of low-lying residences within several blocks of shoreline possibly needed.	
4	Extreme	Shrubs and trees blown down; all signs down. Extensive damage to roofing materials, windows, and doors. Complete failures of roofs on many small residences. Complete destruction of mobile homes. Flat terrain 10 feet or less above sea level flooded inland as far as 6 miles. Major damage to lower floors of structures near shore caused by flooding and battering by waves and floating debris. Low-lying escape routes inland cut by rising water 3 to 5 hours before hurricane center arrives. Major erosion of beaches. Evacuation of all residences within 500 yards of shore and of single-story residences within 2 miles of shore possibly needed.	Hurricane Andrew (1992)
5	Catastrophic	Shrubs and trees blown down; considerable damage to roofs of buildings; all signs down. Very severe and extensive damage to windows and doors. Complete failure of roofs on many residences and industrial buildings. Extensive shattering of glass in windows and doors. Some complete building failures. Small buildings overturned or blown away. Complete destruction of mobile homes. Major damage to lower floors of all structures less than 15 feet above sea level within 500 yards of shore. Low-lying escape routes inland cut by rising water 3 to 5 hours before hurricane center arrives. Evacuation of residential areas on low ground within 5 to 10 miles of shore possibly needed.	Hurricane Camille (1969)

subject to a variety of nonhurricane or extratropical storms. Called variously nor'easters, southwesters, and other names depending on wind direction, these winter storms can be devastating in terms of size, frequency, and duration. The Atlantic seaboard, the Pacific coast, the Gulf of Mexico, and the shores of Alaska are all subject to the widespread property damage and loss of life that these storms can cause.

Nor'easters are called extratropical cyclones because they form during the winter in midlatitudes where there is a large temperature gradient between the air flowing over the cold terrestrial environment and the warmer ocean waters. As a low-pressure system moves over the ocean, it can pick up energy from the warmer water and grow into a fully developed nor'easter. As the storm tracks up the Atlantic or Gulf coasts, it can intensify even more (Bush et al., 1996).

The slower-moving nor'easters can be even more damaging than hurricanes because they can remain off a coast for many days. The winds and waves can continually buffet the shore through several tidal cycles, exacerbating shoreline damage. The waves of winter storms can be generated thousands of miles away and arrive at the shoreline on a sunny day with only light local sea breezes (Bush et al., 1996).

The Dolan–Davis Nor'easter Intensity Scale was developed to classify winter storms along the Atlantic seaboard. The scale is based on levels of coastal degradation, not on wind velocity (Table 2.4).

Forces associated with hurricanes and coastal storms include storm surge, heightened wave action, torrential rains, and high winds. Along the Gulf and Atlantic coasts, storm surge can be especially great as a result of the wider continental shelf and gently sloping shoreline, where water can pile up. Storm surge piles up against the land, forcing its absolute height to elevations well above the high tide mark, resulting in severe flooding (Bush et al., 1996). During Hurricane Hugo, for instance, the storm surge at Bulls Bay, South Carolina, was as high as 20 feet above normal tides.

Storm surge and coastal flooding can result in substantial shoreline

Table 2.4. The Dolan–Davis Nor'easter Intensity Scale

Storm class	Beach erosion	Dune erosion	Overwash	Property damage
1 (weak)	Minor changes	None	No	No
2 (moderate)	Modest; mostly to lower beach	Minor	No	Modest
3 (significant)	Erosion extends across beach	Can be significant	No	Loss of many structures at local level
4 (severe)	Severe beach erosion and recession	Severe dune erosion or destruction	On low beaches	Loss of structures at community scale
5 (extreme)	Extreme beach erosion	Dunes destroyed over extensive areas	Massive in sheets and channels	Extensive at regional scale; millions of dollars

erosion and overwashing of barrier islands and, in certain instances, can cause breaches, creating new inlets or reopening historical inlets. For example, a new inlet was formed on Pawleys Island, South Carolina, during Hurricane Hugo in 1989. The rain bands associated with hurricanes can stretch for many miles from the eye of the storm, and even a hurricane that does not take an inland path can cause severe flooding in areas far removed from the point of landfall.

In addition to loss of human life and property damage, hurricanes and extratropical storms can wreak substantial damage to the natural environment. Wind, storm surge, and flooding can damage or destroy plants and animals, alter habitats, and lead to the spread of invasive or exotic plant and animal species. The landscape itself can be destroyed, causing habitat loss and reductions in biodiversity. Natural ecosystems can be disturbed by the loss of old-growth forests, dunes, and swamps. Sediment and pollutant loading of coastal rivers, tributaries, and estuaries and saltwater intrusion into surface water and groundwater can also greatly disturb the balance of coastal ecosystems (Heinz Center for Science, Economics, and the Environment, 2000a). For instance, after Hurricane Floyd in 1999, the salinity of estuarine systems was changed by the huge influx of freshwater from upstream flooding that was caused by torrential hurricane rains inland. Fortunately, the large volume of water also diluted many of the pollutants that entered the riverine system from flooded wastewater treatment plants, hog waste lagoons, chemical storage sites, and other environmentally hazardous facilities. The extent of fish kills and other environmental impacts that were first predicted after Hurricane Floyd did not reach the levels feared, probably because of this dilution effect.

Sea Level Rise

Over geologic time the rise and fall of the sea has been a major force in shaping coastlines. The last major period of sea level rise began approximately 18,000 years ago, at the end of the Pleistocene period, and is a likely explanation for much of the shoreline retreat that has occurred around the world. Sea level rise slowed dramatically some 7,000 years ago, but sea levels have been rising gradually throughout and since the twentieth century, as measured by tidal gauges around the world. This recent historical rate has been on the order of about 1 to 2 millimeters per year, or about a foot per century. Even very small amounts of sea level rise can represent significant shoreline movement in low-lying and gradually sloping coastal areas such as along the East coast of the United States.

Largely in response to global warming, there has been great concern in recent years about the possibility of accelerated sea level rise. As polar ice caps melt, an increased volume of water will enter the world's oceans. Some global warming has been attributed to human activities, and although there is not complete consensus among the scientific community about the extent of human influence, most agree that global warming is a real phenomenon. Much of the scientific disagreement recently has tended to center on the rate and degree of future global warming, not on whether it will happen.

Estimates of future sea level rise have varied widely, but the consensus seems to be developing around a likely range of 0.5 to 2 meters by the year 2100. According to even the lowest predictions, accelerated sea level rise could result in substantial flooding of both the built and the natural environments. Substantial property damage could result, and under various scenarios some coastal areas could lose up to half their land area because of shoreline changes caused by sea level rise. The economic consequences could be astounding.

The potential impacts of sea level rise on coastal biodiversity could also be severe. Coastal areas harbor a disproportionate number of rare and endangered species, and many of these are found only in a narrow band along the coast, especially in coastal wetlands habitats. These species include the key deer, the Perdido Key beach mouse, the California clapper rail, and the loggerhead sea turtle.

The ramifications for coastal management become evident once the process and impacts of sea level rise are understood. Some observers advocate a full retreat from the shoreline in anticipation that parts of the coast will no longer be there in a few decades. At the very least, regulatory measures and resource strategies must take into consideration the long-term and even perhaps the short-term implications of sea level rise and changing coastal dynamics.

Erosion and Accretion

We have already introduced the mechanics of erosion and accretion in the discussion of wind, waves, and currents; these processes move sediment in and out of the coastal system. We have also mentioned that coastal storms and sea level rise play a major role in shoreline change. This section expands upon that discussion to give a brief overview of the impact of erosion and accretion on a coastal area.

All shoreline types (with the exception of crystalline bedrock and certain corals) are susceptible to erosion. In the United States, all 30 coastal states experience localized erosion, some of it severe. Accretion or stability of the coastline is much less common (French, 1997).

Accretion is the seaward buildup of coastal land that occurs when the supply of sediment is greater than the erosive impacts of sea level rise and prevailing wave and wind conditions. It is an unusual phenomenon on barrier islands anywhere in the world other than spits or islands associated with major river deltas (Bush et al., 1996). Sunset Beach, a barrier island in North Carolina, is cited as an exception to this general rule; its remarkable history of accretion is "a problem all oceanfront communities would like to share" (Bush et al., 1996). According to long-term annual rates of shoreline change, the island's midsection experiences accretion of more than 8 feet per year, although the island's ends show net erosion. A substantial dune field has developed because of the accretion. The reasons behind the accretion of Sunset Beach are unknown, but inlet dynamics are a likely influence, and ebb tidal shoals protect the island from some of the force of incoming waves. Changes in local sediment source or a change in wave refraction resulting from the artificial relocation of Tubbs Inlet may also be contributing to the accretion. When conditions change, Sunset Beach probably will become a more typical (i.e., eroding) barrier island (Bush et al., 1996).

Erosion is the landward displacement of the shoreline and is a much more common and problematic process than accretion. Erosion occurs faster in some areas than in others, especially near inlets and capes, where sand shifts rapidly. Some erosion is temporary; that is, the shoreline will return to a previous built-up condition as sediment that is removed is replaced in the natural course of the sand-sharing system. Some sand is lost permanently to local sediment transport systems when it is carried too far out to sea to be available to restore the beach. The waves and storm surge of strong coastal storms can shift sediment in the opposite direction, creating overwash deposits on the back of barrier islands and into the lagoons, although this sand may eventually be blown back into the dunes (Platt et al., 1992b; Bush et al., 1996). Sand can also be removed from the system by human activities, including trucking it away for construction purposes or other uses elsewhere, and by coastal engineering projects such as groins, jetties, and seawalls that interrupt the normal flow of sediment and starve coastal areas downdrift.

Photo 2.9. After Hurricane Floyd in 1999, the dunes on this beach in North Carolina were slowly eaten away by erosion. (Photo by North Carolina Division of Emergency Management.)

It is difficult to quantify the extent to which erosion of vulnerable developed shorelines in the gulf, ocean, and Great Lakes areas affects our society and economy, but the effects are substantial. Thousands of private dwellings and commercial and public structures are at risk of collapse because of erosion (see Photo 2.9). Even when structures are not completely undermined by erosion, exposed septic tanks, water lines, eroded roads, and other infrastructure further inconvenience and endanger populations near the shore. Not only are buildings and facilities at risk, but the land itself, a precious commodity in coastal areas, can disappear. The ramifications for ownership, liability, and economic investment issues are boundless when coastal real estate is lost to the sea. However, as noted by Peter French, "it is the ways in which humans use the coast which cause the problems, not the natural processes" (p. 4). Citing Clayton (1995), French continues, "If humans did not seek to make use of the coastal zone, there would be few problems as a result of the occurrence of coastal erosion; that is, erosion, and the subsequent need for defenses, is considered a problem only because human activities have occurred which make land too valuable to be allowed to erode" (French, 1997, p. 4).

erosion can cause damage to property (so many people at coast)

Coastal Organisms

We have chosen to adopt a process or system-based classification rather than a purely geophysical one when describing individual types of coastal environments because it is the natural processes and the human influences on or responses to those processes that are the focus of this book. A word on the organic component of the coastal system is warranted here because, though often overshadowed in the literature by the geological formations and inanimate processes of sediment and water movement, the biological influence of plants, animals, and microorganisms is a vital and integral part of the coastal world.

Coastal organisms not only rely on and are affected by their physical environment but are often major agents of change themselves. For example, sea oats and other coastal grasses help form sand dunes as they anchor sand deposits. Benthic (sediment-dwelling) organisms play a direct role in sediment dynamics as they burrow, feed, and produce waste. Some biota even dominate their environments, such as the solid framework of coral reefs that is constructed by organic sources (Viles and Spencer, 1995).

Because of the fluidity of the marine environment, impacts of one coastal ecosystem—chemical, physical, and biological—spill over into other ecosystems, following water circulation patterns or traveling through marine food chains. There is also extensive exchange with neighboring terrestrial ecosystems, even many miles upland, with freshwater streams that drain into the coastal zone. This fluid nature contributes to a broad distribution of species within coastal ecosystems. Some marine species may even spend one life stage in one ecosystem and the next life stage in another. Numerous other animals, including seabirds, survive in both the terrestrial and the marine environments (Thorne-Miller and Catena, 1991).

Coastal organisms are subject to both natural and human-induced disturbances. The natural disturbances act as a check on organism productivity and species diversity. Examples of natural disturbances include storms and the invasion of species. For example, the starfish *Acanthaster* poses a significant risk to the coral reefs where it lives and preys on the organisms that make up the reef (Viles and Spencer, 1995). Likewise, coastal organisms are also sensitive to human-induced environmental degradation, including dredging and spoil dumping in bays and coastal wetlands, increased runoff and sediment loads into coastal waters caused by urbanization, and sewage discharge, which introduces a nutrient subsidy in the form of high levels of nitrogen and phosphorus into the ecosystem.

Even though we understand only a fraction of the interactive nature of the biological and geophysical aspects of the coastal zone, it is evident that disturbances to either the organisms or the geomorphology of the coastal zone can have dramatic ramifications for the whole system.

The Great Lakes

The Great Lakes—Superior, Michigan, Huron, Erie, and Ontario—are considered a fourth seacoast in the United States and are a dominant factor in the Canadian industrial economy (Figure 2.7). The lake system spans more than 750 miles (1,200 kilometers) from west to east and is the largest system of fresh surface water on earth, containing roughly 18% of the world supply, second only to the polar ice caps.

Geomorphology

The Great Lakes basin is a young ecosystem, formed in the last 10,000 years. However, its origins are several geologic eras and many millions of years ago. As continental glaciers slid south during the Pleistocene epoch, they scoured the surface of the earth, leveling the hills and deepening the valleys created in the previous era. As the climate of the earth warmed, the glaciers melted, and vegetation and wildlife appeared. Large volumes of meltwater filled the depressions made by the glaciers, creating large glacial lakes. As the glaciers receded, the land rose, and the uplift created dramatic changes in the depth, size, and drainage patterns of the glacial lakes. Although the uplift has slowed greatly, it is still occurring in the northern portion of the basin. This, along with changing long-term weather patterns, indicates that the lakes are a very dynamic system that continues to evolve.

Lake Characteristics

Although part of a single system, each lake is different. Because the watershed is so large, physical characteristics such as climate, soils, and topography vary across the basin. The climate of the northern areas of the basin generally is cold, and the area is sparsely populated. Coniferous forests and rocky shorelines characterize the terrain, and a thin layer of acidic soils covers a granite bedrock. The southern portion of the basin is warmer, with deep soils of clay, silt, sand, gravel, and gla-

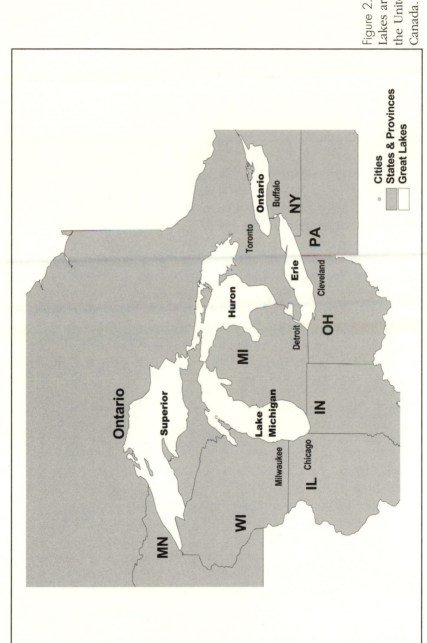

Figure 2.7. The Great Lakes are bordered by the United States and Canada.

cial boulders. The land is generally fertile, and the original deciduous forests have been replaced by agricultural uses and urbanization.

The lakes vary in temperature, depth, volume, pollutant levels, and retention times (retention time is the mean rate of outflow relative to water volume). Lake Superior is the largest, deepest, and coldest of the Great Lakes, with a retention time of 191 years. The cool climate and poor soils make agriculture difficult, and this, along with the heavy forest cover and sparse population, results in few pollutants entering Lake Superior.

Lake Michigan is the second largest of the five and is the only lake entirely within the United States. The northern part of Lake Michigan contains Green Bay, which is one of the most productive of the lakes' fisheries but also receives the waste stream from the world's largest concentration of pulp and paper mills. The southern basin of Lake Michigan is highly urbanized, including the metropolitan areas of Milwaukee and Chicago.

Lake Erie contains the smallest volume of water and is the most urbanized basin. Lake Erie also receives much runoff from the many farms in southwestern Ontario and parts of Ohio, Indiana, and Michigan. Lake Erie is the shallowest Great Lake, with an average depth of about 62 feet (19 meters) and the shortest retention time of 2.6 years.

Lake Ontario is deeper than Erie but smaller in surface area. It receives significant pollution from the major industrial areas of Hamilton and Toronto, although the U.S. shoreline is less urbanized and is not intensively farmed.

Lake Levels

The water levels of the Great Lakes can vary significantly on a short-term, seasonal, and long-term basis. Daily fluctuations are caused by winds that push water to one side of the lake in a phenomenon called wind set-up. Wind set-up usually occurs with major lake storms and can last for several days. Rapid changes in wind direction and barometric pressure can also cause seiche, another extreme form of oscillation on the lakes.

Variations in lake levels occur seasonally based on changes in precipitation and runoff into the Great Lakes. When winter snow and ice solidify the water source, the lake levels are lowest. Evaporation rates tend to be higher in winter when dry winter air masses pass over the lakes, further lowering water levels. In spring the ice and snow thaw, leading to the highest lake levels during the summer.

Long-term fluctuations in lake levels correspond to long-term trends in weather patterns, the causes of which are largely unknown. Periods of heavy rain and snowfall and lower temperatures (which decrease evaporation rates) cause high lake levels. During periods of high lake levels, storms can cause flooding and severe shoreline erosion. Shoreline property is vulnerable to the impacts of flooding and erosion, particularly when development has altered the natural protective features of dunes, wetlands, and shoreline vegetation.

Lake Stratification and Turnover

The Great Lakes form a very dynamic system, and complex processes are constantly changing the nature of the water. As in all deep lakes, changes in temperature cause stratification, or layering, of the Great Lakes. The deepest layers are insulated from the sun's light and warmth and remain cool and dense even during the summer. Surface and foreshore waters are solar heated and form a top layer that is warmer and less dense. The warmer top layer supports most of the life in the lake and is richest in oxygen. In the winter, the ice cover causes the water below to remain warmer than the air. During the spring and fall, as water temperatures rise and fall, a mixing or turnover of the entire lake occurs.

The processes of stratification and turnover are significant for water quality in the Great Lakes. Turnover disperses oxygen throughout most of the lakes on an annual basis as the oxygen-rich water of the surface is mixed with the deeper, oxygen-deprived layers. This prevents anoxia, or complete oxygen depletion. The stratification of lake water in summer can prevent the dispersion of effluents from tributaries, resulting in higher concentrations of pollutants in the foreshore waters.

Wetlands

The Great Lakes basin contains four major types of wetland: swamps, marshes, bogs, and fens. Swamps are characterized by wet organic soils that are flooded most of the year and support trees and shrubs. Ponds and protected bay areas house marshes, where aquatic plants form thick stands. Most of the swamps and marshes are found in the southern and eastern regions of the Great Lakes basin.

Sphagnum moss grows in the shallow stagnant water of bogs, often forming thick mats that decompose slowly. Fens usually are fed by groundwater and develop in shallow, slowly moving water. Small shrubs and trees, as well as peat, sedges, and grasses, grow in fens.

Fens and bogs, also called peatlands, are found in the northern and northwestern regions of the Great Lakes basin.

The wetlands of the Great Lakes serve many important ecological, economic, and recreational functions in the basin's ecosystem. A wide variety of flora and fauna, some unique to the Great Lakes basin, are found in the wetlands. Wetlands provide food, resting places, and seasonal habitats for many migratory bird species. Most fish species found in the Great Lakes use the wetlands as nursery habitat. Organic matter found in the peatlands is extensively exploited and sold as peat moss. Wetlands also buffer the impacts of erosion and flooding and help to dilute point and nonpoint source pollution entering the Great Lakes from land-based activities.

Pollution and Toxic Contaminants

Despite their large volume of water, the Great Lakes are highly susceptible to the adverse impacts of pollutants that enter the system from a variety of sources. Runoff of soil and chemicals from surrounding farms, urban waste, industrial discharges, and leachate from disposal sites all affect the lakes' water quality. Direct atmospheric pollutants from rain and snowfall also collect in the lakes because of their large surface area.

The Great Lakes are particularly vulnerable to pollution because the outflow from the lakes is small (less than 1% per year) compared with the total volume of water. Pollutants that enter the lakes—whether by direct discharge along the shores, through tributaries, from land use, or from the atmosphere—are retained in the system and become more concentrated with time. Pollutants also remain in the lakes because of resuspension of sediment and food chain cycles.

Some toxic contaminants accumulate and become magnified as they move through the food chain, posing a threat not only to aquatic life and other wildlife but also to human health. Top predators, including lake trout and fish-consuming birds, can be exposed to very high levels of toxins. Concentrations of toxic substances can be millions of times higher in animals and fish than in the water. Therefore, although the water may remain safe for humans to drink, eating exposed fish and wildlife could be harmful.

Studies of contaminated species have discovered mutations such as cross-bills and thin eggshells in birds and tumors in fish. The degree of danger to humans from long-term exposure to low levels of toxins is

unknown, but it is certain that risks to health will increase if toxic contaminants continue to accumulate in the Great Lakes ecosystem.
Impairment to reproductive and immune systems could occur, with the
risk especially high for developing children. Toxic contaminants may
also cause some cancers.

Climate Change and the Great Lakes

Throughout geologic time, the Great Lakes basin has been variously
covered by ice and tropical forests. Today, however, unprecedented
rates of change in the climate of the Great Lakes region may be attributed to increasing carbon dioxide emissions from human activity. Scientific models have indicated that at twice the carbon dioxide level, the
climate of the basin will be warmer by 2 to 4°C centigrade and slightly
damper than at present. Warmer climates will cause an increase in
evaporation from the surface of the lakes and evapotranspiration from
the land surface of the basin, thereby increasing the percentage of precipitation that is returned to the atmosphere. The resulting net basin
supply, the amount of water contributed by each lake basin to the overall hydrologic system, will be decreased by up to 50%. The lake levels
could decrease from 0.5 to 2 meters.

Such a drastic change in lake levels could have severe economic
and environmental repercussions for the Great Lakes area. The shipping industry, hydroelectric power generation, and harbors and marinas could be severely affected. Disturbances in weather patterns,
drought, and changes in growing seasons could affect crops and food
production in the basin. Habitats and fisheries could also be affected in
ways as yet unknown. Although the precise rate and degree of change
remain speculative, it is clear that global warming may have long-term
ramifications for the Great Lakes basin and its inhabitants.

Conclusions

This chapter has provided a general introduction to the physical characteristics and natural processes present in the coastal environment.
This environment is highly dynamic and also very ecologically productive. It is clear that any attempt at coastal management must begin with
an understanding of the coastal environment, including an understanding that the coast is subject to a host of natural forces and dynamics

and that interfering with these natural processes can backfire. Special care must be taken in building in dynamic coastal areas to minimize negative impacts on the ecosystem and reduce exposure of people and property to unnecessary risks such as shoreline erosion, hurricanes, and other manifestations of the forces of nature.

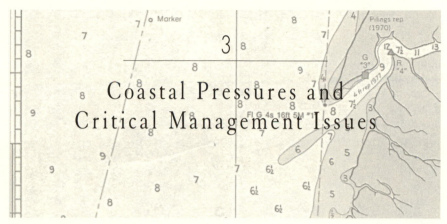

3

Coastal Pressures and
Critical Management Issues

Demographic trends suggest that coastal areas around the world, including those in the United States, are undergoing serious population growth pressures. Already, more than half of the U.S. population resides along the coast and in coastal watersheds. Bookman et al. (1999) predict that by the year 2015, the U.S. coastal population will grow to 166 million. This represents more than a 50% increase from the coastal population in 1960. By 2025 it is believed that almost 75% of the U.S. population will be living along the coast (Hinrichsen, 1999).

Coastal states are among the nation's fastest growing and will experience much of the absolute growth in population in the decades ahead. Several coastal states are predicted to experience especially high population growth rates, in particular California, Florida, Texas and Washington (Culliton, 1998). The Pacific, Gulf of Mexico and Southeast coastal regions of the U.S. are expected to experience the most population and development growth.

As Table 3.1 makes abundantly clear, the coastal counties of this country have continued to grow rapidly over the last ten years, by about 12% during this period (U.S. Bureau of Census, 2000). Growth along the U.S. coast, even within the states and regions, is not uniform, and particular coastal counties are projected to experience very high growth rates. For example, the southern California counties (Los Angeles, Orange, and San Diego) and the counties around Miami (Dade, Broward, and Palm Beach) are expected to experience very rapid growth. Of the nation's 20 fastest growing counties, 17 are coastal.

Population density is another measure of the stresses placed on

Table 3.1. Coastal County Populations, 1990 and 2000

	1990	2000	Percentage increase
Alabama	476,923	540,258	13.28
Alaska	466,410	538,332	15.42
American Samoa	46,773	63,781	36.36
California	21,859,530	24,260,099	10.98
Connecticut	2,030,017	2,120,734	4.47
Delaware	666,168	783,600	17.63
Florida	12,356,550	15,982,378	29.34
Georgia	386,415	439,154	13.65
Guam	133,152	151,968	14.13
Hawaii	1,108,229	1,062,860	−4.09
Illinois	5,659,040	6,021,097	6.40
Indiana	711,592	741,468	4.20
Louisiana	2,044,880	2,170,717	6.15
Maine	885,703	944,847	6.68
Maryland	3,339,056	3,592,430	7.59
Massachusetts	4,494,398	4,783,167	6.43
Michigan	4,640,981	4,842,023	4.33
Minnesota	212,496	216,754	2.00
Mississippi	312,368	363,988	16.53
New Hampshire	350,078	389,592	11.29
New Jersey	6,978,509	7,575,546	8.56
New York	15,026,340	16,036,955	6.73
North Carolina	710,903	826,019	16.19
Northern Mariana Islands	43,345	69,216	59.69
Ohio	2,752,987	2,767,328	0.52
Oregon	1,085,935	1,326,072	22.11
Pennsylvania	2,949,974	2,946,892	−0.10
Puerto Rico	3,008,274	3,808,610	26.60
Rhode Island	1,003,464	1,048,319	4.47
South Carolina	833,519	981,338	17.73
Texas	4,447,727	5,281,168	18.74
U.S. Virgin Islands	101,809	119,615	17.49
Virginia	3,861,122	4,440,709	15.01
Washington	3,389,033	4,070,515	20.11
Wisconsin	1,907,789	1,992,393	4.43
TOTAL	110,283,479	123,301,942	11.80

Source: Data from 1990 U.S. Census compiled by OCRM. Data from 2000 U.S. Census based on counties wholly or partially within the state's legally defined coastal zone.

Photo 3.1. Coastal areas have been experiencing tremendous growth pressure, and scenes like this one on St. George Island, Florida, are very common. (Photo by Tim Beatley.)

coastal areas. Even in 1960, coastal population densities were much higher than in other parts of the country. In that year the average population density for the nation as a whole was 62 people per square mile, compared with 248 people per square mile in coastal counties. This coastal population density was up to 277 people per square mile by 1997, about three times the national average (Bookman et al., 1999). It is projected to rise to 327 people per square mile by 2015 (Culliton, 1998).

Indeed, although more than one-half of the American population lives in coastal areas, this population occupies only a narrow coastal band and a relatively small 17% of the contiguous U.S. (Culliton, 1998). In California, some 80% of the population resides on or near the coast (only one-quarter of the state's land area), and in Florida 60% of that state's population lives within 10 miles of the coast.

Increases in coastal development and population growth in the United States mirror global trends as the planet as a whole becomes more coastal. Indeed, some two-thirds of the planet's population lives in a narrow 400-kilometer coastal band (1999). As Nichols Hinrichsen, notes, 20 of the world's 30 megacities in 2010—cities with populations of 8 million or more—will be located in coastal areas (1995).

Some statistics are also available on the extent to which the U.S. population is using coastal areas for recreational purposes. Some 180 million Americans visit the coast every year (Marlowe, 1999). National Park Service data suggest that visitation to national parks, national seashores, and national monuments has risen markedly in recent years. Coastal tourism is an economic engine now. For instance, 77 million Americans engage in recreational boating (Bookman et al., 1999), and recreational boat sales have gone up dramatically in the last two decades (Pogue and Lee, 1999).

Land Use Patterns and Human Alterations of the Coastal Zone

Historically, and for obvious reasons, settlement of the United States began along its coastlines. Since early settlement days the U.S. coastline has been used in a number of ways. Largely for transportation reasons, major industrial and commercial centers developed around port cities. Cities such as Norfolk, Virginia, and Seattle, Washington, remain important ports. The American coastal zone remains the location of major cities and urban agglomerations. According to Bookman et al. (1999), 14 of the nation's 20 largest cities are located in the coastal zone.

In more recent decades, uses of the coastline have shifted to include more recreational and conservation uses. Recreational and resort developments have increased rapidly. Resource uses of the coastal zone remain significant, including agricultural and fishing industries and oil, gas, and mineral extraction. Coastal areas are economic engines, generating some $54 billion in goods and services and 28 million jobs, according to Marlowe (1999).

There are increasingly serious signs that these economic uses of our coast are undermining their long-term sustainability. The bounty of the sea is a dramatic example, discussed further in this chapter, and is showing signs of absolute limits, as individual overfishing is exhausting and depleting fisheries around the world. Fears about offshore oil and gas development and its impact on beach and coastal environments reflect similar concerns. Beach closures and contaminated shellfish grounds are similar signs of stress.

Accompanying the increased tourism and recreational appeal of coastal areas has been a dramatic development and building boom. It is estimated that more than 750,000 dwelling units are constructed each year along the coast (Bookman et al., 1999). Homes are becoming larger and more consumptive of resources. Much of this new construction occurs in the most vulnerable locations, with an estimated 50,000 new homes built on barrier islands each year.

The value of property along the coast has skyrocketed. In New Jersey alone, the value of oceanfront property has tripled in the last 30 years, today exceeding $34 billion (Gaul and Wood, 2000). These development trends have damaged the coastal environment in a number of ways. Development has resulted in the destruction of forests and wetlands and degradation of water quality; moreover, the natural coastal environment has in many areas been replaced with a heavily human-managed landscape through the construction of seawalls and revetments, groins and jetties, and dams and other flood control projects. These issues are described in more detail later in this chapter.

Patterns of Ownership and Control

The U.S. coastal zone represents a complex pattern of ownership and control. There are several important jurisdictional zones extending seaward from the land. The following is an excerpt from *Coastal Challenges: A Guide to Coastal and Marine Issues:*

> The language that defines the marine environment from "the coast" to the "open ocean" reflects centuries of international conflict and compromise over jurisdiction. Typically, coastal countries have attempted to set limits on other nations' access. These coastal countries wanted to protect what they perceived as their own economic and military interests. This approach usually meant that coastal countries declared waters within a certain distance from their coasts as territorial waters. Other nations would be allowed to pass through these waters, but would be prohibited from fishing or engaging in other economic or military activities.
>
> By the early 1900s, the world was a crazy quilt of irregular territorial zones. Some countries claimed their zones extended three miles from their shoreline out to sea; others claimed six miles or more. In 1945, President Truman proclaimed the United States had exclusive control over its continental shelf, the underwater extension of the North American continent that stretches more than 200 miles beyond the

U.S. shoreline. This proclamation followed the discovery of rich stores of oil and mineral resources on the continental shelf.

Luc Cuyvers, in *Ocean Uses and Their Regulation,* wrote that Truman's proclamation, "called the world's attention to the notion that there was something of great value besides fish in the sea, and that nothing in international law prevented a coastal state from claiming it" (Cuyvers, 1984, p. 148).

Other countries followed the U.S. lead and declared control over broader ocean territories. The crazy quilt of zones became even more irregular. The United Nations responded by recommending that its member nations confer. In 1958, the first United Nations Convention on the Law of the Sea (UNCLOS), held in Geneva, Switzerland, attracted representatives of 86 countries. At the convention, delegates hammered out four agreements, or conventions, that began to define sea rights and responsibilities. A second meeting in 1960 expanded on the earlier agreements.

Finally, a third conference was convened in 1973. This conference (UNCLOS III) proved to be the most difficult, complicated, and comprehensive. It began with more than 400 draft articles. Conference delegates spent nearly 10 years whittling these articles down to about 320 articles and 9 annexes, forming a manageable convention that defines ocean boundaries and the rights and responsibilities of the world community in using the oceans.

This convention, more than any of its predecessors, specifically addressed ocean pollution, making it each country's duty to protect the ocean environment and conserve living resources. It mandated cooperation among neighboring coastal states to control ocean pollution from all sources.

During the previous two decades, the ocean's great mineral wealth beyond oil had come to light. Capturing that sea-bottom wealth, which included fields of manganese nodules, would be technologically challenging and expensive. But industrialized countries, such as the United States, anticipated that as technology improved, those fields could be mined economically in the near future. The UNCLOS convention placed deepwater seabeds outside the jurisdiction of any individual country and within the jurisdiction of a new institution, the International Seabed Authority.

In 1982, the United States voted against the convention, primarily because of concerns that provisions regarding deep seabed mining would restrict U.S. access to valuable seabed minerals. Despite U.S. opposition, in 1982 the majority of the conference delegates voted to adopt UNCLOS. The Deep Seabed Mining Implementing Agreement of July 1994 addressed U.S. concerns about potential mining restrictions. As a result, on 29 July 1994 the United States signed UNCLOS. Although the United States upholds all the provisions of the convention, the United States remains a provisional member. U.S. ratification will be possible once the U.S. Senate has provided its advice and consent.

At the time the United States signed the convention, it was still not in force. Sixty eligible nations had to ratify UNCLOS before the convention could enter into force. That goal was not achieved until 16 November 1994. By January 1998, the convention had been adopted by 123 parties.

Territorial Sea

This zone may extend out to 12 nautical miles (1 nautical mile equals 1,852 meters, or 6,076 feet), measured from a baseline on a country's coast. The territorial sea is considered part of a country's sovereign territory, although ships may pass through as long as passage is innocent (i.e., not done to harass, attach, or exploit the host country or its resources).

Contiguous Zone

This zone extends an additional 12 nautical miles from the territorial sea. A host country has rights to control immigration, customs, sanitary, and pollution regulations in its contiguous zone.

Exclusive Economic Zone

A country may declare an exclusive economic zone (EEZ) extending from the outer boundary of the territorial sea to 200 nautical miles from the coast baseline (i.e., the maximum EEZ width would be 188 nautical miles from the coast where the territorial sea is 12 nautical miles). Within this zone, the coastal country does not have complete sovereignty. Other countries may fly over it, navigate through it, or lay pipes or cables. However, the coastal host country has all rights to control the resources in these waters, including fisheries and mineral resources. It also may assert jurisdiction (which the United States has not) over scientific research conducted in these waters. In March 1983, the United States declared its own 200-mile EEZ through presidential proclamation.

Continental Shelf

UNCLOS provides a complex definition of the continental shelf. This zone extends a minimum of 200 nautical miles from the coastal baseline and may extend up to 350 nautical miles in special circumstances. The coastal country has exclusive jurisdiction over the mineral resources of its shelf, including oil. Up to 7 percent of the profits from mineral development beyond the 200-mile line from shore must be shared with the international community. The coastal country is obligated to protect the continental shelf's marine environment from negative consequences of oil development.

High Seas

This maritime zone extends beyond areas of national jurisdiction and is generally open and freely available for use by all. No country may interfere with the justified and equal rights of other countries on the high seas. The seabed under the high seas, home to certain mineral beds, is the common heritage of humankind, according to part of the convention. Mineral resources of the seabed are under the jurisdiction of the United Nations International Seabed Authority.

(Reproduced from *Coastal Challenges: A Guide to Coastal and Marine Issues* from the National Safety Council's Environmental Health Center, October 2000.)

The territorial sea (which originally, under international law, was measured by the distance of a cannon shot) of the United States was 3 miles from mean high water (MHW), and this area was given to the states by Congress under the terms of the Submerged Lands Act of 1953. In 1988 President Reagan extended the territorial sea to 12 miles by proclamation, but this did not generally extend the states' rights,

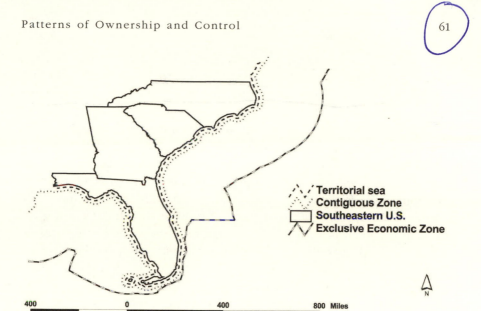

Territorial sea
Contiguous Zone
Southeastern U.S.
Exclusive Economic Zone

400   0   400   800 Miles

Figure 3.1. Federal and state boundaries. (From Ocean Planning Information System, NOAA.)

although Texas and Florida have established claims beyond 3 miles. In 1976 Congress passed the Fishery Conservation and Management Act (the Magnuson Act), extending an exclusive fishery conservation zone to 200 miles, and in 1983 President Reagan proclaimed a 200-mile EEZ (Figure 3.1).

As coastal states become increasingly involved in ocean management, it is likely that they will seek to extend their control and management beyond the existing territorial limit. For instance, the state of Oregon, under its Ocean Resources Management Program, has established an Ocean Stewardship Area, which extends seaward to the base of the continental margin (extending from 35 to 80 miles seaward) and in which management and planning activities are focused. At least for purposes of planning coordination, coastal states are increasingly likely to want to expand their influence beyond the 12-mile limit.

Layered on top of these zones are additional rights of public use created through a combination of federal and state laws, constitutions, and judicial interpretations. Under the federal doctrine of navigational servitude, the federal government protects the right of movement along navigable waters and exercises regulatory control over structures and activities that may impede this right.

At the state level, common-law doctrine has played an important role in establishing public rights of access to coastal resources. In a majority of coastal states the public trust doctrine (or a similar doctrinal basis) ensures the public's right to walk along and use the shoreline (or a certain portion of it). The boundary of this public right varies from state to state, but seaward of MHW is the typical boundary, thus protecting access to the wet beach.

In some states, notably Texas and Oregon, the public trust boundary is the first natural line of vegetation, thus encompassing a sizable portion of the dry beach as well (Kalo, 2000). This line of demarcation has been interpreted by the courts to be dynamic and subject to periodic movement, as in response to natural erosion or coastal storms. Thus the line is a "rolling public easement" with many implications for coastal homeowners. A major example of such implications became apparent after Hurricane Alicia, which struck the Galveston, Texas, shoreline in 1983 (Godschalk et al., 1989). Because the first line of vegetation was moved landward by the hurricane, buildings that were once landward of this line were located seaward after the storm. Homeowners with heavily damaged structures were prevented from rebuilding by the state because such reconstruction would then have been located on the public beach. Several landowners sued the state, claiming that the restrictions amounted to unconstitutional takings by the state. However, the state supreme court found in favor of the state, upholding the public's ownership of the dry beach under the doctrine of customary use.

Many state coastal management programs have delimited regulatory zones in which certain permits are required before development or use of these areas can proceed. Under North Carolina's Coastal Area Management Act, for example, proposed development in Areas of Environmental Concern is subject to a variety of controls. Larger structures built along the ocean (within so-called ocean erodible zones) must be set back a minimum distance of 60 times the average annual rate of erosion for that stretch of shoreline. As a further example, the state of New York has designated shoreline erosion zones that restrict new construction to movable structures only. Most coastal states apply some degree of coastal regulation and management to wetlands, beaches, and sensitive coastal resources.

Actual ownership patterns along the coast are a mixture of public and private. Public ownership occurs, to some extent, at all government levels. At the federal level, ownership of conservation units consists of national seashores (such as Cape Hatteras National Seashore), national recreation areas (such as the Oregon Dunes National Recreational Area), national wildlife refuges (such as the Alligator River National Wildlife Refuge), national monuments, and national forests (such as the Francis Marion National Forest on the South Carolina coast). Extensive federal military facilities also exist (e.g., Camp Pendleton Marine Base).

Planning and management of these different federal units are splintered. For example, the U.S. Fish and Wildlife Service (FWS) has authority over national wildlife refuges, while the National Park Service has control over national seashores and monuments. The U.S. Forest Service, on the other hand, has authority over the management of national forests.

State ownership includes state parks, wildlife management areas, and state historic sites. Extensive local ownership of coastal lands is less typical. However, it is not uncommon for coastal localities to own beachfront parks and recreational facilities. The city of Myrtle Beach, South Carolina, for instance, owns a major strip of beachfront land.

Critical Coastal Management Issues: The Challenge of Sustaining the Coast

The population and development pressures that coastal areas experience generate a number of critical problems and policy issues and raise serious and difficult challenges for coastal planners. What follows is a brief identification of some of the more critical of these contemporary management issues facing America's coastal areas and a discussion of some of the policy and planning options available to address them.

Each of the following issues represents one aspect or dimension of the broader challenge of sustainably managing America's coasts. Although we discuss the issues separately, they are clearly interrelated and part of a complex and interwoven planning and policy matrix.

Coastal Storm Mitigation

As discussed in Chapter 2, the U.S. coastline is subject to a variety of natural hazards. Along the Gulf and Atlantic coasts, hurricanes and tropical storms are a normal and regular occurrence. Although the chances of any one location being struck are fairly small, the physical forces are severe and the impacts potentially catastrophic, forcing coastal states and localities to resolve how best to cope with these threats. In addition to hurricanes, the East coast regularly faces severe nor'easters, and the Pacific coast and other parts of the U.S. coastline face similar storms.

Hurricanes can cause major loss of life and property destruction. The Galveston Island hurricane of 1900 resulted in some 6,000 deaths. Because of the development of a reliable hurricane tracking and warning system in the United States, the number of deaths from hurricanes has declined gradually over the last century. However, property destruction has increased markedly. Between 1899 and 1998 there were an estimated 342 named landfalling storms. The majority are smaller storms, with only about 18 in category 4 or 5 on the Saffir–Simpson scale. These large hurricanes cause the most property destruction, however. Indeed, only about one-quarter of the landfall hurricanes are in categories 3 to 5, yet these larger storms account for some 85% of property damage.

Hurricanes cause substantial property and economic losses as well as loss of life and human suffering. Recent hurricanes to hit the U.S. illustrate this well; for instance, Hurricane Floyd damaged a large area of North Carolina, affected some 5 million residents, and caused 49 deaths. Hurricane Andrew remains the most damaging, most costly storm on record, with more than $27 billion in property destruction. Some 63,000 homes were destroyed in the event, with another 110,000 experiencing damage. Had the hurricane hit Miami only a few miles north, the damages would have been much greater, probably $50 billion or more.

Damages from hurricanes and coastal storms have risen in recent years at an alarming rate. Whether we are already experiencing heightened storm activity and frequency as a result of global climate change is debatable, but there can be little doubt that dramatic rises in coastal population and wealth have accounted for increases in damage levels from storms. Roger Pielke and Christopher Landsea (1998) have effectively demonstrated this by "normalizing" hurricanes that have struck the U.S. mainland over the period 1925–1995—that is, by adjusting not only for inflation but for increasing coastal population growth and increasing societal wealth. Table 3.2 presents the top 30 hurricanes, by damage level, during this period. A large hurricane such as the storm that hit southeastern Florida and Alabama in 1926 would have caused a startling $72 billion damage if it had hit these coastlines in 1995, more than twice the estimated damage level from Hurricane Andrew. Pielke

Table 3.2. Top 30 Damaging Hurricanes, Normalized to 1995 dollars

Rank	Hurricane	Year	Category	Damage (billion U.S.$)
1.	SE Florida/Alabama	1926	4	72.303
2.	Andrew (SE FL/LA)	1992	4	33.094
3.	SW Florida	1944	3	16.864
4.	New England	1938	3	16.629
5.	SE Florida/Lake Okeechobee	1928	4	13.795
6.	Betsy (SE FL/LA)	1965	3	12.434
7.	Donna (FL/Eastern U.S.)	1960	4	12.048
8.	Camille (MS/LA/VA)	1969	5	10.965
9.	Agnes (NW FL, NE U.S.)	1972	1	10.705
10.	Diane (NE U.S.)	1955	1	10.232
11.	Hugo (SC)	1989	4	9.380
12.	Carol (NE U.S.)	1954	3	9.066
13.	SE Florida/Louisiana/Alabama	1947	4	8.308
14.	Carla (N & Central TX)	1961	4	7.069
15.	Hazel (SC/NC)	1954	4	7.039
16.	NE U.S.	1944	3	6.536
17.	SE Florida	1945	3	6.313
18.	Frederic (AL/MS)	1979	3	6.293
19.	SE Florida	1949	3	5.838
20.	Alicia (N TX)	1983	3	4.056
21.	Celia (S TX)	1970	3	3.338
22.	Dora (NE FL)	1964	2	3.108
23.	Opal (NW FL/AL)	1995	3	3.000
24.	Cleo (SE FL)	1964	2	2.435
25.	Juan (LA)	1985	1	2.399
26.	Audrey (LA/N TX)	1957	4	2.396
27.	King (SE FL)	1950	3	2.266
28.	E Florida/Georgia/S. Carolina	1947	2	2.263
29.	SE Florida	1935	2	2.191
30.	Elena (MS/AL/NW FL)	1985	3	2.064

Source: Pielke and Landsea (1998).

Note: Normalized to 1995 dollars by inflation, personal property increases, and coastal county population changes (1925–1995).

and Landsea estimate that annual hurricane damages are about $4.8 billion, much higher than previously estimated.

Although some in the scientific community dispute that global climate change can be seen in increased hurricane frequency, changes in natural hurricane cycles are of more immediate concern. Professor

William M. Gray, of the Department of Atmospheric Science at Colorado State University, has done much work analyzing relationships between hurricane activity and other important weather and global environmental trends and conditions. His annual predictions of hurricane activity are based on a complex interplay between such things as surface ocean temperatures, upper atmospheric wind patterns, and drought conditions in West Africa. In 1999, Gray testified before Congress about what he believes is a decadal shift in the direction of increased hurricane activity. Noting a "major reconfiguration of the 'thermohaline' circulation of the Atlantic Ocean leading to alterations in surface pressure and sea surface temperature throughout much of the Atlantic basin" (Gray, 1999, p. 1), Gray believes the result will be a return to climate conditions that existed in the 1940s and 1950s. He believes we are cycling out of a period of low hurricane threat (1970–1994) and probably are "entering a period of intense hurricane activity" with destruction rising to "unprecedented levels" (p. 1). Gray's conclusions about our readiness for this shift are somber: "Sadly, the large threat posed by landfalling major hurricanes has yet to be fully recognized, either by the general public or by most U.S. government officials" (p. 2).

The threat from hurricanes and other coastal storms has increased substantially because the amount of development and number of people now in high-risk coastal zones have risen dramatically. Much of this development has occurred since the 1950s during an unusual lull in major storm activity. Only a small percentage of the coastal population has actually experienced a hurricane or major storm; surveys show that about 70% of the present coastal population has not.

To protect coastal property, states and localities have a number of policy options. Discussed in greater detail in later chapters, these options include:

- structural reinforcement (e.g., seawalls)
- "soft" shoreline reinforcement (beach renourishment)
- hazard zone avoidance (e.g., coastal setbacks, density restrictions)
- building codes and elevation

A major policy distinction can be made between strategies that seek to avoid exposure (e.g., keeping buildings out of high-risk coastal hazard zones) and those that seek to buttress against the forces of nature (e.g., seawalls).

Evacuation is also a major policy issue in most coastal areas, espe-

Photo 3.2. In 1999 Hurricane Dennis had an unusual track, shown here. It developed over the Bahamas and remained just off the coast of North Carolina for a day in late August. In September it returned as a tropical storm, causing significant erosion and storm surge damage. (Photo by the State Climate Office of North Carolina.)

cially on barrier islands, where population growth has resulted in substantial increases in the time it takes to evacuate residents in the event of an oncoming storm. On Galveston Island, Texas, for instance, evacuation times are estimated at 24 to 36 hours, and they are rising. Substantial rises in evacuation times can be seen in the Outer Banks of North Carolina and the Florida Keys, among many other coastal locations. Moreover, most hurricane experts admit that we have reached a plateau in the ability to predict the future direction of a hurricane and to warn coastal communities of an oncoming storm. The National Hurricane Center in Coral Gables, Florida, is very good at tracking hurricanes, but the unpredictable nature of these events means that they often do not go where they are expected to go. Hurricane Dennis in 1999 is a case in point (Photo 3.2). The tracking map for this event illustrates how unpredictable hurricanes can be, changing directions and speed several times and largely confounding predictions about its likely landfall.

Similarly, Hurricane Hugo veered from its predicted path, assuming a track much farther landward than predicted. Thus, although the National Hurricane Center says it can provide approximately a 12-hour warning before a strike, evacuation times in many communities are much longer. This often presents a dilemma for coastal officials, who must decide to call for an evacuation many hours before they know whether the storm will actually strike their location.

In planning for evacuation, coastal states and communities have many options, including:

- horizontal evacuation (e.g., roads and bridges with enough capacity to allow effective evacuation; adequate warning and preparedness systems)
- vertical evacuation (housing a significant number of coastal residents in engineered structures during a storm)
- growth caps (e.g., limits on the amount of development to not exceed evacuation capability, such as the approach taken by Sanibel Island, Florida)

Vertical evacuation has not been heavily used in coastal areas. However, many experts believe that in areas where population and development continue to increase, this approach may be the only option available. There are a number of potential difficulties in vertical evacuation, however. One is simply finding engineered structures that can survive during a hurricane or major storm. Recent structural surveys are discouraging on this point, indicating that few buildings are safe enough to serve as shelters during a storm. Potential legal liability is another concern that has not yet been resolved. Some critics of vertical evacuation have charged that its use may serve as a way to justify even greater development and growth in coastal areas (Salmon, 1984).

Shoreline Erosion and Sea Level Rise

Many coastal areas are facing chronic long-term shoreline erosion problems. This is especially a problem along the low-lying barrier island systems of the Gulf and Atlantic coasts. Average erosion rates are 6 feet per year along the Gulf and 2 to 3 feet per year along the Atlantic. Some coastal areas may be accreting in the short term, but the general trend is in the direction of shoreline retreat. Historically, the U.S. barrier island system has been gradually moving landward, largely in response to gradual sea level rise (Pilkey et al., 1998; Bush et al., 1996; Titus, 1998).

Few national assessments of the shoreline erosion problem have been undertaken. The first comprehensive assessment of the extent of

Table 3.3. Nationwide Estimate of Structures Susceptible to Erosion[a]

Variable	Atlantic coast	Gulf of Mexico	Pacific coast	Great Lakes	Total
Length of coastline					
Miles	2,300	2,000	1,600	3,600	9,500
% of total	24%	21%	17%	38%	
Structures within 500 feet of shoreline					
Number	170,000	44,000	66,000	58,000	338,000
% of total	50%	13%	20%	17%	
Structures within 60-year erosion hazard area (EHA)[b]					
Number	53,000	13,000	4,600	16,000	87,000
EHA structures as % of those within 500 feet of shoreline					
	31%	29%	7%	28%	
Structures within 60-year EHA assuming all open lots are filled					
Number	76,000	5,200	>16,000[c]	>120,000	

Source: Heinz Center (2000b).

[a]All estimates exclude structures in major urban areas. The analysis assumes that these structures will be protected from the erosion hazard.
[b]The 60-year EHA is determined by multiplying local erosion rates by 60 years.
[c]Data on open lots not available for the Great Lakes.

coastal erosion in the United States was conducted by the Heinz Center for Science, Economics, and the Environment in 2000. They conclude that an astounding 350,000 structures are located within 500 feet of the shoreline in the lower 48 states and Hawaii (Heinz Center, 2000a). Some 87,000 structures were found to be located within a 60-year erosion area and therefore especially susceptible to coastal hazards (Table 3.3). This pattern of development suggests substantial economic costs; the Heinz study estimates annual property losses from erosion at $500 million.

A variety of human alterations can affect shoreline erosion and accretion patterns. The construction of jetties and groins can interrupt normal littoral drift, depriving downcoast areas of sand sediment and causing erosion. One of the places where this impact has been most dramatic is in Ocean City, Maryland. Here, a jetty system was constructed to keep the Ocean City inlet open. The jetty on Fenwick Island (the Ocean City side) has interrupted sand movement to Assateague Island to the south, causing severe erosion there. Construction of seawalls and revetments has also been found to exacerbate shoreline erosion by reflecting wave energy and steepening offshore profiles (Pilkey, 1989).

The damming and diverting of rivers has also caused erosion by depriving coastal areas of important fluvial sediment. This is most dramatic in coastal Louisiana, where extensive wetlands are subsiding and disappearing because of the diversion of replacement sediments from the Mississippi River. Another example is found in the Santee River delta in South Carolina.

Global warming has the potential to cause significant acceleration of sea level rise, as described in Chapter 2, with even greater levels of shoreline erosion and retreat predicted. The Third Assessment Report of the Intergovernmental Panel on Climate Change (IPCC), released in early 2001, makes even stronger conclusions about the causes of global warming and projection for the future. "In the light of new evidence and taking into account the remaining uncertainties, most of the observed warming over the last 50 years is likely to have been due to the increase in greenhouse gas concentrations" (IPCC, 2001, p. 10). Average global surface temperatures are projected to increase by 1.4 to 5.8°C between 1990 and 2100, with resulting sea level rises of 0.09 to 0.88 meters.

These predicted ranges of sea level rise would result in the inundation of coastal communities such as Charleston, South Carolina, and Galveston Island, Texas, causing extensive property damage. Sea level rise would also result in major flooding and destruction of coastal wetlands as well as other negative impacts on the coastal environment (e.g., exacerbating saltwater intrusion; see Edgerton, 1991). With increasing global temperatures, more extreme weather events are likely, according to the IPCC, including more intense precipitation events and increases in peak wind intensities and precipitation associated with tropical cyclones (IPCC, 2001, p. 15).

Policy options available to coastal states and localities in dealing with these issues are several and have already been mentioned. At a fundamental level, coastal jurisdictions can choose to resist these coastal forces (e.g., by reinforcing the coastline with seawalls and other coastal works) or they can choose to engage in strategic retreat from the shoreline. These options are described in greater detail in the next section.

Long-term shoreline erosion and sea level rise are major future challenges for coastal states and localities. While a number of states and localities have adopted some measures to address erosion (e.g., coastal setbacks), few have explicitly incorporated potential sea level rise effects into their planning and policies, although states are clearly beginning to think about the issue (Klarin and Hershman, 1990).

It is often argued that federal programs and subsidies have encouraged risky patterns of development along coastlines. It can be argued that the federal government has created a system of perverse incentives that have encouraged dangerous and irrational building patterns. These subsidies include federal flood insurance, disaster assistance, and casualty loss deductions under the federal income tax code. These programs are discussed in more detail in later chapters.

Strategic Retreat or Coastal Reinforcement?

Given the forces of long-term erosion, hurricanes and coastal storms, and sea level rise, some argue that a policy of strategic retreat is in order. State and local setback restrictions, restrictions on rebuilding after storms, and programs and policies to promote landward relocation can all promote retreat. Some coastal management programs, such as New York's erosion management law, prevent the construction of immovable structures in high-erosion zones. Some proponents of strategic retreat believe that if a building or improvement cannot be moved, it should be allowed to fall into the ocean.

Such positions obviously are controversial and not well received by coastal homeowners and local government officials. They argue that such a radical retreat policy ignores the large amount of public and private property at risk and the inefficiency of not protecting it from the forces of nature. Several options for protecting public and private property are advocated, such as structural approaches including seawalls and revetments, groins and jetties, offshore breakwaters, and other shore-armoring devices. Although these devices may temporarily block flooding and erosion, their economic and environmental impacts are substantial. Continuing seawalls can exacerbate erosion, block normal landward migration of barrier islands, and eventually result in a highly engineered shoreline with no natural beach. This is a process described by Pilkey as "New Jersization" of the shoreline (Pilkey et al., 1980, 1998; Bush et al., 1996).

A dramatic recent example of the debate over coastal retreat is the moving landward of the Cape Hatteras lighthouse, on the North Carolina Outer Banks. When this symbol of coastal North Carolina was built in 1803 it was located some 1,500 feet landward. Over time, however, as Hatteras Island migrated landward, the lighthouse was nearly in the surf zone, and sea waves were lapping at its foundation. A protracted debate ensued about how to address the problem. The U.S.

Photo 3.3. Looking southwest, you can see the Hatteras Lighthouse nearing the 75% point of its journey inland. (Photo by the National Park Service.)

Army Corps of Engineers proposed structural protection, imagining an extensive seawall surrounding the lighthouse. A National Academy of Science panel came to a different conclusion and recommended that the lighthouse be moved. During the summer of 1999, the relocation was completed, gradually moving the lighthouse on tracks, demonstrating that even a 207-foot structure could be moved. The decision to relocate Hatteras Lighthouse represented to many a symbolic victory for strategic retreat and a dramatic demonstration of the merits of this approach to coastal management.

These lessons can be applied equally to other more typical forms of coastal development, such as businesses and homes. A recent study by Edward J. Kaiser, funded by the North Carolina Division of Emergency Management, suggests that a barrier island community can enhance its beach-based economy by carefully managing redevelopment so that it retreats from the hazardous shoreline but not from the entire island (Kaiser, 2001).

An increasingly popular middle ground solution is beach renourishment or replenishment. Here, typically offshore sand deposits are dredged and pumped onto eroding beaches. Beach renourishment can restore the recreational beach and protect (to some extent) shoreline

Photo 3.4. Ocean City, Maryland, has undertaken a major beach renourishment initiative. Although it is expensive, city officials argue that the city's beach economy more than justifies the cost of renourishment. (Photo by Tim Beatley.)

structures from erosion and storm forces. However, recent studies of beach renourishment projects suggest that the practice is very expensive and short-lived. The length of time before additional renourishing is necessary has been consistently overestimated (especially by the U.S. Army Corps of Engineers, which carries out extensive beach renourishment projects). The strategy of renourishing commits a community to a never-ending and expensive process. Even so, it appears to be defensible in coastal communities such as Virginia Beach, Virginia, and Ocean City, Maryland, where millions of dollars of property is at risk and where maintaining a recreational beach supports extensive economic activities (e.g., beachfront hotels, boardwalk businesses).

The use of beach renourishment has increased tremendously over the last two decades as a response to shoreline erosion and storm protection. Trembanis et al. (1999) estimate that along East coast barrier beaches, where the greatest amount of renourishment has occurred, 345 million yards of sand has been placed on 147 beaches.

The costs of these renourishment projects are high and rising. Trem-

taxes!

banis et al. (1999) estimate the annual cost at more than $100 million (perhaps as high as $150 million), and that more than $3 billion has already been spent nationally. Because renourishment projects often do not last as long as predicted, there are substantial long-term upkeep costs, as high as $6 million per mile over a 10-year period.

For Orrin Pilkey and other advocates of strategic retreat, it is important to have more accurate estimates of the real long-term costs of renourishment. These more accurate cost estimates may help put alternatives, such as shoreline retreat, in a more favorable and realistic light:

> In a time of rising sea level and intensifying coastal development, beach renourishment must not be viewed through rose-colored glasses. If beaches are to be preserved for future generations, restrictions to nourished beachfront population density and the relocation alternative must be fairly and realistically compared to the standard practices of hard stabilization and beach nourishment. (Trembanis et al., 1999, p. 339)

Paying for this beach renourishment will be a major challenge in the years ahead. A majority of renourishment projects have involved federal funding, and significant future questions have emerged about the fairness and appropriateness of such a heavy federal subsidy for these projects. Partly in response to these concerns, the Bush administration has proposed to modify the present federal–state or local cost share from 65% federal, 35% state and local to 35% federal, 65% state and local. Finding the resources at state and local levels to fund long-term renourishment costs will be a significant task in the years ahead.

Protection of Coastal Wetlands and Resourcelands

As observed in Chapter 2, loss of coastal wetlands has been a significant problem in the past. Indeed, nearly half of all coastal wetlands have been destroyed since pre-Columbian times. Threats to wetlands have included draining and filling for agriculture, road construction, and urban and recreational development. Degradation through nonpoint pollution remains a significant problem. In the future, sea level rise may be the most serious long-term threat to wetlands, and sizable portions of coastal wetlands would be inundated even under moderate scenarios.

Losses of coastal wetlands have slowed dramatically in the last two decades, largely as a result of tougher federal and state coastal wetland protection laws. At the federal level, wetlands are protected through Section 404 of the Clean Water Act. Most coastal states have adopted coastal wetland protection laws, often stricter and more comprehensive than the federal provisions. Major large-scale projects of filling and draining of coastal marshes have mostly stopped.

However, the coastal wetlands picture is not a completely rosy one. Major losses continue to occur in Louisiana as a result of rapid land subsidence and diversion of the Mississippi River, for example. Although large-scale wetland destruction has nearly stopped, destruction of wetlands for roads, marinas, seawalls, and other development is still occurring through the existing regulatory framework. At the federal level, the Section 404 program contains significant implementation loopholes, and recent efforts have been made by the Bush administration to redefine what legally constitutes a wetland, reducing substantially the area over which federal permit control would exist. At the state level, whereas some states have stringent provisions, others, such as Texas, have essentially no control over private wetlands.

Furthermore, federal and state wetlands programs typically do not prohibit all development or use of wetlands but merely place restrictions on the types of uses permitted and the conditions under which these uses can occur. One issue involves the notion of so-called water-dependent uses. Many state wetlands laws prohibit destruction of wetlands for uses or activities that are not water-dependent. Such uses clearly include such things as marinas, but do they also include seafood restaurants wanting marshfront locations or hotels or motels wanting to capitalize on impressive shoreline views? Wetland destruction typically is allowed only where no feasible or "practicable" alternative locations exist, raising similarly difficult interpretation questions.

Although large-scale coastal wetland loss is less common, there remains the problem of incremental and piecemeal losses and the concern that the wetlands resource base is slowly being "nickeled and dimed to death" (Reid and Miller, 1989, p. 55). The cumulative ecological impact of these incremental wetlands losses is not well understood. Furthermore, many states cannot or do not keep track of the number of acres lost each year or the quality of these losses. Some states have only recently started to monitor and keep a running tally of these losses (e.g., see Institute for Environmental Negotiation, 1991).

When applicants are permitted to fill or otherwise destroy natural wetlands, they are often required, either through the federal 404 program or state laws, to mitigate these losses. Often this mitigation takes the form of requiring the applicant to compensate for or replace the wetlands with newly created wetlands or restore degraded wetlands. A number of "mitigation banks" have been established to facilitate this process, allowing an applicant for a wetland permit to purchase a credit or share of a larger mitigation project (e.g., see Congressional Research Service, 1997).

Wetland mitigation remains a controversial practice. Such forms of wetland compensation are essential to achieving "no net loss," a well-accepted national goal. Yet a recently issued National Research Council (NRC) study on wetland mitigation raises doubts about the ability to achieve this goal. Some wetlands and wetland functions are inherently difficult to restore or replace, and the NRC report recommends avoidance in these cases. The NRC, among other reports, also recommends that mitigation and compensation should be guided by watershed needs, should take place simultaneously with or preferably before wetland filling is permitted, and should incorporate a much longer timeframe for monitoring and stewardship.

Protection of Coastal Waters

Protection of coastal waters is a major goal of coastal management programs. Bays, estuaries, and other coastal waters are subject to a variety of pollutants, both point and nonpoint sources. Historically, industrial point sources were a significant problem as factories and other manufacturing activities located along water bodies. Not surprisingly, recent studies of the water quality in the waters around several major cities find high concentrations of pollutants in shellfish and other aquatic life and in sediments. Many coastal waters are not fishable or swimmable.

Nonpoint pollutants from agriculture are also a major problem, generating excessive levels of nutrients, especially nitrogen and phosphorus, which are found in fertilizers and animal manure. In the Chesapeake Bay, for example, excessive nutrient levels have resulted in high algal growth, clouding waters and reducing oxygen availability for aquatic life (Horton, 1991). The dead zone in the Gulf of Mexico is another dramatic example, having grown to an astounding 7,000 square miles.

Urban nonpoint sources include runoff from roads and other impervious surfaces; leachate from septic tanks, which is also a major problem in coastal areas; and construction sites, which generate a substantial amount of sediment runoff.

States and localities have sought to control these and other nonpoint pollutants through best management practices (BMPs). Agricultural BMPs include contour plowing, crop rotation, filter strips, animal waste control, and retirement of highly erodible land. Urban BMPs include stormwater collection ponds, infiltration basins and swales, use of porous asphalt, and restrictions on impervious surfaces. Construction BMPs include phased land clearance, filter fencing, protection of trees and vegetation, grading restrictions, runoff diversions, and location and design of road beds.

Some of the more promising approaches to controlling nonpoint pollutants involve maintaining, to the extent possible, the ameliorative capabilities of the coastal ecosystem. For instance, maintaining natural forested lands along the shore's edge helps to filter pollutants and to take up excess nutrients. A number of state and local coastal programs mandate shoreline buffers along rivers and water bodies (e.g., Virginia's Chesapeake Bay Preservation Act). Maintaining as much unpaved land as possible and placing restrictions on the percentage of land in development projects that is impervious (where percolation and infiltration of rainwater is not possible) will further reduce amounts of urban and rural runoff (Thurow et al., 1984).

Although the federal Clean Water Act has done much to reduce major point sources, it does not adequately address nonpoint source problems. Controlling nonpoint pollution is a major policy issue in most coastal areas, and in recent years there has been greater emphasis on nonpoint sources. The federal Coastal Zone Management Act has as a major centerpiece the control of nonpoint pollutants, with important (though controversial) requirements for coastal states in this area.

Placing controls on agricultural activities is especially controversial in coastal areas, and agriculture, historically exempted from many environmental provisions, has been able to secure a preferred status among land uses. For coastal managers, putting into place effective controls on agricultural activities is a major challenge.

There has also been great concern in recent years over the water quality impacts of oil and gas development and transport. Offshore oil and gas development has become increasingly unpopular, especially in California and Florida, and new restrictions have been placed on these activities in these and other coastal states. The potential impact of oil spills is also a major concern, heightened by the *Exxon Valdez* spill, which resulted in the discharge of 11 million gallons of crude oil into the sensitive ecosystem of Prince William Sound. Although this spill led to significant new restrictions on tanker design and procedures (requirements for double hulls, for instance), the number of damaging oil spills in the coastal environment remains high. The Coast Guard estimates that in 1999 alone, more than 8,500 spills were reported in U.S. waters, discharging some 1.2 million gallons of oil and petroleum (www.uscg.mil).

Energy Development and the Coast

The 2001 energy crisis in the United States has focused attention on our coasts and oceans as the source of new oil and gas production. The Bush administration energy plan proposed significant new offshore drilling, but these proposals have been controversial in affected states, ironically pitting Governor Jeb Bush, who opposes drilling off the Florida coast, against President Bush. Responding to the concerns of some coastal states about oil spills and potential environmental damage, Congress has banned new drilling under the Great Lakes and in Florida and California. At this writing, however, the House of Representatives has approved an energy bill to permit exploration and development along the northern coast of Alaska, in the Arctic Natural Wildlife Reserve, and a compromise has been reached that will permit drilling on 1.5 million acres in the Gulf of Mexico (supported by the other Gulf states of Alabama, Mississippi, and Louisiana), indicating that continued priority is to be given to solving the nation's energy and dependence in this way.

It remains to be seen whether, as proponents contend, offshore exploration and drilling can occur without damaging beaches and coastal environments (increasingly valuable for tourism and recreation). Opponents argue that the risks are unnecessary because other options exist, including conservation. Ironically, the same energy bill approved by the House of Representatives endorsing further drilling failed to raise fuel efficiency standards for sport utility vehicles, which would have saved more oil than can ever be expected from new drilling in Alaska or the Gulf of Mexico (Overholser, 2001).

Thinking beyond oil and gas development will be a major challenge for coastal planners and policymakers, and coastal regions will represent new opportunities to address energy needs in other ways. A number of renewable, less environmentally damaging sources of energy represent important opportunities in coastal and ocean environments. These include offshore windmills, wave energy systems, and tidal power. Portions of the U.S. coast are especially well suited to specific technologies. Tidal power has great potential in states such as Maine and Alaska, where large tidal differences occur, and wave power systems have potential along the northern California coast. Few of these technologies have been applied in the United States, but as renewables become a more important part of the nation's energy mix, they will probably grow in promise and potential.

Offshore wind farms have been built or are being built in Denmark, the Netherlands, and elsewhere, and have the potential to generate large amounts of energy at increasingly competitive prices. The first offshore wind farm in the United States is in development, planned for a site off the coast of Nantucket. When completed in 2004, it is expected to generate some 420 megawatts at its peak. Though more environmentally sustainable, such projects will also be controversial. Already concerns about the Nantucket project's impact on ocean views are being expressed (Krasner, 2001).

Biodiversity and Habitat Conservation

As noted in Chapter 2, coastal areas are home to tremendous biological diversity. *Biodiversity* refers to the diversity of species, but it also refers to the diversity within species and the diversity of broader ecological communities and processes. Coastal areas do very well on all measures of diversity (Reid and Miller, 1989; Reid and Trexler, 1991).

As Reid and Trexler (1991) note, coastal jurisdictions contain a disproportionate number of rare and endangered species. Moreover, coastlines are important habitat for numerous species that may not be endangered. Many forms of life rely entirely or partially on coastal shorelines. A recent study by the Florida Game and Freshwater Fish Commission found that of the state's 668 taxa of native vertebrates, coastal habitats were of high importance for vulnerable taxa, particularly for reptiles, birds, and mammals (Millsap et al., 1990).

As development of coastal areas continues, habitat loss remains as a significant problem. There are numerous examples of direct conflicts between demands for resort development, second homes, and other development proposals and the habitat needs of an endangered species. In the Florida Keys, the endangered key deer is threatened by increasing development, automobile traffic (road kills are a major factor), gradual habitat loss, and the interference of development with essential movement corridors. Along the California coast, the California gnatcatcher and other species indigenous to coastal sage scrub habitat are increasingly threatened. Habitat for the threatened Florida black bear has been declining as a result of coastal development pressure,

Photo 3.5. The piping plover is a shorebird that is listed on the FWS Endangered Species List. (Photo by U.S. FWS.)

including a recently proposed mobile home park in Pasco County. Along Virginia's coast, barrier coastal development (e.g., on Cedar Island) threatens the piping plover. Expanding shoreline development has taken away nesting sites for endangered sea turtles, and extensive lighting of coastlines has led to serious disorientation of newly hatched turtles. Extensive and growing recreational boating in south Florida commonly results in severe cuts to manatees (despite efforts to institute slow zones). The conflicts between marine life and human development and use of the coastal zone are innumerable.

Efforts are under way to protect coastal biodiversity. In the United States many of these efforts have resulted directly from the stringent requirements of the federal Endangered Species Act, which generally prohibits the taking of listed species (except under certain limited circumstances). Species conservation efforts have occurred in the coastal zone, including the preparation of habitat conservation plans, which seek to balance development and conservation interests (e.g., see Beatley 1994). Recent trends include preparing multiple-species plans and plans that seek to protect larger ecosystem units and broader patterns of diversity.

Land acquisition remains an important strategy for preserving coastal biodiversity and has occurred through federal, state, and private means (e.g., the Nature Conservancy). For example, the state of Florida has been a leader in acquiring and setting aside sensitive lands through its Conservation and Recreation Lands program. There is also a growing recognition that to ensure long-term ecological viability of protected lands, sufficient linkages and corridors must be provided. This is especially true for species such as the Florida panther that need large blocks of habitat. As coastal development continues, habitat fragmentation remains a growing concern.

Marine and Fishery Management

Although many coastal conservation efforts have focused on protecting terrestrial habitats, there is also a growing need to strengthen protections for marine and ocean habitats and species. As mentioned, some unique marine habitats such as coral reefs have been lost, and pressures on them are increasing. The decline in fisheries worldwide is another indication of these negative trends. Of marine fish populations monitored in U.S. waters, more than 40% have been overfished, with larger migratory species such as tuna, swordfish, and shark all in decline (Center for Marine Conservation, 2001). As catches of large predator fish decline, fishing further down the food chain occurs. As Wilder et al., (1999, p. 59) note, such practices both reduce the value of catches and undermine the integrity of marine ecosystems: "Both biodiversity and resilience decline as the balance of predators disappears."

The causes are many, but overfishing and lax regulatory and management regimes are largely to blame. The current and future management challenges here are tremendous and probably include a combination of stronger restrictions on fishing, more conservative sustainable catch levels, and the creation of a coherent network of marine protected areas that include no-take zones as a major element (Wilder et al., 1999; Center for Marine Conservation, 2001).

Coastal states are starting to take important actions on their own in this area. California enacted the Marine Life Protection Act in 1999 to expand and strengthen its network of marine reserves and conservation areas (which now comprises only 0.2% of its coastal waters). The act requires the state's Department of Fish and Game to prepare a marine master plan by July 2002 and may result in the addition of 80 new fishing-restricted areas. At the time of this writing, the state is holding a series of regional workshops to discuss preliminary concepts and receive comments from the public. Though admirably ambitious and strongly supported by the conservation community, the act has already angered supporters of recreational fishing who object to closing off new areas to this sport. In the words of one, "This is all being driven by people who want to turn the ocean into one big aquarium" (Stienstra, 2001, p. E2).

The Coast as a Recreational Commons: Protecting Access to Beaches and Shorelines

The coast is an immense recreational resource enjoyed by millions each year. Yet as coastal growth and development continue, public access to the coastline or the beach may itself become difficult. Substantial conflicts arise between the desires of coastal developers, resort owners, and private property owners to secure and protect shoreline locations and the goal of ensuring public access to and enjoyment of coastal areas. As noted earlier, most state common law protects at least the right of the public to walk along the wet beach unimpeded. However, in many coastal areas a wall of private development exists, and actual access to the beach is quite limited.

Many parts of the coast have been developed or are being developed as restricted or gated developments. Private barrier island developments, such as Hilton Head and Kiawah Islands, restrict shoreline access to property owners or guests. Although the public is entitled to visit and walk on the beach, there may be no physical way to reach these areas (except by boat). Should such private developments be able to appropriate this collective resource? Should public beach access be required, as it is now in some states and localities, as a condition of development approval?

Other types of actions or policies can also effectively restrict access. For instance, some beach communities impose fees or restrict parking for nonresidents, in turn reducing public access. Increasingly, coastal states are establishing minimum access requirements that localities must satisfy before they are eligible for certain types of state monies (e.g., state beach renourishment monies).

Social Equity in Coastal Planning

Social equity is also a major issue in contemporary coastal planning and management (and related to the earlier issue of beach access). Many recent coastal communities have tended to develop as upper-income resort or vacation communities. The result is that coastal land values often rise, displacing low- and moderate-income residents. Paradoxically, environmental regulations, beach access requirements, and other coastal management requirements sometimes are accused of contributing to the high cost of living in coastal areas and, especially, the high cost of housing. Over time, there has been a gentrification of the coastal zone.

In many coastal states there are sharp spatial distinctions between newer and often exclusive beachfront resort communities and the surrounding rural communities. The latter areas often are quite poor and exhibit lower income and education levels and, generally, lower housing and living conditions. Debate sometimes centers around the extent to which these poorer surrounding communities benefit economically from recent coastal development and whether these spatial inequalities represent a major social injustice. Although poorer residents are valued as service workers, it is often difficult or impossible for them to locate affordable housing in these resort communities. Mobile homes are a major source of affordable housing but often are prohibited or severely restricted in resort communities. Providing affordable housing is a major policy issue that must be confronted in the coastal zone.

Housing affordability is a special problem in many coastal areas. In seasonal resort communities such as Nantucket, housing increasingly is beyond the reach of all but the wealthy. The price of housing there has reportedly risen by 75% in the last 5 years (Aquatic Resources Conservation Group, 2000), with average home prices more than $1 million.

Many coastal communities are attempting to address the lack of affordable housing. A number of examples of different techniques can be cited. Some communities, such as the Martha's Vineyard Commission, apply affordable housing exactions for developments over a certain size. Zoning regulations have been changed in some communities, as on Cape Cod, to make it easier to create accessory housing units and to encourage housing above shops and retail establishments. Other coastal towns have adopted graduated building permit fees to encourage small homes.

State governments can and should play an important role in promoting more inclusive and affordable coastal communities. Some state coastal permitting programs have contained minimum affordable housing requirements, and in states such as Oregon and New Jersey, all localities (including those in the coastal zone) are required to accommodate a mix of housing types and a "fairshare" of affordable housing. Other state initiatives include tax credits for affordable housing, low-interest loan programs, and, as in Maryland, financial support for those who choose to live close to where they work. In California, a minimum of 20% of all redevelopment monies are to be used for affordable housing. Together, these state-level initiatives can make a difference.

Displacement of poor and minority residents by new coastal development has also been a major issue in some areas. Concerns have been expressed that development pressures on Hilton Head, Daufuskie, and other prime barrier island development sites have substantially raised land values and displaced many minority families whose ancestors have lived in these areas since the 1800s.

In addition to providing affordable housing to those who work in the coastal zone, another, perhaps even more significant issue is the low- and moderate-income people and families who simply want to visit the shore. Beach accessways are important for those who live within an easy commute to the beach, but out-of-town visitors need overnight accommodations to enjoy the shore. State and national parks offer some opportunities to camp, but increasingly they require reservations far in advance. This problem will get worse before it gets better.

Some coastal communities are beginning to address this aspect as well. The City of Santa Monica, for example, has enacted a Low Cost Lodging Mitigation Fee Ordinance, intended to address the problem of the gradual loss of affordable places to stay along the coast. Adopted in 1990, the intent of the ordinance is to "ensure that there is a balanced mix of visitor and recreational facilities providing an opportunity for all economic sectors to enjoy the coastal zone" (City of Santa Monica, 2000). The mitigation fees are assessed on projects that involve the loss of affordable lodging, and can be used to underwrite the renovation of older lodging or the construction of new units.

Coastal Sprawl, Land Use Pressures, and Quality of Life

Coastal localities and regions around the country are facing severe development and land use pressures, which are threatening the very qualities that make coastal areas attractive places to live in and visit. The pressures are great, including an estimated 9,000 new single-family homes built along the coast each week (Bookman et al., 1999). Moreover, coastal homes are getting larger and are being built on larger lots. Much coastal growth is in the form of *sprawl:* scattered, low-density, car-dependent development. Traffic congestion, rising public service costs, and loss of greenspace and natural lands are all significant problems associated with coastal sprawl. Wasteful development patterns that threaten traditional farming, fishing, and resource-based industries are a consistent concern of coastal managers.

Loss of forested land and other changes to the natural qualities of places can be seen in many coastal regions. A study by the Woods Hole Research Center of land use changes on Cape Cod over a 40-year period shows substantial loss of forested land and a tripling of land devoted to urban and commercial development. On Cape Cod, forest cover decreased from 71% in 1951 to 43% in 1990, and the region also witnessed a 75% reduction in agricultural land.

Many of the coastal management issues and problems mentioned in this chapter are directly related to patterns of coastal sprawl, including habitat destruction, water quality problems, and growing vulnerability to coastal hazards. The latter is a good case in point and is well illustrated by the flooding and damages associated with Hurricane Floyd, which hit eastern North Carolina in 1999. Although larger amounts of rain actually fell during events in the 1950s, the substantially less altered watershed meant that less flooding occurred. Stanley Riggs (2000) argues persuasively that the flood crisis in eastern North Carolina was a result of the "systematic modification of our watersheds during the last several decades" (p. 94–97). Over time, many coastal watersheds have been seriously overdeveloped and developed in ways that have fundamentally altered natural hydrologic features and dynamics. Coastal watersheds generally are less resilient to the force of hurricanes and storms, as urbanization has gradually replaced wetlands, forests, and open land with highways, parking lots, and paved surfaces. This is another significant and serious result of unchecked coastal sprawl.

Protecting the character and flavor of coastal communities is an important issue in many areas. Many coastal communities contain impressive historic buildings and resources that they want to protect. A number of localities have sought to protect community character by instituting urban design review standards and processes. The coastal community of Canon Beach, Oregon, for instance, has outlawed the building of "formula food restaurants" (e.g., McDonald's, Pizza Hut). Other communities, such as Hilton Head, have enacted certain requirements for color, materials, and architectural style (they are proud that they now have a Red Roof Inn without a red roof). Increasingly, coastal communities are placing restrictions on billboards and signage and imposing more stringent vegetation standards and requirements for visual buffers.

In new coastal developments there has been a renewed interest in incorporating the planning and design features that characterized early American towns and communities. These design features include grid streets, central public buildings and common spaces, pedestrian orientation, and the mixing of land uses (interspersing commercial and residential uses). Such a design philosophy has been called neotraditionalism and is strongly evident in such highly acclaimed coastal developments as Seaside on the Florida Gulf coast.

Dramatic increases in the population growth rates of coastal communities translate into a host of other serious environmental and resource demands, from energy and water consumption to the materials needed to build homes and buildings. Such issues, though related to land use patterns, extend beyond them and suggest the need for attention to broader patterns of resource sustainability. As discussed in Chapter 8, there are many opportunities for coastal cities, counties, and towns to operate much more sustainably and tread more lightly on the environment.

Private Property versus the Public Interest in Coastal Planning

One of the most significant policy dilemmas in contemporary coastal management is determining the appropriate balance between government police power regulations of coastal lands and the sanctity of private property. Coastal property owners affected by coastal regulations (e.g., coastal setbacks, restrictions on filling wetlands) often claim that such regulations violate the Fifth Amendment of the U.S. Constitution (as well as similar provisions in state constitutions).

The Takings Clause of the Fifth Amendment provides that "private property shall [not] be taken for public use, without just compensation." In 1971, Joseph I. Sax wrote the following in his excellent article in the *Yale Law Review:*

> Few legal problems have proved as resistant to analytical efforts as that posed by the Constitution's requirement that private property not be taken for public use without payment of just compensation. Despite the intensive efforts of commentators and judges, our ability to distinguish satisfactorily between "takings" in the constitutional sense, for which compensation is compelled, and the exercise of the police power, for which compensation is not compelled, has advanced only slightly since the Supreme Court began to struggle with the problem some eighty years ago. (p. 149)

Almost 30 years later, land use lawyers are still in a quandary. After the most recent land use law case (*Palazzolo vs. Rhode Island*) decided by the Supreme Court, Timothy J. Dowling, Chief Counsel of the Community Rights Counsel, said, "After lamenting that its prior opinions failed to provide specific guidance on how the Takings Clause applies to regulations that protect our communities, the Court once again has handed down a ruling that muddles takings law and threatens community protections" (Dowling, 2001). However, there are a few things about takings law that coastal management programs, as well as all public managers, must be aware of:

- The physical occupation of private land by a unit of government, except under extreme circumstances, is a taking (e.g., building a city hall on the front yard of a private residence).
- A government regulation that removes all economic value of privately owned land is a taking (e.g., zoning a piece of privately owned property for a public park).
- A government regulation that regulates the use of land that has no rational connection to a valid public purpose is a taking.

The Fifth Amendment does not deny the government proper exercise of its police power. States and municipalities may regulate property and its uses without the owner necessarily being entitled to compensation. The government's police power involves the power to legislate to further the health, morals, safety, or welfare of the community, even where that legislation imposes a burden on the use and enjoyment of private property.

The courts have yet to articulate a clear and definitive set of criteria for determining when a taking has occurred, and different judicial approaches and theories have contributed to the confusion about how far restrictions on coastal development and land use can go.

Several significant coastal cases highlight the ethical and legal disagreements that arise over the takings issue and the significance of this issue for coastal management. In *Lucas v. South Carolina,* David Lucas owned two beachfront lots in the Wild Dunes subdivision on Isle of Palms, a barrier island community east of Charleston. After he acquired the lots, the South Carolina legislature enacted the Beachfront Management Act, which prohibited construction seaward of certain lines. Both of the Lucas lots were seaward of this point and thus were unbuildable under the law. Lucas sued the South Carolina Coastal Council, claiming that a taking had occurred. The trial court agreed and awarded Lucas $1.2 million. The Coastal Council appealed and won in the South Carolina Supreme Court, which concluded that the state was merely preventing a public harm, so compensation was not required. Lucas appealed this decision to the U.S. Supreme Court, which reversed the South Carolina Supreme Court decision. The U.S. Supreme Court reinforced the notion that where a regulation precludes all economically viable use of land, a taking has occurred. However, the Court did suggest that certain regulations might constitutionally preclude all economic use if all that the state or local regulations are doing is effecting a pre-existing common law restriction, particularly the common law of nuisance.

A more recent takings opinion was issued by the U.S. Supreme Court in *Palazzolo v. Rhode Island* and further highlights the controversy and confusion surrounding the takings issue (121 S.Ct. 2448 [2001]). Here a landowner, Anthony Palazzolo, held 18 acres of coastal marshland and, citing *Lucas,* claimed an unconstitutional taking as a result of that state's wetlands regulations. The Court reversed in part the Rhode Island Supreme Court's decision that a taking had not occurred and remanded for reconsideration. The court concluded that the mere existence of the wetland regulations before Palazzolo obtained ownership did not constitute a defense by the state against takings. On most other points, little change from the substantive standards of *Lucas* and previous cases can be seen in the opinion, and the justices actually agreed with the lower court that all economic use of the property had not been denied because Palazzolo retained some upland land that could support construction of a house. Nevertheless, the *Palazzolo* decision is likely to embolden coastal property owners to further challenge coastal regulations and fuel the battle over what constitutes legitimate and reasonable regulation of coastal development.

These cases highlight the centrality of the takings issue in coastal management, important in a legal, political, and philosophical sense. Key questions remain, including under what circumstances it can be said that all economic uses have been extinguished. In the South Carolina case, for instance, Lucas still had the right to use his land, to erect a temporary structure, and to sell it to an adjoining landowner.

Conclusions

Coastal areas in the United States have been experiencing substantial growth in population and development in recent decades. Coastal counties are expected to have grown by more than 50% between 1960 and 2015. With these development pressures come a host of environmental and land use conflicts and issues. Some of the more critical of these management issues have been identified and described here, and some clearly involve very different notions of how the coastal zone ought to be used by the human species. The problems and challenges facing coastal managers are substantial. However, there is a regulatory and management regime in place to address many of these issues, as well as substantial management activity at federal, state, regional, and local levels. The next several chapters attempt to briefly describe the main contours of this framework, the types of coastal management programs and policies in place, and the extent to which they are effective at accomplishing coastal management goals.

4

The Coastal Management Framework

Coastal management in the United States involves a wide variety of actors in both the public and the private sectors. In this chapter we introduce these actors and briefly describe their role in managing the coastal zone of the United States.

In the public sector, responsibility for coastal management in the United States is scattered among a number of agencies at all three levels of government. At the federal level, several federal agencies have management responsibilities, including the National Oceanic and Atmospheric Administration (NOAA), especially the Office of Ocean and Coastal Resources Management (OCRM), the U.S. Environmental Protection Agency (EPA), the U.S. Army Corps of Engineers (COE), the Federal Emergency Management Agency (FEMA), and several agencies within the Department of the Interior including the National Park Service, the U.S. Fish and Wildlife Service, the Minerals Management Service, and the Bureau of Land Management. These diverse agencies and the laws they are charged with implementing are listed in Table 4.1.

Although the OCRM (within NOAA) has primary responsibility for implementing the federal Coastal Zone Management Act (CZMA), each agency has important responsibilities and can significantly influence activities that occur in the coastal zone. The OCRM mission is exclusively coastal zone management, but its authority is limited. It depends almost entirely on the initiative and management programs of state agencies to carry out programs encouraged by the CZMA.

No single agency at the federal level has exclusive control over coastal management, and there is no single or unified national coastal zone policy or strategy that guides or coordinates federal actions or programs. Although the CZMA is an attempt at the federal level to

Table 4.1. Federal Agencies and Legislation Affecting the Coastal Zone

Agencies	Primary coastal management activities	Authorizing legislation
Office of Ocean and Coastal Resource Management (OCRM within NOAA)	Implements coastal zone management program; works with states in developing and implementing their coastal zone programs	Coastal Zone Management Act (CZMA)
U.S. Army Corps of Engineers (COE)	Implements Section 404 wetland permit program; provides technical assistance and funding of shoreline protection and beach nourishment and dredging of navigable waters	Federal Flood Control Acts (of 1917, 1936, 1945, 1955, 1968); Section 404, Clean Water Act
Environmental Protection Agency (EPA)	Has joint responsibility with NOAA for Section 6217 of Coastal Nonpoint Source Pollution Control Program; oversees Section 404 wetland permit program; establishes emission standards for air pollutants and effluent standards for water pollutants	CZMA, Clean Air Act (CAA), Clean Water Act (CWA)
Federal Emergency Management Agency (FEMA)	Implements National Flood Insurance Program (NFIP); provides pre- and postdisaster assistance to coastal states and local governments	National Flood Insurance Act, Flood Disaster Protection Act, Stafford Disaster Relief and Emergency Assistance Act, Disaster Mitigation Act of 2000
National Park Service (NPS), within Department of the Interior (DOI)	Maintains and manages national seashores and NPS units; oversees Coastal Barrier Resources System (CBRS)	Site-specific legislation; Coastal Barrier Resources Act (CBRA)
U.S. Fish and Wildlife Service (FWS, within DOI)	Enforces federal wildlife and endangered species laws; prepares and implements species recovery plans; establishes and maintains system of national wildlife refuges	Endangered Species Act (ESA)
National Marine Fisheries Service (NMFS, within DOI)	Manages fisheries; protects marine mammals	Marine Mammal Protection Act

establish national goals for coastal management, it falls short of providing a management framework for federal activities that affect the coast. Thus, coastal zone management responsibilities are fragmented and dispersed at the federal level.

This fragmented system consists of three types of policy. First, it includes policy that *directly* affects the coastal zone, that is, policy that was designed specifically to affect the coastal zone and little else (e.g., CZMA). Second is policy that is *connected* to the coastal zone, although it was designed to affect an issue that extends well outside the coastal zone (e.g., the Clean Water Act [CWA]). Third is de facto coastal management policy, which affects the coastal zone although it is highly unlikely that the coastal zone was considered in its formulation. Its effect on the coastal zone is an unintended consequence of the policy. For example, the federal tax code can have a significant influence on coastal land use and development patterns. The code currently includes provisions that subsidize hazardous development patterns. For instance, the casualty loss deduction allows coastal property owners to deduct the cost of uninsured damages resulting from hurricanes and coastal storms. Other tax code provisions include the interest and property tax deductions allowed for second homes and accelerated depreciation for seasonal rental properties. Although these tax benefits tend to be more obscure, they nevertheless influence development patterns.

In many cases, federal funds for highway construction have made coastal areas more available for development. Other federal activities that may influence coastal development include grants and loan guarantees provided by the Department of Housing and Urban Development and the Department of Veterans Affairs. The Rural Utilities Service (electricity) and the U.S. EPA (public wastewater) have also played a role in providing infrastructure necessary for development.

In this fragmented system, the programs and policies of different federal agencies often work at cross-purposes. For instance, FEMA has historically viewed its role as one of helping communities and states recover from disasters. It provides extensive relief after hurricanes and other coastal disasters. Although hazard mitigation has gained importance in recent years, it can be argued that providing disaster relief and flood insurance, another very important program administered by FEMA, has encouraged development in hazardous areas, thus working at cross-purposes with EPA, OCRM, and other agencies. The COE's focus on funding and constructing shoreline protection (e.g., seawalls, jetties) and beach renourishment programs is perceived to work against the objectives of coastal resource protection.

Responsibilities within a single program may also be shared between agencies. For instance, the Clean Water Act Section 404 wetland permitting program is jointly administered by the COE and the EPA (the COE issues permits in accordance with EPA guidelines, and the EPA holds veto power over them). The Clean Air Act is an example of shared responsibilities between the EPA and state governments. Some policy, especially cross-cutting policy, is designed to work in concert with other policies (e.g., the Coastal Barrier Resources Act and the National Environmental Policy Act). Thus, important coastal management programs and authorities are dispersed among a number of different federal agencies, and there is no unified national strategy for managing the coastal zone. Although this body of policy was not designed as a system, it is important that it be considered as a system because that is the way it works in the coastal zone.

Role of State and Local Governments

The U.S. coastal management framework is clearly one of shared management between federal, state, and local jurisdictions. The federal government plays a major role in coastal management. However, most of the responsibility for managing development in the coastal zone lies with coastal states and localities.

Effective, comprehensive coastal management involves management and control of the use of land, powers reserved under our federal system to state government. Historically, there has been substantial opposition to and suspicion of federal efforts to impose land use controls in the coastal zone or elsewhere.

States play an important role in coastal management, described in greater detail in Chapter 6. Each coastal state and territory exercises some degree of control over the coastal zone within its jurisdiction. The states, like the federal government, have policies that *directly* affect the coastal zone (e.g., the North Carolina Coastal Area Management Act, or CAMA), are *connected* to the coastal zone in that they clearly affect it but also affect other areas of the state (e.g., water quality programs), or affect the coastal zone as an unintended consequence of the implementation of the policy (e.g., state department of transportation highway and bridge location and construction).

States also exercise control over the coastal zone under CZMA. Almost all eligible jurisdictions, including oceanfront and Great Lakes states, territories, and commonwealths, have OCRM-approved coastal management programs (33 out of 35 states, with Indiana in development and Illinois inactive) and are implementing coastal management programs and policies with OCRM assistance. These programs include direct regulation and control of shorefront development (e.g., through an erosion-based setback standard imposed by North Carolina's CAMA), development in other sensitive coastal lands (e.g., coastal marshes), acquisition of coastal lands and provision of beach access and recreational facilities, and other policies.

Historically in the United States, the authority to manage land use and development has been delegated by the states to local governments. Typically, coastal localities have authority (and indeed in a few states are required) to adopt at least basic land use management tools, some of which include comprehensive or land use plans, zoning and subdivision ordinances, capital improvement programs, historic district regulations, land acquisition programs, targeted taxation assessments, impact fees, and annexation programs.

Enactment of state coastal management programs often involves imposing new planning requirements on local governments. Under North Carolina's CAMA, for example, coastal localities are required to prepare local land use plans. These plans must satisfy certain minimum state standards and be approved by the state. Some coastal local governments have gone beyond these minimum state requirements. Several of the more progressive of these are described in later chapters.

Coastal ecosystems rarely follow international, state, or local jurisdictional boundaries and, as a consequence, suggest the need for special regional substate or multistate management programs. A coastal bay or estuary may encompass a large area and many different local jurisdictions (as in the case of San Francisco Bay), or even several states (as in the case of the Chesapeake Bay). Examples of substate management and regulatory bodies include the San Francisco Bay Conservation and Development Commission, the Puget Sound (Washington) Regional Water Quality Management District, and the South Florida Regional Planning Council. There has been much interest at the federal level in promoting regional, ecosystem-based management efforts. These programs have included the National Estuary Program, the CWA, the National Estuarine Research Reserve System, and the preparation of Special Area Management Plans under the CZMA.

Photo 4.1. Satellite photo of San Francisco Bay in California showing sediment flow into the bay. (Photo by U.S. Army COE.)

Stakeholders in Coastal Management

Coastal policy and its outcomes clearly are the result of political processes in which different factions and interest groups compete for attention and resources. Coastal management must be understood to occur within a political process. Actual coastal management decisions are very much the result of the interplay of these different groups.

The stakeholders in coastal management policy include major interest groups that seek to influence or are influenced by the allocation of coastal resources. Coastal policy in the United States is shaped in large part by and for these stakeholders, who make up a network of public and private organizations. Of course, the entire body of stakeholders is much larger than these groups and their membership. It includes all people who, regardless of their place of residence, spend time at the coast renting, camping, boating, fishing, swimming, or just relaxing. It includes all those who eat seafood, expecting it to be healthful and free from toxins or other harmful pollutants. It includes all the people who

have some relationship with the coast. Some would argue that the major stakeholders—biodiversity and future generations—do not even vote or belong to a single nongovernmental organization. It is the breadth and depth of this body of stakeholders that make coastal management of special importance because of the responsibility to ensure that all their values are fairly and adequately represented.

This network shapes our coastal policy and also is important in the implementation of resource management and water and land use regulation. Coastal management in the United States is carried out by a unique blend of government and nongovernment organizations, for-profit and nonprofit groups, and development and environmental advocates. Often policy coalitions compete with one another, each seeking to secure its own piece of the coastal resource pie. Despite the disparate viewpoints and multiplicity of agendas, a dynamic process creates a working system of policies, plans, and programs that affect the conservation and development of coastal areas and resources.

The first group of stakeholders is made up of the coastal states, the majority of which are officially part of the national coastal management program through the CZMA. The managers of the state programs get together regularly to discuss issues of common interest with one another, OCRM staff, and the Coastal States Organization (CSO). The CSO, made up of gubernatorial delegates, also represents states' interests. The CSO was formed in 1970 to ensure state representation in developing national coastal policy, and it continues to serve this purpose.

Coastal states are interested primarily in controlling coastal management initiatives within their jurisdiction by ensuring that any federal coastal policies remain flexible and allow individual states discretion over policy implementation. Many analysts believe the success of the CZMA results in large part from its voluntary nature. National standards are set by NOAA in some substantive areas, but whether and how to participate are left up to individual states.

Coastal states also have a strong interest in ensuring that the incentives for CZMA participation remain in place. One of these incentives is undoubtedly financial; the CZMA-authorized grants (Secs. 306, 306A, 309, and 6217) have encouraged many states to initiate and continue innovative and effective programs for their coastal regions. The second major incentive is the consistency doctrine of CZMA (Sec. 307). By creating enforceable policy as a part of approved coastal programs, the states are assured that federal activities within the states' jurisdictions will not undermine state regulatory and management initiatives. Such a promise of federal consistency makes participation in the national coastal management system attractive to many states. These two incentives, federal financial assistance and consistency, have led to almost unanimous participation by the coastal states.

A second important group of stakeholders in the coastal policy formation process includes coastal environmentalists. Private organizations such as the Natural Resources Defense Council, the Sierra Club, the Nature Conservancy, the Center for Marine Conservation, and other environmental and public interest groups are influential in setting national priorities for coastal policy. These national organizations, as well as state and local organizations, are a powerful force and often are quite visible and vocal in presenting their agendas.

Coastal development interests make up another stakeholder group whose influence cannot be overstated. This group is composed of powerful energy organizations such as the American Petroleum Institute, which calls for greater latitude in areas such as offshore oil exploration and drilling. Development organizations such as the National Association of Homebuilders push for less regulation of private property to allow more development in coastal regions. These interest groups often are supported by local economic development advocates and chambers of commerce, which are anxious to see their communities grow.

Some government agencies are also important stakeholders, most notably the U.S. Army COE. Although the corps is given regulatory responsibility over certain coastal wetlands, it also plays a major role in maintaining the navigability of coastal waters by dredging harbors, deepening channels, constructing bulkheads, and renourishing beaches.

Congress, congressional committees, and staff are important stakeholders because they are the authors of national coastal legislation, and they play a vital role in formulating coastal policy. This group includes program-oriented career civil servants, their politically appointed chiefs (whose agendas may be at odds), and the elected members of Congress. Staff members play a vital role in implementing the CZMA and work with national interests in mind. OCRM is also responsive to pressures from state, environmental, development, and congressional coalitions.

The CZMA was created originally to be collaborative in nature and immune from one interest group or faction gaining complete control and dictating coastal policy for the nation.

Most stakeholders agree that managing growth to balance environmental protection and development in the coastal zone is a national priority, one that is best served by maintaining the voluntary, incentive-based intergovernmental program that has been created thus far. Most actors in the coastal policy process also believe that the states should be given discretionary power and autonomy in defining their individual coastal programs to deal with their particular needs. National interests should also be a part of each state plan, with some universal standards applicable to all participants. Most stakeholders would agree with the operation of the consistency doctrine, requiring that federal activities within the coastal zone be consistent with approved state plans.

Despite consensus on some issues, the stakeholders certainly do not agree on all elements of the national coastal program. There has been persistent conflict between the interest groups that want increasing latitude and flexible standards, with freedom to develop and use coastal resources to the maximum extent feasible, and those that argue for more stringent regulation of development affecting the natural environment and for the requirement of more explicit standards in all state plans. The result is a constant process of balancing between flexibility and rigor, development and conservation, regulation and laissez-faire.

When discussing stakeholders, it is crucial to consider the groups and individuals who do not reach the forefront of policymaking and yet have a definite stake in the coastal region. Many whose very livelihood depends on the viability of coastal ecosystems may not be recognized as stakeholders and therefore are not invited to the discussion table when coastal policy is being formulated. Local populations along the coast often fall into this category of unrecognized stakeholder. The fisher who depends on healthy waters to support his catch, the clam digger who relies on mudflats left untainted by upriver pollution, the beachfront cottage owner who comes seasonally for rest, relaxation, and a beautiful view—all these people have come to depend on the coast as a way of life, and yet too often such people are not involved in the high-stakes discussions that affect their futures.

We must include in our discussion of stakeholders the elected official. Certainly at the local level, and at the state and federal levels as well, representatives of the people must champion the cause of coastal management for both the economic health of local communities and the preservation of the ecosystem. Through their representatives in government, residents, workers, visitors, and others with an interest in the coastal regions of our nation should have their voices heard as coastal policy is formed.

Conclusions

This chapter has provided a broad overview of the coastal management framework in the United States. Coastal management occurs in a fragmented framework, with responsibilities and authorities shared by federal, state, and local government bodies. At the federal level, agencies such as the OCRM, the U.S. Army COE, FEMA, and the EPA are major actors. However, much of the actual on-the-ground management in the U.S. framework occurs at state and local levels. Local governments historically have had the primary responsibility for land use planning and community land use decisions, although increasingly states have exercised direct control over development and other activities occurring in the coastal zone.

Coastal zone management is very much a political process and involves a number of key actors and interest groups in addition to government agencies. These different coastal stakeholder groups have different perspectives on coastal management, and coastal management decisions often are the result of the interplay of these different groups.

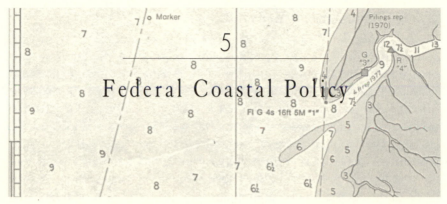

5
Federal Coastal Policy

As discussed in Chapter 4, the federal government plays an integral role in coastal zone management.

The federal role in managing the coastal zone expanded in the early 1970s when Congress passed the Coastal Zone Management Act (CZMA). With the passage of this act, Congress declared that the coastal zone of the United States contains resources of tremendous national value and that the existing management programs were not adequate to protect the coastal zone for the nation.

Although the CZMA is an important element of federal involvement in managing the coastal zone, the program it created is but one piece of the federal coastal policy mosaic. In this chapter we review in some detail the major components of this mosaic, including the CZMA. This policy mosaic is made up of three types of coastal policy: direct, connected, and de facto coastal policy. Direct coastal policy includes the CZMA, Coastal Barrier Resources Act (CBRA), the National Marine Sanctuary Act, and other legislative acts that have as their purpose the conservation of coastal and marine resources. Connected coastal policy includes environmental policy that affects the coast through federal laws aimed at maintaining the quality of critical resources such as water and air and reducing the impacts of disasters and natural hazards, all of which affect the coastal zone. De facto coastal policy includes federal actions, such as road and bridge building, taxation, and housing policy, that have consequences, often unintended, for the coastal zone.

Direct Coastal Policy

Coastal Zone Management Act

In many ways the CZMA is the cornerstone of federal efforts to protect and manage our nation's coastlines. Enacted in 1972, the act grew out of a growing public concern for the environment, including ocean and coastal resources. The Stratton Commission's 1969 report, *Our Nation and the Sea,* was instrumental in focusing the attention of citizens, politicians, and scientists on the importance of the coastal zone and the lack of effective management. Several coastal management bills were introduced in Congress after issuance of the Stratton Report; most of the legislation emphasized *either* development *or* conservation. Passed in 1972, the act is a unique combination of goals: The National Oceanic and Atmospheric Administration (NOAA) in the Department of Commerce would administer a voluntary, grant-in-aid program that would encourage but not require coastal states to achieve a balance between development and the environment through coastal land use planning, management, and other programs.

A Collaborative Strategy

The CZMA is a unique federal–state collaboration. The act provides incentives for coastal states to prepare and implement coastal management programs, through cost-sharing grants, the consistency doctrine, and technical assistance. Sections 302 and 303 of the act set out congressional findings and policy that lay a solid foundation for federal involvement in the management of the coastal zone and the direction that involvement should take. Under Section 305, federal grants are made available to states to prepare coastal management programs (CMPs). Section 306(d)(2) sets out the program elements that a state coastal management program must have to be approved, which include the following:

- a definition of the boundaries of the coastal zone to which the program applies
- a definition of areas of particular concern within the coastal zone
- a definition of permissible land and water uses within the coastal zone and the "identification of the means by which the state proposes to exert control" over them
- a description of the organizational structure for the implementation of the program

- a planning process to provide protection of and access to public beaches
- a planning process to lessen the impact of shoreline erosion

Once the coastal management program has been approved, a state is eligible for annual matching grants to administer its program. The amount of the annual grant is based on "the extent and nature of the shoreline and area covered by the program" and its population.

As Table 5.1 indicates, federal funds provided to states from the program's inception in 1972 through the 2001 fiscal year for Section 305 (program development) exceed $72 million, and Section 306 (program administration) funds exceed $844 million. Through a process described in Section 312, state programs must be periodically reviewed and approved by the Office of Ocean and Coastal Resources Management (OCRM). The secretary of commerce has the authority to suspend or withdraw funding, or even withdraw approval of the state's management program, if a coastal state fails to adhere to "the terms of any grant or cooperative agreement."

Section 306A was added to the original CZMA to make matching grants available to the states to encourage them to do more than merely administer their CMPs. Allowing the states to become more involved than had been authorized under 306, these bricks-and-mortar grants are available to help the states achieve the following coastal management objectives defined by Congress:

- to preserve and restore areas valued for recreational, ecological, or aesthetic purposes
- to redevelop urban waterfronts and ports
- to provide access to public beaches and other coastal areas
- to develop a coordinated process to regulate aquaculture

Table 5.1. Coastal Program Expenditures, Fiscal Years 1972–2001

Section		Amount ($ million)
305	Program development	72.1
306	Program administration	844.1
308	Coastal zone management fund	10.9
309	Coastal zone enhancement	79.1
310	Research and technical assistance	4.9
315	National Estuarine Research Reserves	130.1
6217	Coastal Nonpoint Pollution Program	29.7
P.L. 92-532	Marine sanctuaries	9.9

In 1990, Congress again expanded the CZMA with the addition of Section 309, the Coastal Zone Enhancement Program, which encourages the states and territories to make changes in their CMP that, as defined by Congress, "support attainment" of one or more of the "coastal zone enhancement objectives." Unlike the federal grants available pursuant to Sections 306 and 306A, the Coastal Zone Enhancement Program does not require state matching funds and is competitively awarded to the coastal states. The coastal zone enhancement objectives defined by Congress include the following:

- to protect, restore, enhance, or create coastal wetlands
- to eliminate development in hazardous areas and anticipate sea level rise
- to expand beach access opportunities
- to reduce marine debris
- to control cumulative and secondary impacts of development
- to formulate and implement Special Area Management Plans (SAMPs, which are discussed further in Chapter 6)
- to plan for the use of ocean resources
- to formulate a process to facilitate siting energy facilities
- to adopt procedures to facilitate siting aquaculture facilities

In 1992, the states and territories with approved CMPs assessed their objectives, and with OCRM's approval, the states developed 5-year strategies to improve their managerial programs in the objective areas agreed on. In 1997, a similar process was initiated that gave the states the opportunity to revise their strategies to reflect current priorities.

In addition to the enhancement grant program, the Coastal Zone Reauthorization Amendments of 1990 added to the CZMA Section 6217, a coastal nonpoint source pollution control program. Synthesizing the nonpoint source pollution programs of Section 319 of the Clean Water Act (CWA) and the land use planning program of the CZMA, Section 6217 requires that each approved coastal state prepare a Coastal Nonpoint Pollution Control Program. The program shall "implement management measures for nonpoint source pollution to restore and protect coastal waters." Each state 6217 program must be coordinated with state and local water quality plans developed pursuant to the CWA and the state's CMP. It also requires that each state 6217 program follow the guidance formulated by the Environmental Protection Agency and NOAA and contain the following elements:

- Identification of land uses that may degrade coastal waters.
- Identification of critical coastal areas within which land use controls are required.
- Management measures that are necessary to achieve CWA requisite water quality standards.
- Technical assistance to local governments and the public.
- A public participation process.
- Administrative coordination between state agencies and between state and local agencies.
- State coastal zone boundary modification. "The Secretary [of Commerce], in consultation with the [EPA] Administrator . . . shall . . . review the inland coastal zone boundary of each coastal state . . . and evaluate whether the State's coastal zone boundary extends inland to the extent necessary to control the land and water uses that have a significant impact on the coastal waters of the State . . . [and] shall recommend appropriate modifications . . . to the affected State."

The coastal nonpoint source pollution program has proved to be very difficult to carry out. Preparing the programs as they were originally conceived was not easy, and most of the states felt that the funds made available to them were not adequate. In addition, it was not until October 1998 that the EPA and NOAA completed the guidelines to help states prepare their programs. However, by the summer of 1999, all the state programs had been conditionally approved (the programs met the requirements but needed work in one or more areas).

A major incentive provided to the states through Section 307 of the CZMA requires that all "federal agency activity within or outside the coastal zone that affects any land or water use or natural resource of the coastal zone shall be carried out in a manner which is *consistent* to the maximum extent practicable with the enforceable policies of approved state management programs." Federal activities that fall within this consistency doctrine include the following:

- Direct action: activities and projects carried out by a federal agency or their agents
- Indirect action: activities and projects not carried out by a federal agency but for which a federal permit, license, or other form of approval is required, including the approval of grants and loans to state and local governments

Examples include navigational and flood control projects, CWA Section 404 wetland permits, highway development, airport plans, waste-

water treatment facility funding, military activities, and fishery management. The purpose of the consistency doctrine is to ensure that all
direct and indirect action by federal agencies likely to affect the coastal
zone complies with the approved CMP of the relevant state. Ideally,
federal agencies consult with the state coastal management program
early in the process of planning the action that will be subject to the
consistency requirement. But in any case, the federal agency submits a
consistency statement to the CMP when the action is ready to move
forward. The state then determines whether the action is consistent. If
it is determined to be consistent, the activity may proceed. Findings of
inconsistency may be appealed to the secretary of commerce.

Through federal consistency, many states see the opportunity to
gain an increased measure of control over federal actions and policies
in the coastal zone. Implementation of the consistency doctrine generally has been successful. The body of consistency decisions by the
secretary of commerce appears to strike a balance between state interests and national economic and security interests. Based on this
record, it is clear that federal development projects in the coastal zone,
as well as private development projects for which a federal permit is
required, are subject to state coastal management policies and may be
substantially modified at the insistence of the states to conform to
these policies.

Coastal Barrier Resources Act

The CBRA was enacted by Congress in 1982 in an attempt to shift some
of the ill effects of federal subsidies, such as flood insurance and infrastructure assistance, away from coastal barriers, including barrier
islands. A product of conservative political times, CBRA was intended
to reduce threats to people and property and to minimize the expenditures of the federal government that typically encourage the development of hazardous, sensitive areas of the coast.

The act designated a Coastal Barrier Resources System (CBRS), originally comprising 186 undeveloped barrier island units, including
453,000 acres and 666 miles of shoreline. After October 1983, a number of federal subsidies would no longer be permitted in these designated areas, including the issuance of new flood insurance policies and
the expenditure of federal money for roads, bridges, utilities, erosion
control, and nonemergency forms of disaster relief. The Department of
the Interior has responsibility for administering the program, with the
U.S. Fish and Wildlife Service as its lead agency.

Coastal barriers were defined in the act to include depositional geologic features (barrier islands, barrier spits) and "associated aquatic habitats" (e.g., adjacent marshes, estuaries; see P.C. 97-348; 16 U.S.C. 3501-10). Criteria for determining whether a coastal barrier was undeveloped, and thus should be included, were as follows (Godschalk, 1987):

- less than one walled and roofed building per 5 acres of land
- absence of urban infrastructure (vehicle access, water supply, wastewater disposal, and electrical service to each lot)
- not part of a development of 100 or more lots

A coastal barrier is not considered undeveloped if it has been perturbed in one or more of the following ways:

- extensive shoreline manipulation or stabilization
- widespread canal construction and maintenance
- major dredging projects and resulting sedimentary deposits
- intensive capitalization projects, such as condominiums, that effectively establish a commitment to stabilize the area even when there are few actual structures

The CBRA does not require an entire coastal barrier to be included as a unit in the system. An undeveloped portion of a coastal barrier may be included. For such CBRA units a boundary line is drawn along the break in development.

The Department of the Interior initially prepared maps in 1981, under the Omnibus Budget Reconciliation Act of that year. In consultation with landowners and others, Congress modified the boundaries of units, initially reducing the oceanfront area covered by the CBRA provisions. The CBRS was later expanded in 1990 under the Coastal Barrier Improvement Act to include 560 units, 1.27 million acres, and 1,200 shoreline miles (GAO, 1992). Most of the units added in 1990 were designated Otherwise Protected Areas, units such as local, state, and national parks that were already in public ownership. In addition, under the 1990 act, the Department of Interior was directed to map all undeveloped coastal barriers along the Pacific coast (eventually to be forwarded to Congress for inclusion in the CBRS).

Several studies have sought to evaluate the effectiveness of CBRA at discouraging barrier island development. In 1984, Godschalk conducted one of the first exploratory studies (1984, 1987). Using telephone interviews and mail surveys, this pilot study assessed the viewpoints of developers, government officials, and conservationists in three states (North Carolina, South Carolina, and Florida) and included two case studies (Topsail Island, North Carolina, and Hutchinson Island, Florida). The results of the study were mixed but raised serious questions about the effectiveness of CBRA. These limited case studies showed that at least initially the loss of subsidies slowed development. However, the cases also indicated that, especially for larger developments, developers probably would be able to find replacement insurance and would also be able to replace other subsidies (e.g., through state funding for bridge construction).

A 1990 study by the National Wildlife Federation examined aerial photographs to determine the extent of new development occurring after the enactment of CBRA (Jones and Stolzenberg, 1990). Specifically, structures were analyzed for 157 barrier island units, encompassing about 95,000 acres of fastland (solid land along the shoreline that is not subject to erosion). These results show that much development occurred after the enactment of CBRA. The study counted 594 additional (post-CBRA) structures, or an increase of more than 40%. The development activity was particularly high in certain states. Development in Florida accounted for about 52% of the total counted. Significant numbers of additional structures were also found in North Carolina, South Carolina, Alabama, Delaware, and Texas.

The U.S. General Accounting Office (GAO) undertook an assessment of CBRA in 1992. The GAO study examined 34 CBRS units (from the original 186), comparing aerial photographs over time with field visits and building permit data (GAO, 1992). The study also included extensive interviews with agency personnel and a random sample of property owners to determine whether restrictions on flood insurance were being complied with. The resulting conclusions of this study are similar. Of the 34 units analyzed, the GAO found that 9 had undergone new development since 1982. About 1,200 new residential units had been constructed in these 9 units, and additional development is planned for the future.

Yet the study also concluded that the CBRA restrictions have had some positive effect:

> CBRA's prohibitions of new federal expenditures and financial assistance have slowed, delayed, or stopped development in some CBRS units. For example, the principal owner of the CBRS unit at Deer Island, Mississippi, told us that he

[handwritten in left margin: CBRA not effective in preventing development]

could not proceed with his development plans without federal flood insurance and other forms of federal assistance. In an effort to proceed with plans to build about 160 condominium vacation cabins, a swimming pool, tennis courts, roads, and a marina, he has been trying to get the unit removed from the CBRS. He wants to develop the unit despite a history of hurricane damage that devastated previous structures on the island. (GAO, 1992, p. 17)

Despite the act's ability to slow down and discourage development in some units, the study does conclude that further development is likely unless stronger controls are pursued. In the study's words,

Additional future development in 9 of the 34 CBRS units included in our review is planned and likely to occur with or without federal financial assistance. Other CBRS units that are accessible and/or suitable for development and investment may undergo similar development. While the availability of accessible coastal land is limited, populations of coastal areas are expected to increase by tens of millions by the year 2010. This population increase will further spur market demand, providing an incentive for developers, owners and investors to assume the risks associated with owning and building in these storm-prone areas. Stronger protective measures may be needed if further development is to be discouraged. (GAO, 1992, p. 24)

The GAO study also uncovered other problems with CBRA implementation. The study's random sample of property owners found that about 9% of them were able to obtain flood insurance even though they were ineligible under CBRA. (These problems appear largely associated with write-your-own companies; see GAO, 1992, p. 26.) The Federal Emergency Management Agency (FEMA) identified a more recent example, finding that after Hurricane Fran in 1996, about 100 property owners in North Topsail Beach, North Carolina, were issued National Flood Insurance Program (NFIP) policies in error. The 1992 GAO study also identifies problems with the certification process established to ensure that federal agencies comply with the act, although it concludes that federal agencies generally are adhering to the restrictions.

The most recent study published by Salvesen and Godschalk (1999) and funded by the Coast Alliance, comes to similar conclusions. A major part of the study involved a random sample of parcels in three states, within and outside of CBRS areas, and comparing the percentage of these parcels that were developed. Sampled parcels located in the CBRS were found less likely to be developed (19% of CBRS parcels compared with 36% of non-CBRS parcels). The authors also analyzed the development experiences of four barriers in more detail. Generally, the authors conclude that, consistent with earlier studies, the CBRA limitations do seem to make a difference, although they note that substantial amounts of development are still occurring within CBRS units (for instance, the authors found a 300% increase in development in one North Carolina unit). The authors also conclude that the actions of state and local governments can make a significant difference: "Where state and local policies reinforce the objectives of CBRA, development is less likely to occur. The converse is also true" (Salvesen and Godschalk, 1999, p. 39).

Recommendations offered by Salvesen and Godschalk are similar to those of earlier studies, highlighting the need to strengthen CBRA (e.g., by codifying the density criterion), to include additional lands in the CBRS, to work with state and local governments to further reduce development subsidies, to reinforce the NFIP, and to accelerate the public acquisition of sensitive barrier island lands (see pp. 43–44). Jones and Stolzenberg (1990) recommend removal of the remaining forms of federal subsidy allowable under the current federal income tax code (casualty loss deductions, interest and property tax deductions for second homes, and accelerated depreciation for seasonal rental properties), prohibition of all loans made by federally insured banks and lending institutions (originally waived under Section 11 of CBRA), prohibition of federal block grants, and prohibition of federally funded projects occurring outside designated units yet affecting them.

Other recommendations include requiring that people who buy properties in CBRS units be notified by the seller in advance that they will be ineligible for certain federal subsidies. Also, it has been suggested that states should adopt provisions and policies consistent with the CBRA, which would prevent the state from encouraging development in the CBRS and similar areas. Several states (e.g., Maine, Florida, and Alabama) have already done this.

Photo 5.1. Blue whales surface in the Gulf of the Farallones National Marine Sanctuary. (Photo by NOAA.)

National Marine Sanctuary Program

— create sanctuaries in areas of importance

The National Marine Sanctuary Program (NMSP) was created in 1972 by Title III of the Marine Protection, Reserve and Sanctuary Act (MPRSA) and is administered by NOAA. The program was established to create and manage marine sanctuaries in areas of national significance to protect coastal and marine resources and to encourage scientific research in pristine waters. Sites selected must exhibit unique ecological, historical, research, educational, recreational, or aesthetic qualities.

Thirteen marine sanctuaries have been designated thus far: Stellwagen Bank in Massachusetts Bay; *U.S.S. Monitor* (North Carolina); Gray's Reef (Georgia); Florida Keys; Flower Garden Banks (Texas and Louisiana); Channel Islands, Cordell Bank, Monterey Bay, and Gulf of the Farallones (California); Olympic Coast (Washington); Fagatele Bay, American Samoa; Hawaiian Islands Humpback Whale Sanctuary; and the newest sanctuary and the first on the Great Lakes, Thunder Bay National Marine Sanctuary and Underwater Preserve in Lake Huron. Each sanctuary is managed according to a site-specific management plan prepared by NOAA.

The stated policies of MPRSA (16 U.S.C. §1431) are to:

- identify marine environment areas of national significance because of their resource or human use value

- provide authority for comprehensive and coordinated conservation and management of these marine areas that will complement existing regulatory authorities
- support, promote, and coordinate scientific research and monitoring of the resources of these marine areas
- enhance public awareness, understanding, appreciation, and wise use of the marine environment
- facilitate, to the extent compatible with the primary objective of resource protection, all public and private uses of the resources of these marine areas not prohibited pursuant to other authorities
- develop and implement plans to protect and manage the designated area and facilitate intergovernment coordination
- create models and incentives for ways to conserve and manage the designated areas
- cooperate with global programs that encourage conservation of marine resources
- maintain, restore, and enhance marine species that depend on the designated areas to survive

The concept of multiple use was introduced in this program to accommodate the various activities that are demanded of the sanctuary's resources. These include recreational and commercial fishing, scuba diving, vessel traffic, and oil exploration and drilling. Allowing sanctuaries to be used for purposes other than research made the designation of some areas more politically and economically feasible.

Another problem facing the NMSP is the enforcement and jurisdictional mechanisms in place. Multiple agencies at all levels of government exercise regulatory authority within each designated sanctuary, causing a lack of coordination and cooperation at some sites.

For instance, in addition to NOAA, the National Marine Fisheries Service has authority to enforce regulations at all sanctuaries; the National Park Service and various state agencies often are involved in regulatory enforcement. Conflict has been known to arise between the various agencies involved. However, there has been a concerted effort at intergovernment coordination on some levels. For example, the Coast Guard and NOAA are directed to coordinate enforcement activities in designated sanctuaries. Furthermore, since the 1992 reauthorization and amendments, NOAA has the power to review all federal agency actions that affect the sanctuaries.

Public participation and education are two important aspects of the NMSP. The educational programs accompanying some sanctuaries have been especially successful. The programs have taught members of the public, including many schoolchildren, have been made aware of the value of our marine resources, the fragility of marine ecosystems, and the threats they face. Public education has tended to bolster protection and enforcement efforts.

Local citizens are encouraged to participate in the NMSP at all stages. The selection and designation process is open to public comment, and citizens and other interested parties have opportunity to give testimony regarding plans that have been proposed by NOAA.

Critics of the NMSP have pointed out that the program can never reach its stated goals given the limited funding it receives. The selection and designation of new sanctuaries is lengthy and entails the preparation of an environmental impact statement, a management plan, and resource assessments. The operation of a sanctuary includes financial support for educational programs, regulatory enforcement, and sanctuary maintenance. Unlike the National Estuarine Research Reserve System, the NMSP does not operate on a cost share budget with the states; federal funds must cover all the financial needs of the NMSP. Funding for the NMSP has increased over time with the inclusion of more sanctuaries, but there are limited opportunities for existing programs to grow at current funding levels.

Another criticism of the NMSP is that the designation of individual, small areas of the ocean as sanctuaries does not provide adequate protection for those areas or for the ocean as a whole. Designated sanctuaries are not immune to external forces such as oil spills, nearby dredge spoils, intensive fish and shellfish harvesting, and other events that affect the health of the resources within sanctuary borders. The program has no mechanism for regulating such activities beyond jurisdictional boundaries and therefore cannot safeguard the entire area. However, despite these criticisms, the NMSP has thus far provided an effective management framework for preserving some of our nation's most unique and valuable natural marine resources.

The Florida Keys National Marine Sanctuary has incorporated some innovative techniques into its management plan. In 1990, Congress enacted the Florida Keys National Marine Sanctuary and Protection Act. According to the act, the Key Largo and Looe Key National Marine Sanctuaries, established in 1975 and 1981, respectively, were incorporated into the new Florida Keys Sanctuary. The sanctuary is now the second largest of its kind in the United States, encompassing 120 protected sites and approximately 3,800 square miles.

The act lays out certain rules for the sanctuary, including restricting commercial vessel traffic within an internationally designated "area to be avoided." In addition, the large size of the new sanctuary affords the opportunity to set up differing regulations for separate areas within its borders, similar to a system already in place at the Great Barrier Reef Marine Park of Australia. "No-take" ecological preserves have been established in coral reefs to allow these areas to recover from overuse and overharvest. A system of zones with varying levels of restrictions to ensure protection of resources is incorporated into the comprehensive management plan for the sanctuary. A 1997 management plan created five zones: the previously mentioned ecological preserves, wildlife management areas, existing management areas, sanctuary preservation areas, and special-use areas. Some areas, such as the existing management zones, can continue to be used in the accustomed ways, whereas other areas including special-use zones can be designated for preservation, restoration, or scientific research. Still other areas, such as the Dry Tortugas Ecological Preserve in the Florida Keys National Marine Sanctuary, are more restrictive. The Dry Tortugas Reserve is the largest no-fish zone in the United States.

The National Estuarine Research Reserve System

Section 315 of the Coastal Zone Management Act (CZMA) of 1972 establishes the National Estuarine Research Reserve System (NERRS). The secretary of commerce was directed to "acquire, develop, or operate estuarine sanctuaries, to serve as natural field laboratories in which to study and gather data on the natural and human processes occurring within the estuaries of the coastal zone." The CZMA also created the system to "acquire lands to provide access to public beaches and other public coastal areas of environmental, recreational, historical, aesthetic, ecological, or cultural value."

These purposes were to fulfill the perceived need for more information about the functions and processes of estuarine ecosystems and humans' effects on them. The value of the nation's estuaries had been realized, but before the institution of NERRS fewer undisturbed or non-polluted estuarine areas were available for scientific study and public education. Therefore, the NERRS was established to create estuarine "field laboratories."

Governors of the coastal states nominate estuaries for inclusion in the system. The areas must be "representative estuarine ecosystems suitable for research." The state must provide sufficient protection to foster a suitable environment for research, which can require fee-simple acquisition but can also be provided through conservation easements or land regulation.

Funding of the NERRS operates on a 50–50 federal–state cost share basis. Three types of matching grants are available. These include the preacquisition award for site selection and preparation of draft management plans; the acquisition and development award for land acquisition, minor construction activities (such as nature trails and boat ramps), and program development; and the operation and management award for assistance in implementing the research, educational, and administrative programs that are detailed in the individual research reserve management plans. There are 25 NERRS-designated estuaries in 21 coastal states. A systemwide monitoring program monitors water quality and atmospheric variables within the NERRS sites.

National Estuary Program

Created in a 1987 amendment to the CWA, the National Estuary Program (NEP) aims to identify, restore, and protect nationally significant estuaries. The EPA administers the program adapting the ecosystem approach used in the Chesapeake Bay Program for 28 estuaries in the United States. The NEP is a voluntary program that provides funds on a 75–25 federal–state share and technical assistance to designated estuary projects. The EPA identifies estuaries that are threatened by pollution, development, or overuse and assists these projects in preparing a Comprehensive Conservation and Management Plan (CCMP) (Imperial and Hennessey, 1996). The CCMP must address three management areas:

- water and sediment quality
- living resources
- land use and water resources

To prepare a CCMP, NEP projects are developed through a management conference process involving a policy committee and a management committee.

The management conference generally is headed by a policy committee made up of the following:

- the EPA
- the state governor (or governors, in cases where estuary boundaries cross state lines)
- state agency officials

The policy committee members direct the activities of the management conference, but the management committee is the consensus-building body. The management committee identifies and defines environmental problems in the estuary, advises the policy committee, and guides the development and approval of the CCMP (Imperial and Hennessey, 1996). The CCMP contains an action plan that addresses problems identified by the management conference. Action Plan Demonstration Projects test on a small scale the effectiveness of strategies and technologies that may be incorporated in the CCMP.

The planning process used by the NEP holds promise for the future of ecosystem-based management. Challenges include clarifying how changes and modifications to the CCMPs will be made, overcoming intergovernment obstacles (such as an estuary in multiple states), and obtaining a stable source of implementation funding (Imperial and Hennessey, 1996).

Marine Protected Areas

In May 2000, President Clinton signed Executive Order 13158, which strengthened and expanded the U.S. system of Marine Protected Areas (MPAs), calling for the development of scientifically based, comprehensive national MPA system that represents diverse marine ecosystems and U.S. natural and cultural resources.

A globally accepted concept, MPAs are broadly defined in the executive order as "any area of the marine environment that has been reserved by Federal, State, territorial, tribal, or local laws or regulations to provide lasting protection for part or all of the natural and cultural resources therein." In the framework proposed in the executive order, MPAs should be managed by the Departments of Commerce and the Interior, which were required to establish a Marine Protected Area Center in Santa Cruz, California. The center serves as both a training center and a clearinghouse of MPA information.

MPA proposals have often raised controversy, particularly when a no-take reserve area is proposed. The process of establishing MPAs includes the following four steps (National Research Council, 2001):

- evaluate conservation needs at local and regional levels
- define objectives and goals
- describe key biological and oceanic features of the region
- identify and choose sites that have the highest potential for implementation

Beach Renourishment and Shoreline Protection

Significant subsidies have been provided in the form of funding and technical assistance from federal and state agencies for flood control and oceanfront property protection. These subsidies have been provided for both the installation of "hard" devices, such as seawalls, revetments, groins, jetties, and breakwaters, and "soft" approaches, such as beach renourishment and dune building. A comprehensive study of erosion in the United States found that coastal erosion may claim one out of every four houses within 500 feet of the U.S. shoreline over the next 60 years (Heinz Center, 2000a).

At the federal level the U.S. Army COE has had primary responsibility for shore protection programs. The COE has shifted its focus from hard stabilization projects to soft approaches such as renourishment. Beach nourishment can provide storm protection in situations where it is technically feasible (i.e., adequate and compatible sand supply) provided that (National Research Council, 1995):

- Erosion rates are a component of project design.
- Engineering standards are used for the planning, design, and construction of the project.
- Projects are maintained according to design specifications.

Photo 5.2. Sand is pumped onto a beach on Tybee Island, Georgia, as part of a beach renourishment project. (Photo by U.S. Army COE.)

Establishing a federal management strategy for beach renourishment has proved difficult because erosion rates and sand supplies vary greatly along the U.S. coastline. Because maintaining the renourishment projects is critical to their success, long-term commitments must be made by the COE and state and local partners. The Water Resources Development Act of 1999 reduced the federal cost share for shore protection projects to 50%, placing more responsibility directly with the states and local governments. Table 5.2 shows that through 1996, nourishment along the East and Gulf coasts and the Great Lakes exceeded $2 billion.

A number of states now provide funding for local renourishment projects, often through the issuance of bonds and often in combination with federal subsidies. In New Jersey, for instance, the state legislature created a Shore Protection Fund to help implement the state's Shore Protection Master Plan. The fund is designed to be the nonfederal share of any state–federal renourishment project (NOAA, 2000). The state of Maryland has provided substantial funding for beach renourishment in Ocean City (some $60 million) under its Shore Erosion Control Program (SECP). Also under the SECP the state provides interest-free loans and technical assistance to shorefront property owners experiencing erosion problems for, among other things, the construction of bulkheads and riprap (Pito, 1992). Maryland also provides 50% matching funds to property owners who undertake nonstructural erosion control (e.g., grass planting).

Beach renourishment remains a controversial approach to the coastal erosion problem. Such projects are very expensive; for example, Miami Beach spent $5 million per mile in 1981 (Pilkey and Dixon, 1996). Such projects also have been shown to have much shorter life spans than are typically estimated (e.g., see Pilkey and Clayton, 1987; Pilkey, 1989). A single nor'easter or other significant coastal storm can wipe out millions of dollars in renourishment expenditures (which is what has happened in Ocean City, Maryland). A 1982 $5.2-million renourishment project in Ocean City, New Jersey, lasted only 2.5 months (Pilkey and Clayton, 1987). Coastal geologist Orrin Pilkey concluded from a major 1987 study of beach replenishment that coastal engineers have remained unjustifiably optimistic in predicting the lifetime and costs of beach nourishment projects (Pilkey and Clayton, 1987). Beach renourishment policy in the United States must consider the possibility that the projects can be a temporary fix to a long-term problem. The federal government should

Table 5.2. Regional and State Summary of Beach Renourishment Costs through 1996: New England, East and Gulf Coasts, and Great Lakes

State	No. of projects	Total estimated cost[a]	Total adjusted cost (in 1996 dollars)[b]
Alabama	2	$1,461,977	$1,870,000
Connecticut	44	$12,387,418	$48,259,564
Delaware	33	$20,600,000	$46,895,882
Florida	257	$499,686,113	$667,957,408
Georgia	8	$25,735,544	$34,062,300
Louisiana	16	$39,704,045	$54,529,849
Maine	15	$3,643,612	$6,778,180
Maryland	6	$51,280,869	$65,977,063
Massachusetts	81	$18,150,531	$56,410,146
Mississippi	13	$19,738,060	$56,052,218
New Hampshire	8	$3,914,808	$25,575,329
New Jersey	124	$188,424,101	$312,720,819
New York	73	$183,243,307	$523,099,957
North Carolina	108	$93,553,601	$146,156,213
Rhode Island	11	$1,481,946	$3,255,838
South Carolina	28	$53,538,342	$90,034,254
Texas	14	$19,833,383	$24,637,623
Virginia	48	$38,559,116	$78,814,630
Great Lakes			
Erie	54	$40,461,571	$77,905,646
Huron	26	$3,881,448	$5,168,858
Michigan	280	$65,842,448	$100,804,089
Ontario	3	$1,283,000	$2,847,266
Superior	53	$7,381,267	$9,551,403
TOTAL	1,305	$1,393,786,507	$2,439,364,535

Source: Data adopted from the Duke University Program for the Study of Developed Shorelines.

[a]Total estimated costs include both known costs and estimates for projects with unknown costs. Estimates were determined by using the mean cost by funding category or by the mean regional cost, in project-year dollars.
[b]Total adjusted cost is the total estimated cost adjusted to 1996 dollars.

consider ways to incorporate exit strategies in their shore projects to reduce taxpayer burden in cases where renourishment clearly is not meeting expectations.

Federal Environmental
Policy That Affects the Coast

The connection between coastal zone management and other federal environmental policy is strong, despite the fact that much of the environmental policy was not prepared exclusively for the coastal environment. In this section, these connected federal policies are examined.

National Environmental Policy Act

The National Environmental Policy Act (NEPA) became law on New Year's Day 1970. The congressional objectives were spelled out in Section 2 of the act:

> To declare a national policy which will encourage productive and enjoyable harmony between man and his environment; to promote efforts which will prevent or eliminate damage to the environment and biosphere and stimulate the health and welfare of man; to enrich the understanding of the ecological systems and natural resources important to the Nation; and to establish a Council on Environmental Quality.

NEPA strives for agencies of the federal government to consider the environmental ramifications of their actions by requiring all federal actions, in the coastal zone as elsewhere, to prepare an assessment of the effect of those actions on the natural environment. Environmental impact assessments are used as a screening device and can produce a finding that the federal action will not significantly harm the environment, or a finding of no significant impact. If a federal project is deemed a "major federal action," NEPA requires that a detailed environmental impact statement be prepared. The statement documents the environmental impact of the proposed action, including any adverse environmental effects that cannot be avoided should the proposed project be implemented, and alternatives to the proposed action.

NEPA is a policy act, setting course for government action, but it lacks the regulatory muscle of other federal environmental statutes (Caldwell, 1998). It requires an assessment of the impact of proposed actions but does not go any further, even when the impact is horrendous. Authority to prevent an action must be found in some place other than NEPA. As a policy act, however, NEPA has succeeded as an information dissemination device, forcing the documentation of impacts. NEPA supporters contend that the act's most enduring legacy is a framework of collaboration between federal agencies and those who bear the environmental, social, and economic impacts of agency decisions (CEQ, 1997).

Clean Water Act

The CWA contains several key programs and provisions that have had a substantial management influence on the coastal zone. These include a shared system of federal–state control of point source pollution, local stormwater management, a nonpoint program, restrictions on wetland dredging and filling (Section 404), and the NEP.

The centerpiece of the CWA's pollution prevention strategy is the National Pollutant Discharge Elimination System (NPDES), which is administered by the EPA. Under the NPDES program, a permit is required from the EPA or an authorized state for the discharge of any point source or end-of-pipe pollutant into U.S. waters. The NPDES permit requirement extends to federal oil and gas leases beyond state jurisdictional boundaries.

Urban stormwater runoff, often highly polluted, is carried by storm sewer systems and discharged into streams and rivers without treatment. Because of stormwater's potential effects on water quality, the CWA requires that local governments obtain an NPDES permit for stormwater discharges. The NPDES phase I stormwater permit program, created in 1990, applied only to communities or counties of 100,000 or more and 11 categories of industrial activity, including construction activity that disturbs 5 or more acres of land. In the winter of 1999, the EPA promulgated NPDES phase II, which extended the permit requirement to all small stormwater systems not covered by phase I and reduces the size of regulated construction activities to include projects between 1 and 5 acres of land disturbance. Local governments are required under phase II to develop a stormwater management program consisting of six elements:

- public education and outreach
- public participation and involvement
- illicit discharge detection and elimination
- construction site runoff control
- postconstruction runoff control
- pollution prevention and good housekeeping

Section 319 of the CWA is the nonpoint source (NPS) program. States are required to develop management programs to address NPS runoff, including the use of best management practices (e.g., detention or retention ponds, swales, and check dams). The NPS program authorizes grants to assist the states in implementing their management programs. One of the most important sections of the federal CWA is Section 404, which represents the cornerstone of federal efforts to protect wetlands. Specifically, Section 404 restricts the discharge of dredge and fill materials into U.S. waters, requiring permit approval from the U.S. Army Corps of Engineers (COE) or, in some cases, from the state. The COE must approve, deny, or modify such permit requests consistent with its own public interest review and the Section 404(b)(i) guidelines promulgated by the EPA. (The EPA also has final veto authority over the issuance of 404 permits.) Under the 404(b)(i) guidelines, the COE can issue a permit only where it concludes that there are no practicable alternative sites for the proposed use (no water-dependent uses are assumed to have practicable alternatives) and where impacts are mitigated to the maximum extent. Mitigation requirements can include the creation of new wetlands or the enhancement or restoration of degraded wetlands.

The 404 program has suffered from a number of problems and limitations, including a limited set of activities over which it has control (i.e., it pertains only to discharges), problems with conflicting definitions of wetlands, the perceived ease with which the COE has issued permits (statistically, few permit requests are denied), the inconsistency with which wetland mitigation and compensation are required, and the failure to designate in advance wetlands where discharges would and would not be appropriate. In the 2000 case *Solid Waste Agency of Northern Cook County v. Army Corps of Engineers et al.,* the Supreme Court found that the COE permit authority regarding wetlands does not extend to "isolated" wetlands that are not adjacent to navigable waterways. Many states have a regulatory framework (e.g., stormwater management) that protects isolated wetland areas, but others have been forced to scramble to try to retain control over isolated wetlands.

The 404 program, then, exercises much control over development in coastal areas. Clearly, however, the program could be strengthened in a number of ways, which would permit it to more effectively reduce coastal risks and take into account future sea level rise.

Clean Air Act

The Clean Air Act (CAA), first passed in 1970, regulates air emissions from area, stationary, and mobile sources. Under the CAA, the EPA is authorized to establish National Ambient Air Quality Standards (NAAQS). The CAA is implemented by the states themselves through state implementation plans. The NAAQS sets maximum pollutant levels for the following seven criteria pollutants:

- ground-level ozone (smog)
- volatile organic compounds
- nitrogen dioxide
- carbon monoxide
- particulate matter
- sulfur dioxide
- lead

Areas that do not meet NAAQS standards for one or more of the criteria pollutants are considered "nonattainment areas" by the EPA. It has been estimated that about 90 million Americans live in nonattainment areas.

Nonattainment areas are required to reduce air pollution levels so they may reach NAAQS standards and come into attainment. Since there is a relationship between air pollution and water pollution, as the nonattainment area's air quality increases, there may be a corresponding increase in water quality. Hence, regulation of air quality through the CAA may affect water quality in the coastal zone.

Endangered Species Act

The purpose of the Endangered Species Act (ESA) is to conserve and recover endangered and threatened species and the ecosystems on which they depend. An endangered species is one that is in danger of extinction throughout all or a significant portion of its range. A threatened species is likely to become endangered within the foreseeable future. As of October 2001, 1,249 species were listed as endangered in the United States (509 animals and 740 plants).

The act requires that all federal agencies use their authority to conserve listed species and to consult with the U.S. Fish and Wildlife Service, which administers the act to ensure that their actions do not threaten the continued existence of a listed species.

Section 6 of the act encourages each state to prepare conservation programs for threatened and endangered species found therein. Section 9 prohibits any person from "taking" a listed species. The term *take* means to "harass, harm, pursue, hunt, shoot, wound, kill, trap, capture, or collect" and has been interpreted to include significant habitat modification or degradation. However, private landowners who want to develop property that is inhabited by an endangered species can receive an incidental take permit that allows them to develop the land if they prepare and implement a habitat conservation plan providing for conservation of the species in question.

National Flood Insurance Program

Under the National Flood Insurance Program (NFIP), federally subsidized flood insurance is made available to owners of flood-prone property in participating communities. Coverage is available both for the structure itself (up to $250,000 for a single-family structure) and for its contents (up to $100,000). Administered by FEMA's Federal Insurance Administration, the program requires participating communities to adopt certain minimum floodplain management standards. Other standards include a requirement that new structures in the 100-year flood zone be elevated to or above the 100-year flood level (generally known as base flood elevation, or BFE), and a requirement that subdivisions be designed to minimize exposure to flood hazards. For high-hazard coastal zones (velocity zones, or V zones), additional standards are imposed, including the requirement that buildings be elevated on pilings and that all new development be landward of mean high water; the BFE includes potential wave heights, and new development must not damage dunes or dune vegetation. FEMA recently introduced the concept of a coastal A zone, which is differentiated from the inland A flood zone by the effect of waves, storm surge, and erosion, albeit to a lesser degree than in the V zone (FEMA, 2000b). Although program participation is entirely voluntary, strong incentives exist. Because of limited participation in the early years of the program, the 1973 Flood Disaster Protection Act mandated flood insurance for all federally backed mortgages (e.g., Veterans' Administration, Federal Housing Administration) and mortgages and loans obtained through federally insured and regulated financial institutions. Also, disaster assistance grants (public assistance) are not available to local governments not participating in the program (individual property owners need not have flood insurance to be eligible for individual and family grants, however). As a result, community participation has been high, with about 19,000 localities participating.

Although participation rates for owners of flood-prone property have been fairly low (about 25% of those eligible), this amounts to a large federal financial liability. There are approximately 4.1 million flood policies in effect. The NFIP is the second largest financial obligation at the federal level (Social Security being the largest). It is estimated that almost 60% of the NFIP policyholders are located in coastal communities, with many of these located in the most hazardous locations (Platt, 1999). Some 84,000 policies are in V zones (FEMA, 2000a).

Historically, the NFIP has suffered from a number of problems and has been the subject of much criticism. A major point of contention between supporters and detractors of the program is whether it is actuarially sound and thus pays for itself. The program has generated deficits over much of its lifetime. As shown in Table 5.3, between 1986 and 1997 the program generated a $1.1-billion deficit (Platt, 1999).

Another significant concern about the NFIP as it functions in coastal areas is its failure to take into account long-term erosion. At current enrollment rates, the NFIP will pay $80 million per year for erosion-related damage. This represents about 5% of all premiums (Heinz Center, 2000a). Long-term erosion trends generally are not taken into account in current FEMA floodplain mapping. The V zones, or velocity zones, are the closest flood zone to a shoreline erosion zone, yet they are often narrowly drawn and "frequently exclude adjoining areas with

Table 5.3. National Flood Insurance Program: Policies, Coverage, and Net Income or Loss, FY 1986–1997

Fiscal year	No. of policies (1,000s)	Coverage ($ billion)	Net income (loss)
1986	2,075	133	$29.7 mill.
1987	2,079	158	$171 mill.
1988	2,101	169	$183 mill.
1989	2,200	179	($146 mill.)
1990	2,378	203	$73 mill.
1991	2,506	219	$169 mill.
1992	2,561	229	($20.4 mill.)
1993	2,725	254	($602 mill.)
1994	2,804	274	$269 mill.
1995	3,264	325	($576 mill.)
1996	3,546	369	($536 mill.)
1997	3,811	422	($117 mill.)
1986–1997 (CUMULATIVE TOTAL)			($1.1 billion)

Source: Adapted from Platt (1999).

virtually indistinguishable hazard characteristics" (National Research Council, 1990, p. 75), hence the addition of the coastal A zone. A report on coastal erosion issued by the Heinz Center for Science, Economics and the Environment recommends that the cost of expected erosion be included when setting flood insurance rates in coastal areas (Heinz Center, 2000a). Another problem is the infrequency with which flood insurance maps are revised and updated. It has been estimated that FEMA is able to remap communities on average every 9 years. In 1997, FEMA developed a Map Modernization Plan to update and digitize the entire U.S. floodplain map panel inventory. Unfortunately, lack of funding has hindered the Map Modernization Plan efforts. Many participating communities are rapidly growing, and substantial development and building in the floodplain can modify local flood hazards. State and local governments are likely to become more involved in the floodplain mapping process in the near future. In the aftermath of the 1999 Hurricane Floyd disaster, the state of North Carolina became FEMA's first state with responsibility for mapping its own floodplains. Also in 1999, the joint government of Charlotte–Mecklenburg County, North Carolina, used a FEMA-approved hydrology model to remap its floodplains at ultimate buildout of each watershed and establish floodplain extents accordingly. Such higher standards probably will remain a solely local activity for the foreseeable future.

For new construction occurring in flood hazard zones, the NFIP has imposed stronger building standards, notably through elevation requirements. Newer elevated structures on pilings have clearly performed better in coastal storms, and in this sense the NFIP has had a positive effect. Under the NFIP these new construction standards are also imposed during reconstruction under its "substantial improvement" provisions. FEMA administers another program called the Community Rating System (CRS), which seeks to reward communities for the additional activities and programs they undertake, beyond the minimum requirements of the NFIP, that minimize flood damages. Specifically, the insurance premiums of property owners within these communities are reduced to take into account these local activities. Participation in CRS is voluntary, and local governments are responsible for documenting implementation of these creditable activities.

Federal Disaster Assistance

The federal government has been involved for many years in assisting state and local governments in responding to and recovering from disasters. Such financial assistance acts as another form of incentive for development in hazardous coastal locations by subsidizing the risk of public and private actions. The federal disaster assistance framework was substantially revamped in 1988, when Congress passed the Robert T. Stafford Disaster Relief and Emergency Assistance Act, which provides greater emphasis and financial support for mitigation activities.

Several major forms of disaster assistance are available through FEMA. Such assistance generally falls into two categories: individual and family assistance and public assistance.

Under FEMA's Individual and Family Grants (IFG) program, grants of aid up to $14,400 can be made to individuals and families to cover disaster-related expenses (e.g., replacement of personal belongings such as furniture and appliances). Under FEMA's public assistance program, states and communities can receive grants, usually at a 75–25 federal cost share, to cover the cost of damages to public facilities and infrastructure. Eligible projects include repair and replacement of roads, bridges, sewer and water systems, and recreational facilities and replacement of artificial public beaches. Communities not participating in the NFIP are not eligible for public assistance funds. Applicants under the IFG program need not be in a participating community or have purchased federal flood insurance (although they must agree to purchase it as a condition of receiving such grants).

Precisely how much of an impact federal disaster assistance has in encouraging (or failing to discourage) hazardous and damaging coastal development is uncertain. Amounts of federal disaster assistance in recent years have been substantial.

Disaster assistance is seen by states and communities as an entitlement and something deserved regardless of the extent or cause of the damages or the ability of these jurisdictions to assume these costs. In theory, presidential disaster declarations are to be issued only where the resources of affected states and local governments are clearly exceeded. Yet presidential declarations have been increasingly viewed as pro forma and have occurred even where damage levels are modest and where state and local governments could have assumed the cost with little burden.

In an update of the Stafford Act, the Disaster Mitigation Act of 2000, FEMA stepped up its emphasis on hazard mitigation by requiring that communities have a hazard mitigation plan in place to receive some types of federal disaster aid. The Stafford Act required states to prepare a Section 409 hazard mitigation plan. An assessment of earlier state plans demonstrated that many of the state 409 plans lacked some of the baseline requirements of the original act (Godschalk et al., 1999). The

Disaster Mitigation Act of 2000 offers the incentive of increased mitigation funds if states will prepare an enhanced hazard mitigation plan.

Part of the Stafford Act is the Hazard Mitigation Grant Program, which provides federal matching funds for state and local mitigation projects. These grant funds are tied to disaster declarations and are limited to 10% of the federal share of the public assistance monies made available.

National Park System

The National Park System was created by the National Park Service Organic Act of 1916 to manage lands under the control of the Department of the Interior. The National Park Service's stated purpose is to "conserve the scenery and the natural and historic objects and wildlife" within national parks, monuments, and reservations and "provide for the entertainment of same in such manner and by such means as will leave them unimpaired for the enjoyment of future generations." A proposed unit of the National Park System must meet four standards:

- The area is an outstanding example of a particular type of resource.
- It possesses exceptional value or quality in illustrating or interpreting the natural or cultural themes of our nation's heritage.
- It offers superlative opportunities for recreation, public use and enjoyment, or scientific study.
- It retains a high degree of integrity as a true, accurate, and unspoiled example of the resource.

The National Park System encompasses more than 83 million acres of land and includes national seashores on the Atlantic, Gulf, and Pacific coasts and national lakeshores on the Great Lakes. Each park unit is established and administered by site-specific congressional legislation. Including the National Park System, the federal government is the largest landowner in the country (Table 5.4).

Table 5.4. Federally Owned Lands, United States, 2000

Agency	Program	Total acreage (millions)
Bureau of Land Management	National Landscape Conservation System	39.1
National Park Service	National Parks, Seashores, and Lakeshores	83.3
U.S. Department of Agriculture Forest Service	National Forests and Grasslands	192
U.S. Fish and Wildlife Service	National Wildlife Refuges	93

Photo 5.3. Sleeping Bear Dunes National Lakeshore, Empire, Michigan. (Photo by NOAA.)

Brownfields

Brownfields are defined as "abandoned, idled, or under-used industrial and commercial facilities where expansion or redevelopment is complicated by real or perceived environmental contamination" (EPA, 2001). The EPA provides incentives for brownfield development. Falling under the Comprehensive Environmental Response, Compensation, and Liability Act (CERCLA, commonly known as the Superfund program), the EPA administers the Brownfields program.

The Brownfields program is related to coastal zone management because many former industrial sites can be found in our nation's coastal communities, especially because shoreline access helps maximize access to water for better transport, cooling, and power. Over time, many of these facilities have been abandoned. The expense of redeveloping such areas can be very high, so communities have been reluctant to do so. The Brownfields program provides funding and incentives to clean up these areas, thereby aiding in the revitalization of coastal communities. Brownfields can be converted into public beach access areas and parks, thereby allowing improvement of coastal resources. Wyandotte, Michigan, converted a former BASF plant into a waterfront park complete with a walkway and observation decks, picnic areas, jogging trails, a rowing club, and a public golf course (Walker, 1997).

De Facto Coastal Policy

As described earlier, federal policy that has unintended consequences that affect the coastal zone is considered de facto coastal policy. In other words, de facto coastal policy is that which is created with objectives that are unrelated to coastal zone management but nonetheless influences management of the coast. Such policy is administered by the Department of Energy (DOE), the Internal Revenue Service, the Department of Transportation (DOT), the Department of Housing and Urban Development (HUD), and other agencies.

Department of Energy — power plants

Among other things, the DOE determines where energy facilities, such as nuclear power plants, pipelines, and refineries, are located. It also determines how existing facilities will be operated and what happens to closed facilities. When such facilities are located in the coastal zone (or a corresponding watershed), their presence can affect pollutants in the coastal region and development patterns to support the facilities. Therefore, the decisions that the DOE makes regarding facility placement greatly affect the coastal zone and necessary steps for protection.

Internal Revenue Service — subsidies

Coastal development subsidies are provided in the form of tax expenditures, or deductions, and other subsidies contained in federal and state tax codes. For example, the tax code encourages construction and development in the coastal region by making mortgage interest on second homes tax deductible. Because the coastal zone, especially beachfront property, often is inhabited by seasonal populations, the incentives for purchasing a second home affect the demand for homes in the coastal zone.

The casualty loss deduction allows coastal property owners to deduct the cost of damages resulting from hurricanes and other natural disasters. Allowable deductions are determined by subtracting the poststorm value of the property from its prestorm value, less insurance received. The deduction is allowed only where losses exceed 10% of adjusted gross income.

Coastal Development Subsidies

The DOT has provided extensive funding for the construction of highways, roads and bridges, and other improvements that have served to make many otherwise remote coastal areas readily accessible. What's more, because bridges and roads contribute to stormwater runoff, DOT policy decisions affect nonpoint source pollution in coastal regions, which in turn affects how the coast must be managed, preserved, and protected.

HUD administers programs and develops policies that influence coastal development patterns. HUD provides Community Development Block Grants to communities for a variety of renovation and restoration projects as long as a percentage of the projects benefits low-income citizens. HUD also provides guaranteed home loans and has teamed up with FEMA to provide disaster assistance to public housing authorities after presidentially declared disasters.

Funding decisions for infrastructure construction also affect the coastal zone because development follows infrastructure. If an undeveloped coastal area has been granted funds for public facilities, development will inevitably occur. Once a community agrees to spend money on wastewater treatment plants and sewer systems, dense development follows that can harm the coastal environment and put more people and property at risk from natural coastal hazards.

In large degree, these coastal development subsidies are largely hidden, so estimates of their aggregate cost are hard to come by. However, there is little doubt that the extent of the public costs brought to bear from these subsidies is substantial.

Conclusions

This chapter has briefly reviewed several of the primary federal programs, laws, and policies that influence the coastline. The federal CZMA was introduced here; the state programs initiated under the CZMA are discussed in Chapter 6.

This review of key programs and laws leads to several important conclusions about federal coastal policy in the United States. First, as the review indicates, policy is fragmented and dispersed over several different federal agencies and departments. There is no single federal agency in charge of coordinating these different programs and laws, and there is no comprehensive, unified national coastal management plan or program. Moreover, the review of programs illustrates that federal policy can and does influence the coast and coastal development in numerous ways. Historically, the federal government has provided a number of different subsidies to coastal development, including making available federally subsidized flood insurance, disaster assistance monies, income tax code provisions, and a host of infrastructure subsidies (e.g., funding for roads and highways, sewage treatment plants). At the same time, the federal government has sought to promote conservation and protection of coastal resources, for instance, by acquiring coastal areas for national seashores and wildlife refuges and encouraging coastal states and localities to prepare coastal management plans. We would argue that many federal subsidies should be eliminated or substantially reshaped if sensible and sustainable coastal development is to be achieved. Coastal property owners should be asked to assume, as much as possible, the costs of locating where they choose. This suggests the need to substantially raise NFIP premiums, curtail the issuance of new flood insurance in especially hazardous locations (e.g., within V zones, seaward of a 30- or 50-year erosion line), curtail or substantially reduce postdisaster assistance, and modify the U.S. tax code so that it encourages more rational development patterns, for example.

Many of these federal programs and policies have certain management benefits. As a result of the NFIP, development occurring within the 100-year floodplain must adhere to certain positive mitigative building standards (e.g., elevation and floodproofing). The federal CZMA has clearly resulted in the enactment of state and local management controls that would not have otherwise been undertaken. As a result of Section 404 of the CWA, many thousands of acres of coastal wetlands have received substantial protection from development. Under the ESA, critical habitat in coastal areas has been afforded some protection.

Moreover, this review has shown that many of the federal programs identified have teeth. Federal disaster assistance provisions, especially the Disaster Mitigation Act of 2000, contain substantial authority for FEMA to require that more attention be paid to hazard mitigation by states and localities. Provisions of the federal CWA (especially Section 404) have the potential, if stringently and conscientiously enforced, to reduce coastal hazards and to further minimize coastal environmental degradation. Many of these programs, though perhaps not as directed toward management and mitigation in their present forms, constitute a positive foundation on which to build a more effective and sensible federal coastal management strategy or plan.

It is clear that a great many federal programs play a role in managing the coast. There are those that manage the coast directly by design (e.g., the Coastal Zone Management Act), those that are connected to coastal management by their involvement in larger programs (e.g., the CWA), and those that manage the coast almost by mistake or as an unintended consequence (e.g., the Internal Revenue Code).

It is also clear that these programs often are aimed in different directions and are trying to accomplish different, sometimes conflicting goals. Given the nature of our governments' overlap, confusion and even conflict probably are inevitable. However, it does seem that with some effort, the federal government could formulate a meaningful, comprehensive coastal policy against which other policies could be evaluated. In this way, policy and budgetary proposals could be seen and evaluated within a context of the entire resource. A national coastal policy would have the potential to guide future policy to accomplish more rational development patterns in the coastal zone.

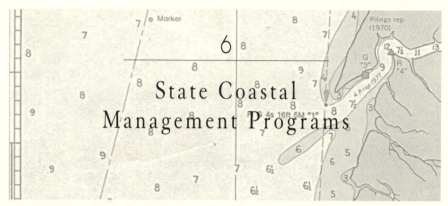

6

State Coastal
Management Programs

As Chapter 5 describes, there are many federal agencies and programs that influence coastal zone development but no single strategy. Moreover, historically in the United States responsibility for land use controls and planning (including coastal areas) has been left to states and localities. In 1972, with the passage of the Coastal Zone Management Act (CZMA), the federal government initiated a new partnership with states to promote planning and management of the nation's coastlines. In this chapter we review the content and focus of state coastal management programs (CMPs) under the CZMA, with profiles of certain states that have undertaken innovative or successful approaches.

As described in Chapter 5, under CZMA, funds are provided on a cost share basis to states to develop and implement their own CMPs. These state programs must meet minimum requirements of the CZMA and must be approved by the Department of Commerce (specifically the Office of Ocean and Coastal Resource Management [OCRM]). Certain subsequent federal actions and policies must be consistent with these state programs to the maximum extent practicable. Thus, the CZMA provides states with the double incentive of financial assistance and greater control over federal actions and policies.

The incentives provided under CZMA have encouraged a high degree of state participation. Thirty-three of 35 eligible coastal and Great Lakes states and American territories now have federally approved coastal programs. Although in some cases the CZMA has provided funding for states to undertake management activities they would have undertaken in any event, most observers believe the act has done much to encourage states to better plan for and manage their coastal zones. There is little doubt that the act has resulted in greater levels of protection for wetlands and estuarine waters, less risky coastal development patterns, and generally greater levels of state and local planning of development and growth.

One of the key features of the CZMA is the flexibility coastal states have in crafting their programs to meet their own unique circumstances and political and cultural contexts. Consequently, there is much variation among the state programs in terms of the organization of their management programs and the types of management tools and techniques used. Some states had little in the way of a management framework before 1972. In North Carolina, for instance, enactment of the Coastal Area Management Act (CAMA) created an entirely new regulatory and planning framework, including the creation of a Coastal Resources Commission (CRC), a permitting system for activities in Areas of Environmental Concern (AECs), and mandated planning in coastal counties and communities. Before CAMA neither the state nor local governments exercised much direct control over development in coastal areas.

Other coastal states have taken a networking approach in which their coastal programs involved pulling together a number of largely preexisting laws and management programs, perhaps with different state agencies taking the lead in one or more aspects of the program. Coastal states exhibiting this pattern include Florida, Wisconsin, Massachusetts, and Maine.

In some states the CMP has been integrated into a much broader state-planning framework. Oregon is perhaps the best example of this approach. Here coastal management requirements are expressed in the form of several statewide goals, part of a set of 19 goals that serve as the basis for a system of statewide land use planning. Local government plans and state agency actions must be consistent with these goals. In other states, coastal management is not well integrated in broader statewide planning. In North Carolina, for instance, the CAMA program applies only to the coastal zone and has little relationship to planning in other parts of the state. The framework for Maine's, Oregon's, and North Carolina's CMPs is discussed in greater detail later in this chapter.

States have also taken different approaches to defining the coastal zone to which regulations and program requirements apply. Florida has defined its entire land area, except for public and Native American lands, as its coastal zone. In North Carolina, the 20 counties that border brackish water make up the coastal zone; in Rhode Island, the coastal zone boundary extends 200 feet inland of a coastal feature; and in Connecticut, the coastal zone includes all lands within the interior contour elevation of the 100-year frequency flood zone, a 1,000-foot setback from the mean high-water mark, or a 1,000-foot setback from the inland boundary of mapped tidal wetlands, whichever is farthest inland.

Not all state CMPs have been completely successful. Two main trouble areas continue to be implementation and enforcement of programs and regulations. For example, Florida's CMP looks good on paper but has suffered persistent implementation problems since its inception in 1978. The Florida program is fragmented by its very nature; it is a networked program, combining 23 laws, eight agencies, and five water management districts. The coordinating function is a difficult challenge, and no one agency has comprehensive responsibility and accountability for the state's coastal program. Furthermore, although Florida has strong requirements for local planning, the approved coastal elements of local plans are not enforced or overseen at the state level.

Overview of State Programs

Part of the appeal of the CZMA is that it encourages each state to craft its own CMP to fit their particular physical, social, and political circumstances. Consequently, the actual components of a CMP vary widely from state to state. Several broad program issues can be identified: shoreline management, retreat, coastal construction practices, coastal wetlands, sea level rise, beach access, cumulative and secondary impacts of development, urban waterfronts, Special Area Management Plans, areas of particular concern, aquaculture, energy facility siting, and ocean management.

Shoreline Management and Retreat

A study of the effectiveness of state CMPs in protecting shorelines, beaches, and dunes found regulatory tools (e.g., setbacks, regulation of shoreline development, and shoreline stabilization) to be the most common tools used nationwide (Bernd-Cohen and Gordon, 1998). Regulatory tools are enhanced by planning, land management and acquisition, and nonregulatory tools such as education and research.

As noted in earlier chapters, shoreline erosion is a significant problem along much of the U.S. coastline. States must deal with the flooding and storm hazards associated with close proximity to the ocean, as well as the prospect of long-term sea level rise. Some states have chosen to address these measures in terms of the desire to engage in a strategic retreat from the shoreline. Other states attempt to "draw a line in the sand." For example, Parsons and Powell (2001) estimate the cost of allowing the beaches of Delaware to retreat inland over the next 50 years to be about $291 million. Therefore, in the short term, the state strategy that may make economic sense to the state of Delaware is beach renourishment as opposed to retreat.

Probably one of the most effective ways to address erosion and other shoreline hazards and promote coastal retreat is through regulatory setback requirements. As Table 6.1 indicates, 25 states and territories now impose some form of coastal setback, requiring new development to locate a certain distance landward of the ocean as measured from mean high water, first line of vegetation, or various other marks (Bernd-Cohen and Gordon, 1998; Platt et al., 1992b; National Research Council, 1990; Houlahan, 1989). Increasingly these setback requirements are calculated according to local erosion rates. For example, North Carolina has one of the toughest erosion-based setbacks.

Specifically, for small-scale development in beachfront areas, new development must be set back a distance of at least 30 times the average annual rate of erosion for that particular stretch of

Table 6.1. Status of State Setback Authorities

State or territory	Setback legislation
Alabama	Yes
Alaska	No
California	Yes
Connecticut	No
Delaware	Yes
Florida	Yes
Georgia	No
Hawaii	Yes
Louisiana	No
Maine	Yes
Maryland	Yes
Massachusetts	No
Michigan	Yes
Minnesota	Yes
Mississippi	No
New Hampshire	Yes
New Jersey	Yes
New York	Yes
North Carolina	Yes
Ohio	No
Oregon	Yes
Pennsylvania	Yes
Rhode Island	Yes
South Carolina	Yes
Texas	No
Virginia	Yes
Washington	Yes
Wisconsin	Yes
American Samoa	Yes
Guam	Yes
Northern Marianas	Yes
Puerto Rico	Yes
Virgin Islands	Yes

Source: Adapted from Bernd-Cohen and Gordon (1998).

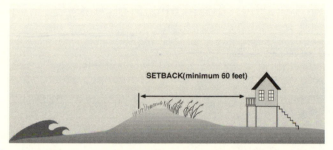

Figure 6.1. North Carolina Division of Coastal Management enforces a setback minimum of 60 feet. (From North Carolina Division of Coastal Management.)

coastline, measured from the first stable line of vegetation (Figure 6.1; see North Carolina Division of Coastal Management, 1988; Godschalk et al., 1989; Platt et al., 1992b). Development must also be landward of the crest of the primary dune and the landward toe of the frontal dune. For larger structures, the setback is doubled to 60 times the rate of erosion.

Other types of shoreline restrictions are also imposed. Under New York's Coastal Erosion Hazard Areas Act, for example, in certain erosion zones (in so-called structural hazard zones) only movable structures are permitted (see Platt et al., 1992b). Specific density limitations are imposed by some states in certain high-risk locations. Under North Carolina's CAMA, for instance, development in inlet hazard zones is restricted to structures of less than 5,000 square feet in size and generally must not exceed a density of more than one unit per 15,000 square feet of developable land (North Carolina Division of Coastal Management, 1988).

Many state coastal programs also impose some form of real estate disclosure requirement, which may be useful in discouraging hazardous shoreline development. Under North Carolina's CAMA permit program, for example, an applicant must acknowledge in writing that he or she is aware of the risks associated with development in the ocean hazard area and of the area's limited suitability for permanent structures (North Carolina Administrative Code, 2002). The potential benefit of this acknowledgment has not fully borne out in practice. Often the "applicant" who signs the notice is the project developer, and the eventual homeowner may never see the notification (Godschalk, 1998). Under South Carolina's modified beachfront management program, similar disclosure provisions are required when a special beachfront variance is issued (see Beatley, 1992).

Restrictions on Shore-Hardening Structures

Some coastal states have also imposed significant restrictions on the building of erosion control structures (e.g., seawalls, revetments, and groins). Some states, including North Carolina, South Carolina, and Maine, have banned the construction of new permanent shore-hardening structures altogether. In the long run, such actions reduce destruction of beaches and put property owners on notice that should a beachfront structure end up subject to erosion hazards, it will not be permissible to construct such protective (yet damaging) structures. States such as North Carolina have managed to resist recent political and legal challenges to such controls, as in the case of the Shell Island Condominium near Mason's Inlet in the Town of Wrightsville Beach, North Carolina (Photos 2.2 and 2.3). Condominium residents have made several requests to build a seawall, which has been rejected by the North Carolina Division of Coastal Management (DCM) and upheld in court based on agency rationale that building a seawall would be detrimental to the sandy beach in the area.

Managing Reconstruction

Many state coastal programs also seek to manage rebuilding and reconstruction after hurricanes or other major flooding events. Most state programs require development permits for rebuilding substantially damaged structures. Hurricanes and coastal storms, though exacting substantial human and economic cost, often are opportunities to rebuild and reconstruct in ways that minimize exposure to future risks (e.g., through relocation, setback requirements, and elevation of buildings).

The South Carolina Beachfront Management Act (BMA), originally created in 1988, contained some of the most stringent reconstruction provisions in the country when Hurricane Hugo hit the coast a year later. In enacting the BMA, the state sought to explicitly implement a long-term shoreline retreat policy (flowing from the recommendation of a blue-ribbon committee on beachfront management). Under the original BMA, habitable structures that were found to be "damaged beyond repair" (two-thirds or more damaged) would be allowed to rebuild only landward of a no-construction zone (the "dead zone"). All structures rebuilt within a larger 40-year erosion zone were also required to move as far landward as possible. Some 159 beachfront structures located in the no-construction zone were found to be damaged beyond repair. Pools and recreational amenities damaged 50% or more also were prevented from being rebuilt. Restrictions were placed on rebuilding erosion control structures damaged more than 50%. Vertical seawalls could be replaced with sloping revetments but only under certain conditions. (For a discussion of the South Carolina Act, see Platt et al., 1992a; Beatley, 1992.) Opposition to the rebuilding restrictions after Hugo was intense, especially by beachfront property owners. Moreover, several takings decisions (e.g., *Lucas v. South Carolina Coastal Council*) suggested that the state's financial liability could exceed $100 million. These political dynamics led to a substantial softening of the law, completely eliminating the dead zone and creating a special variance procedure allowing development to occur even further seaward under certain conditions (seaward of the baseline, or the crest of the ideal dune). Despite creating somewhat stronger rebuilding restrictions for erosion control devices, the 1990 revisions in many ways are a political retreat from retreat (for a discussion of these dynamics, see Beatley, 1992).

It is worth noting that state coastal programs increasingly are requiring that local governments prepare hurricane and coastal storm recovery and reconstruction plans. North Carolina was the first state to impose such requirements, but other states have followed suit (e.g., Florida and South Carolina). Florida makes funds available to communities calculated to match the community's vulnerability in terms of repetitive loss, population, relative risk, and participation in mutual aid agreements with neighboring communities. In accepting the mitigation funds, communities agree to develop a local mitigation strategy using technical assistance from the Florida Department of Community Affairs.

Unbuildable Lots

All coastal managers and planners should be aware of the 1992 Supreme Court case *Lucas v. South Carolina Coastal Council* because of its ramifications for regulatory takings of private property. But a taking does not occur until a disgruntled landowner takes the regulatory official or agency to court, claiming loss of property rights because of an oceanfront setback rule or similar regulation. Coastal planners and managers therefore must be aware of *potential* takings claims before they reach the point of litigation. Such caution is especially important when coastal regulations create "unbuildable lots," as occurred in the *Lucas* case.

In the *Lucas* case, the landowner claimed that a South Carolina regulation had effected an unconstitutional taking of his oceanfront lots. The statute concerned was the 1988 South Carolina BMA, which established an oceanfront setback line and prohibited the construction of any habitable structures seaward of that line. The U.S. Supreme Court held that any regulation that prohibited a landowner from making any "economically beneficial or productive use of his property" constituted a categorical taking that warranted compensation unless the government could prove that the regulation prohibited activities that would be considered a nuisance (i.e., a threat to human health, welfare, or safety arising from "unreasonable, unwarranted or unlawful use by a person of his own property"—*Black's Law Dictionary*).

One reason the Court found that no economically beneficial use was left for Mr. Lucas's property after the application of the setback rule may be that the South Carolina rule prohibited him from building almost any type of structure on his lot. Only a small walkway or deck would have been permissible, although Mr. Lucas had originally intended to build a single-family residence.

Other states have approached this situation differently than South Carolina. For instance, the North Carolina CAMA allows a wider range of structures to be built seaward of the oceanfront setback. These uses include campgrounds, unpaved parking areas, outdoor tennis courts, elevated decks of a certain size, some types of beach accessways, inhabitable gazebos and sheds of proscribed square footage, temporary amusement stands, and swimming pools.

States have taken a variety of approaches to the unbuildable lot situation. In 1986, the North Carolina DCM inventoried all the beachfront vacant lots that were rendered unbuildable by setback regulations. The owners of the lots were informed that their applications for building permits might be denied and that DCM was willing to offer $200 to $5,000 for each lot. The vacant lots would be used to construct public beach access facilities (Ballenger, 1993).

Public reaction to the purchase offer was mixed. Some owners were interested in the offer, but others, shocked to discover that they might be prohibited from constructing any habitable structures, were irate (Ballenger, 1993).

Although lots may have no value as residential property, some have argued that economic value still remains in unbuildable lots. For instance, adjacent landowners may want to purchase the property to construct walkways, decks, or beach cabanas; provide a drain field for a septic tank; or obtain additional parking space. In addition, landowners fearing that the state purchase of the property to provide public beach access could bring an "onslaught of the unwashed masses" might purchase adjacent unbuildable lots precisely to forestall such a possibility. Or owners of motels and multifamily structures not located on the oceanfront might purchase such lots to provide beach access for their guests or lessees (Ballenger, 1993).

Many states that have instituted oceanfront setback requirements include variance or exemption provisions. For instance, Michigan has a system for granting exceptions for construction on substandard lots platted before the adoption of its setback. Special permits are issued with conditions that structures be made readily movable and that all structures be relocated before shoreline erosion damage occurs. The landowner must further agree to follow property engineering standards in design, to use a septic system located landward of the structure rather than a sanitary sewer, and to locate the structure as far landward as the local zoning ordinance will permit, among other provisions (Ballenger, 1993).

The state of Florida allows for a variance under certain circumstances. Single-family homes may be constructed seaward of the setback line if the land was platted before the setback regulations came into effect. However, the landowner may not receive a variance if he or she owns another parcel adjacent to the parcel he or she is attempting to build on. An exception will not be granted under the Florida regulations if the structure will be built seaward of the frontal dunes (Ballenger, 1993).

The North Carolina CAMA also contains a variance provision whereby permission to use land in a manner otherwise prohibited by the regulations will be granted if the landowner can show "practical difficulties or unnecessary hardships." The applicant must further show that the difficulties or hardships result from conditions that are peculiar to the property and could not reasonably have been anticipated when the rules were adopted.

Despite the presence of variance provisions in setback laws, if few to no variances are granted, landowners who have been deprived of all practical use of their property may still have grounds to bring a regulatory takings claim to court. There is a delicate balance between drafting setback regulations that create lots so unbuildable that the courts find that no "economically beneficial or productive use" remains (thus entailing a regulatory taking necessitating compensation) and drafting regulations so broad in their exceptions that nearly all property own-

Lots of diff. state regulations on setback

ers are permitted to build inappropriate structures. Coastal managers and planners who are well versed in the *Lucas* perils that are possible in setback cases may be able to avoid takings claims through careful preparation and drafting.

Building Codes and Construction Standards

Building codes and construction standards are another important component of many state and local risk reduction strategies (though not necessarily an explicit component of a state's coastal program). Coastal structures can be designed to better withstand hurricane winds, wave, and surge. Building codes may be state mandated (as in North Carolina) or a local option (as in Oregon) and can vary substantially in their stringency. Most building codes are based on model building codes such as the International Building Code. The CZMA does not require that states impose building codes. Eleven coastal states have a state-mandated building code for all buildings and occupancy classifications, five (Delaware, Hawaii, Mississippi, Pennsylvania, and Texas) have no state-mandated codes, and two (Maryland and Oregon) allow local amendments that are less stringent than the state-mandated building codes (IBHS, 1999). It is not uncommon for rural areas especially to be without construction standards.

Coastal Wetlands Protection

Approximately 50% of U.S. coastal wetlands have been lost (NCSU Water Quality Group, 2001). Most coastal states have imposed restrictions on development in tidal or saltwater wetlands, and a smaller number of states apply restrictions to nontidal or freshwater wetlands. Good et al. (1998) assessed the potential effectiveness of state CMPs in protecting coastal wetlands and estuaries and found most programs to be "good on paper." States have been effective in protecting tidal wetlands, but the management of nontidal, freshwater wetlands merits attention, particularly in light of a 2001 court decision that exempts isolated wetlands from Clean Water Act Section 404 permit requirements (*Solid Waste Agency of Northern Cook County vs. U.S. Army Corps of Engineers, 200 U.S. 321, 2001*). In tidal wetland areas, states typically require a permit before certain activities can take place in wetland areas and usually include a more expansive list of such potentially damaging activities than those regulated under the federal Section 404 program. Pennsylvania expanded its coastal zone in the Delaware Estuary to include hydrologically connected wetlands, potential mitigation sites, and unprotected natural resource areas. Other states, such as Michigan and New Jersey, have assumed permitting responsibility under the Section 404 program. For a review of state wetland programs, see Salvesen (1990).

Activities regulated under Section 404 of the Clean Water Act typically include discharge of dredge and fill, draining of wetlands, and cutting of trees and destruction of vegetation. These regulations often extend to adjacent buffer areas as well. State wetland standards often incorporate many of the key concepts contained in the EPA 404(b)(i) guidelines, including restricting wetland alternatives to water-dependent uses and forbidding such activities where practicable alternatives exist.

Most state wetland programs also require mitigation when natural wetlands are destroyed or damaged. Mitigation ratios imposed can be quite high, ranging from 2:1 to 7:1 (i.e., amount of created, restored, or enhanced acreage required for each acre of natural wetland destroyed or damaged). Wetland mitigation banking is a market-based conservation concept that is being used with greater frequency. A mitigation bank allows compensation for small wetland losses that would go unmitigated otherwise (Oregon Division of State Lands, 2000). Wetland mitigation banks are wetlands located outside the immediate area of wetland loss that are restored, created, enhanced, or preserved as compensation for unavoidable losses on site. Mitigation banks seem to be a tool to ease cumulative impacts. For a discussion of wetland mitigation banks as a tool for sustainable development, see Etchart (1995).

Acquisition and the restoration of wetland areas remains an option. Massachusetts has passed an Open Space Bond to earmark funds to acquire coastal lands, including wetland resources. Louisiana, which suffers an estimated 80% of coastal marsh loss nationwide, receives funds for restoration from the federal Coastal Wetlands Planning, Protection, and Restoration Act (CWPPRA). Using such funds from the CWPPRA, Louisiana has have saved a wetland area the size of Newark, New Jersey (NOAA, 1998).

Sea Level Rise

Some states have begun to explicitly incorporate consideration of sea level rise into their programs. Klarin and Hershman (1990) report that 17 coastal states have officially recognized the problem of sea level rise and have undertaken assessments of the problem (e.g., through proclamations, legislative findings, research, and impact assessments). Eleven coastal states have initiated new public and intergovernment processes (e.g., forming a sea level rise task force or a policy-setting process), and 13 states already have existing regulations adaptable (or partially adaptable) to future sea level rise (e.g., coastal setbacks, such as those discussed earlier). However, Klarin and Hershman report that only three states have adopted new policies specifically to respond to sea level rise.

Beach Access and Land Acquisition

Nearly all coastal states are grappling with the issue of public access to the shoreline. Although effective demand for recreational shoreline areas is at an all-time high, there is an ever-dwindling supply of lake, ocean, and other waterfront property accessible to the public. Increased private ownership of shorefront property has fenced off many of these places. There is a delicate balance between providing enough public access so that all residents and visitors can enjoy the beach and protecting the rights of owners whose property is adjacent to the public beach area.

Providing access is an area of coastal management that takes a good

Photo 6.1. Along the coast of North Carolina, public beach access is marked by signs such as this one in Kitty Hawk. (Photo by David Brower.)

deal of creativity. Connecticut has chosen to waive development permit fees for projects that propose or include public access as part of the development. Funds from special Long Island Sound license plates go toward installing interpretive signs and public viewing platforms at state-owned access sites. Geographic information systems and the Internet have permitted states to develop online databases of access sites.

Many state CMPs are addressing problems of public access through a wide range of activities, including regulatory, statutory, and legal systems; innovative techniques to acquire, improve, and maintain access sites; coastal public access management plans that target all users and resources of recreational, historical, aesthetic, ecological, and cultural value; and protection measures that minimize the potential adverse impacts of access on coastal natural resources and private property (U.S. Department of Commerce, 1992).

In some states common-law doctrine establishes more extensive public rights to beach access. In Texas, for instance, under the doctrine of customary use the public beach extends landward to the natural line of vegetation, thus encompassing much of the dry beach as well as the wet. The 1959 Texas Open Beaches Act codifies this common law and reinforces the public's right of access to the coastline. Texas law was tested in 1983 when, after Hurricane Alicia, a number of beachfront property owners on Galveston Island were prevented by the Texas attorney general's office from rebuilding because the natural line of vegetation had moved back and their structures were now on the public beach. Because the extent of the public beach is determined by the natural line of vegetation and because this line moves in response to storms and other natural coastal processes, the public right in Texas amounts to a rolling easement. When Alicia moved the natural line of vegetation landward, homes that before the storm were on private beach were now on the public beach. Several property owners challenged the constitutionality of the Texas law, claiming that the actions of the attorney general's office to prevent rebuilding amounted to an unconstitutional taking of property. However, the Texas Supreme Court found in favor of the state, upholding the state's restrictions on rebuilding.

One principal means of securing public access to the shoreline is attaching conditions to development permits issued by the government. Permits are granted only if the developer of shorefront property agrees to set aside a prescribed area for the public to use as an accessway. A recorded fee, easement, or deed restriction can ensure long-term public access for the specified area. Communities that receive U.S. Army Corps of Engineers beach renourishment projects must abide by corps public access policies. For a federally funded renourishment, survey lines are drawn that indicate the extent of the renourished beach. The renourished portion of the beach is treated as public land. States such as Florida have adopted similar requirements for renourishment, including the provision of parking places. Developers and prospective buyers often are not convinced of the fairness of such conditions. However, the logical and legal rationale for requiring shoreline access is not a radical or new concept. In some states, under the Public Trust Doctrine the beaches and oceans have always been considered a public resource. To use this resource effectively, the public must have ready access to it.

However, despite the generally solid legal background, there are obstacles to requiring the provision of public access as a condition for development permits. One major obstacle lies in the Fifth Amendment to the U.S. Constitution (the takings clause). In *Kaiser Aetna v. United States,* the Supreme Court reiterates that the right to exclude the public from one's own land is one of the most fundamental property rights.

Other judicial decisions have limited the extent to which conditions can be placed on development. The Constitution requires that there be the proper "nexus" between the impact of the development and the conditions imposed. This point was made clear in 1987 by the U.S. Supreme Court in *Nollan v. California Coastal Commission,* 107 S.Ct. 3141 (1987). In *Nollan,* the Supreme Court majority, in an opinion by Justice Scalia, held that a condition attached to a permit must "substantially advance" a legitimate government interest, and the government interest must be the same one served by the permit itself. The facts of the case are simple. The Nollans owned a bungalow on the California coast that they wanted to demolish, remove, and replace with a new and larger house. They applied to the California Coastal Commission for a permit. The permit was granted on one condition: The Nollans were required to convey to the public a lateral access easement over their beachfront between their new house and the shoreline. The easement would allow the public to walk along their beachfront between the mean high tide and a preexisting seawall. The Nollans sued, claiming a taking without just compensation.

The Coastal Commission's defense was that the lateral easement was necessary to provide the public with views of the ocean and to help overcome the "psychological barrier" that existing development had created and that would be perpetuated by the proposed development.

The Supreme Court held that this was a taking, emphasizing the character of the government action: physical occupation. The Court said it could not find the required nexus or close fit between the condition imposed (lateral access) and the government interest to be furthered (visual access from the street) because people already on the beach (these were the only people who could have used any lateral access easement on the beachfront side of the house) did not need any encouragement to view the ocean. The Court found that a taking had occurred because the Nollans had lost the right to exclude others from their land.

Land use regulators will do well to heed the lessons of *Nollan*. The Supreme Court implied through the case that people have a right to build on their land and that permits are not to be considered government benefits. Beyond this dicta, however, the specific *Nollan* requirement is not that difficult: Permit conditions must relate directly to impacts caused by development.

Another coastal management strategy that some states are using is acquisition of coastal lands. Some states use acquisition to provide beach access, and other states put the land to other uses, such as safeguarding important habitats or preserving especially sensitive ecological areas.

Although there may be problems associated with public acquisition of coastal lands, such as the limited funds available or the reluctance of some landowners to sell, acquisition often is the most appropriate, the most effective, and sometimes the only way to ensure that large land areas can be added to the inventory of public accessways or conservation areas.

Acquisition can be in the form of fee-simple (outright ownership) or less-than-fee-simple rights. Although fee-simple acquisition is the most complete form of ownership and affords the public a right to use the land in any legal manner, it can also be expensive. Less-than-fee-simple rights often give the public the right of use needed for that particular parcel while the owner retains certain other rights in the property. Florida's Conservation and Recreation Lands (CARL) is one of the nation's most aggressive acquisition programs. As a result of action taken by the 1999 Florida legislature, the CARL program receives $105 million from the sale of bonds for lands to be maintained as parks, recreation areas, wildlife management areas, wilderness areas, forests, and greenways. Easements are a very useful form of less-than-fee-simple acquisition. An easement is the right to use someone else's land in some specifically designated manner. Easements generally are purchased in circumstances in which it is unnecessary or unfeasible to purchase the land itself, that is, in which only some rights to use the land, such as the right to pass over it (e.g., for an accessway), are needed. Conservation easements can also be granted by a landowner, whereby the land is reserved for conservation purposes and the owner agrees not to put the property to any incompatible use. Future owners are also subject to the terms of the easement. Landowners often can be persuaded to grant easements because of the tax consequences involved, through a decrease in the valuation of their property for property tax purposes.

Another type of less-than-fee-simple property interest is development rights. Owners with absolute title to a piece of property have the right to develop the property for whatever purposes one wants within the confines of the local zoning laws. Public purchase of the owner's right to develop the property for certain purposes has been used to prevent the destruction or substantial transformation of historic structures and to prevent the residential or commercial development of certain large open lands.

Development rights may be purchased outright by a public entity and banked in a conservation trust, or they may be purchased by a private developer and used to increase the density in a designated section of an urban area where the right to develop at greater than normal densities is extremely valuable. This latter method is commonly called transfer of development rights (TDR). (See Chapter 8 for further discussion of land ans property acquisition, including TDR.) Thus far, the results from TDR programs are mixed. Because land use is managed at local levels, TDRs can be difficult for state coastal management agencies to initiate.

Another state-level entity that has been at the forefront of using acquisition for resource management is the California State Coastal Conservancy. The conservancy was created in 1976 by the California legislature to allow the state to use acquisition as well as regulation for coastal protection, restoration, and management. The Coastal Conservancy has been especially effective in its use of innovative acquisition techniques, including less-than-fee-simple interests and development rights transfers (including TDRs and transfer of development credits, or TDCs). The California Coastal Plan recognized the Big Sur in Monterey County as an area of statewide significance. Monterey County developed a Big Sur Land Use Plan that imposed development restrictions to preserve scenic viewsheds along Highway 1 (Pruetz, 1997). The Monterey County TDR Ordinance designates donor sites, which must be both buildable parcels and viewshed lots. Designated donor sites must offer a permanent scenic easement to the county. When a parcel is designated a donor site, it receives two development credits, which allow development within a designated receiving site.

Many of these approaches were first initiated in response to funding constraints; it was soon discovered that less-than-fee-simple ownership was just as satisfactory, or more so, for securing coastal resources. California Coastal Conservancy has been particularly creative in using various acquisition approaches as a part of broader program and project implementation efforts. For instance, the conservancy has used less-than-fee-simple methods in conjunction with fee acquisition, lot consolidation, and area planning programs.

The conservancy has acted as a temporary repository for property interests attained and has also acted along with nonprofit land trusts and local governments. This flexibility and adaptability are one reason for the Coastal Conservancy's many successes in California resource management (Grenell, 1988).

Cumulative and Secondary Impacts

As discussed throughout this book, most coastal states are experiencing rapid growth and development along the shoreline. Not only are oceanfront properties being built, but as land costs skyrocket and the demand for waterfront or water-view property increases, other coastal areas are being exploited, such as sounds, estuaries, and even wetlands. States have to confront the pressures on the natural environment caused by the new development itself, and the cumulative and secondary impacts of growth are becoming increasingly apparent.

Cumulative impacts occur when activities that alone may not create significant changes in the environment are added together, producing a much larger effect over time. The cumulative impact of impervious surface (roads, rooftops, parking lots) degrades watershed health. Adverse impacts have been noted in streams at around 10% impervi-

ousness within watersheds (Schueler, 1992). The runoff from such surfaces cause sedimentation and nonpoint pollution.

Secondary impacts occur when roads, bridges, municipal water and
sewer facilities, and other structures are built in the coastal zone,
paving the way for more development in the vicinity of the services
provided. The areas most vulnerable to cumulative and secondary
impacts generally are those where growth is occurring most rapidly and
where particularly sensitive natural resources are located.

Many states currently lack sufficient information on which to base
an assessment of cumulative and secondary impacts, which is an
important first step in measuring and controlling the impacts. As a
result of this gap, coastal states struggle to demonstrate that individual
actions additively affect natural resources and the coastal environment.
With this in mind, some states have included significant projects in their
CMPs designed to address cumulative and secondary impacts. Research
of cumulative impacts of septic tanks in the Florida Keys has led to a
change in the jurisdiction of the state Department of Health and Reha-
bilitative Services. The agency bases permit decisions on water quality
impacts and human health considerations. South Carolina is using a
pilot project in the community of Folly Beach to provide septic tank
maintenance and cleaning on a periodic basis. The advantages of such
a program are twofold. First, if the septic tanks can be maintained in
good working order, impacts on water quality are reduced. Second, it
could prevent secondary impacts from the extension of sewer lines.

An objective of many state CMPs is the development of river basin
and watershed planning. North Carolina is moving toward river basin
planning and management, led by the Division of Water Quality. They
have established riparian buffer guidelines for two of the state's river
basins most affected by nutrient loading: the Neuse and the Tar-Pam-
lico. They also established a 50-foot buffer along intermittent and
perennial streams and lakes, ponds in each watershed. States such as
Maryland and Delaware have also commenced riparian buffer initiatives to protect forest land and streamside vegetation.

Urban Waterfront Development

Governments sponsoring redevelopment must understand that revitalizing urban waterfronts can be expensive. East coast redevelopments in
New York City's Battery Park City and Boston's Charlestown Navy Yard
cost $200,000 to $500,000 per acre in government grants (Gordon,
1997). A wide range of activities has been undertaken by coastal towns

and cities in efforts to develop and redevelop their waterfront districts. A national assessment of state CMPs found that the coastal states that have achieved positive outcomes in revitalizing urban waterfronts aggressively market their assistance programs (Goodwin, 1997). Other successes have been achieved by targeting specific waterfronts for action, responding to local revitalization efforts, reacting to revitalization through the regulatory process, or, in the case of networked coastal programs, delegating authority to state planning and community redevelopment agencies. The most commonly used tools are financial assistance, partnering, and technical assistance (Goodwin, 1997). Specific projects carried out in several communities as a result of revitalization plan implementation include construction of marinas; docks; piers for commercial and recreational fishers; boat ramps; retail, office, restaurant, and condominium complexes; and public access facilities. For instance, in Ponce and San Juan, Puerto Rico, docking facilities for cruise ships are being improved, and in Reedsport, Oregon, moorage for Antarctic research vessels has been designed.

Many state CMPs have contributed to local communities' urban waterfront development efforts through grants of financial and technical assistance. The Michigan CMP was instrumental in assisting with the design and engineering plan for the redevelopment of the City of Wyandotte's waterfront. Some localities have joined with one another and with the state CMP in a collaborative effort to revitalize an entire waterfront area. In New York, the state established the Horizons Waterfront Commission to develop a regional development plan for the entire Erie County waterfront. Representing municipalities, the county, and the state, the commission has bonding authority and eminent domain powers to implement its plan.

Many states are reporting substantial private and public investment taking place in and around refurbished urban waterfronts. For instance, CMP funds were used in Kewaunee, Wisconsin, to plan and construct a 150-slip marina and waterfront park; the development catalyzed significant private investment in the area, in addition to attracting more than 100,000 tourists annually. In Jersey City, New Jersey, a waterfront park and pier project was recently completed, and $2 billion in new-construction condominiums and retail shops now surrounds the new park. The Malaloa Bulkhead project in American Samoa has opened the door for four new marine-dependent businesses operating adjacent to the bulkhead (U.S. Department of Commerce, 1992). Brownfield redevelopment has also been primed by state action. States that are running

Photo 6.2. The waterfront of Seattle, Washington, is an active commercial seaport that also serves as a popular recreation, dining, shopping, and tourist destination. (Photo by NOAA.)

low on developable property in the coastal zone are rehabilitating contaminated properties. For example, the New Jersey Brownfields Reclamation Act reimburses developers for 75% of the costs of site remediation. The city of Glen Cove, New York, which is located on the north shore of Long Island, is transforming a contaminated site into a waterfront resort with a hotel, restaurants, and open space near the city's existing parkway (Newman, 2000).

Special Area Management Plans

The CZMA defines a Special Area Management Plan (SAMP) as a "comprehensive plan providing for natural resource protection and reasonable coastal-dependent economic growth." Such plans are used "to guide public and private users of land and water." Encouraging SAMP preparation is a fundamental goal of the CZMA. SAMPs have been prepared to provide greater specificity in protecting natural resources, economic growth, protection of lives and property in hazardous areas, and increasing reliability of government decision-making (NOAA, 1999e). They are particularly useful in areas with resource use conflicts (e.g., conflicts between habitat and protection and urban sprawl or aquaculture and polluted runoff). Once approved, a SAMP becomes a formal part of a state's coastal zone management program. SAMPs are developed to address many coastal issues, such as waterfront revitalization. Florida's CMP promotes the preparation of inlet and beach management plans and has developed a Waterfronts Florida partnership. Through this partnership, the state offers technical and financial assistance to small waterfront communities to help with revitalization projects.

The Hackensack Meadows District in northeastern New Jersey contains the Meadowlands, the two remaining large tracts of estuarine wetlands in the New York City metropolitan area. In 1988, the Hackensack Meadows Development Commission, the regional planning authority for the district, began creating a SAMP for the Meadowlands, in concert with the U.S. Environmental Protection Agency (EPA), the U.S. Army Corps of Engineers and the New Jersey Department of Environmental Protection (Thiesing and Hargrove, 1996). The proposed SAMP included a land use plan for the district, a wetland mitigation program, preservation through zoning and deed restrictions or conservation easements of the remaining wetland acres in the district not proposed for development, and a transfer of development rights program (Thiesing and Hargrove, 1996).

SAMPs can also be a mechanism to improve intergovernment relations. In South Carolina, a diverse group of city and county governments is collaborating on the Charleston Harbor SAMP in response to rapid growth in the region and potential effects on water quality.

Areas of Particular Concern

Many state CMPs give heightened protection to certain especially sensitive areas of their coastal zones. Coastal programs may define Areas of Particular Concern and impose more stringent development or permit requirements in these designated areas. Often Areas of Particular Concern are defined geographically, according to the natural resources or habitats present, or according to the function performed by a particular coastal feature.

The Florida Environmental Land and Water Management Act of 1972 established Areas of Critical State Concern to protect certain highly sensitive geographic areas (Finnell, 1985). Through the Critical Areas process, the state specifies standards with which land development regulations enacted by the affected local government must comply. The standards apply to the discrete geographic areas designated as Critical Areas by the governor and the Cabinet. If a local government fails to submit adequate regulations, the state prepares and adopts suitable land use regulations to be administered by local authorities. The designation of Critical Areas is subject to legislative review, and land development regulations adopted within Critical Areas are effective only upon such review. The local government is responsible for issuing projects in Critical Areas. The local government's decision to issue or deny the permit is final unless appealed to the Florida Land and Water Adjudicatory Commission (Finnell, 1985).

Marine Debris

Marine debris is "any human-made object of glass, wood, plastic, cloth, metal, rubber, or paper that is present in the marine environment" (Klee, 1999, p. 129). Plastics are particularly problematic because they deteriorate slowly and can become a nuisance for seabirds and other marine life. As part of their CMPs, states have developed recycling programs, creating education programs, and sponsoring volunteer cleanup initiatives. For example, New Jersey has established a Clean Shores Program that uses state and county prison inmates to clean debris from its beaches.

Direct waste dumping is another issue that coastal states grapple with. The number of boaters enjoying coastal waters has increased the impacts of sewage dumped from boats or marinas. Rhode Island has taken regulatory steps to address waste from both vessels and marinas. Consistent with the requirements of CZMA Section 6217, Rhode Island requires all new significantly expanding marinas to develop operation and maintenance plans that develop a management method for debris. The Clean Water Act provides that states can prohibit the discharge of treated or untreated sewage by having areas designated by the EPA as no-discharge areas. Rhode Island has become the first in the nation to receive this designation for all its coastal waters (NOAA, 1999c).

Aquaculture, Energy, and Government Facility Siting

Coastal states must consider the various impacts that industry has on the area, both from an economic as well as environmental perspective. Aquaculture, or the farming of marine and freshwater plants and animals, often necessitates the conversion of land and water areas (Clark, 1996). Shellfish beds and hatcheries often are sources of point and nonpoint pollution. As a result, siting these facilities has been controversial in some locations and subject to the not-in-my-backyard attitude. Connecticut, which is the nation's second largest shellfish producer, had grown from 1 million pounds of shellfish in 1985 to 8.2 million pounds in the early 1990s. The industry has flourished because of improved water quality and aquaculture practices and through an industry–state partnership to restore historic oyster beds (NOAA, 1999b).

Energy demands have contributed to shortages in recent years. With the continued migration to the coastal zone, siting energy facilities in state coastal zones will remain an important issue. Offshore oil and gas exploration may well become a major issue in the future. Siting both onshore and offshore facilities in federal waters often triggers a consistency review by state coastal management agencies. For example, New York faces the dilemma of developing and siting facilities for the disposal of contaminated dredge material from New York Harbor.

Ocean Management

In recent years there has been increasing concern on the part of both coastal managers and the public about activities occurring offshore and the potential impacts on sensitive marine ecosystems. State coastal programs historically have concerned themselves with managing land use activities occurring in and around the coastal shoreline. A number of states are moving in the direction of expanding the geographic and ecological scope of their management programs, taking into account extensive offshore marine habitats. This expansion takes them more squarely into the areas of fisheries, marine mammals, unique marine habitats (e.g., offshore reefs), and proposals for oil and gas development and mineral extraction. Resources and uses of ocean areas under jurisdiction of the federal government and the states are affected by the fragmented management framework mentioned in Chapter 4. The result often is jurisdictional confusion and inefficient decision-making that fails to consider ecosystem effects (NOAA, 1999e).

The challenge for such initiatives in ocean planning is to overcome the differences in jurisdictional points of view about how these areas should be managed. For instance, federal administrations have been inclined to support offshore oil and gas development, often in direct conflict with state officials and citizens. Indeed, much of the impetus behind ocean management programs comes from such federal proposals for oil and gas development.

State Case Studies

As previously discussed, the CZMA provides states with flexibility in coastal program management and implementation. To illustrate the variety, what follows is a brief look at the well-established CMPs in Maine, North Carolina, and Oregon.

Maine

Maine is a predominantly rural state, ranking 40th in the United States in population and 37th in per capita income. Maine's coastal area includes 139 towns, several unorganized territories, 4,568 miles of coastline, and 4,613 islands (Maine SPO, 2000). The economies of many of the state's smaller coastal communities rely heavily on commercial fishing and tourism. Maine's CMP was established in 1978 and is administered by the State Planning Office. The Maine CMP is a network of local, regional, and state agencies that share responsibility for effective coastal management. A small staff at the State Planning Office is responsible for policy development and program enhancement, municipal technical assistance, program administration, outreach and educa-

Photo 6.3. Lobster boat in Portland, Maine. (Photo by NOAA.)

tion, habitat restoration, local grants, municipal comprehensive planning and implementation, federal consistency, public access planning, and the coastal nonpoint source pollution program. The state's environmental and marine resource laws are administered by the Department of Environmental Protection (DEP) and the Department of Marine Resources (DMR).

True today as it was when the program was created, the core activity of the Maine Coastal Program is the administration and enforcement of environmental laws. Maine gained national attention for the early adoption of strong environmental laws such as the Site Location of Development Law (provides for state review of large-scale development), Mandatory Shoreland Zoning (requires districting and setbacks within 250 feet of the water's edge) and Coastal Wetlands Law. The latter has been combined with other laws into the Natural Resources Protection Act (NRPA), which applies to development in or near coastal wetlands and sand dunes, freshwater wetlands, Great Ponds (ponds more than 10 acres in size), rivers, streams, brooks, fragile mountain areas, and significant wildlife habitat. Permits are required for activities in these areas and, in the case of the water resource areas, on adjacent lands where development activity could cause soil erosion or nonpoint source pollution. The Wetland Rules (Chapter 310, NRPA) require compensation for the loss of wetland functions and values for projects that exceed minimum thresholds of wetland disturbance. The Coastal Sand Dune Rules (Chapter 355, NRPA) reflect the state's policy of retreat by prohibiting the construction of new seawalls, restricting the size and height of structures, and requiring that the 100-year shoreline position and sea level rise are considered when siting new development. If the shoreline recedes so that coastal wetlands extend to any part of a structure for 6 months or more, the structure must be removed and the site restored to natural conditions within 1 year.

Recent additions to Maine's suite of regulations include the erosion and sedimentation control law and the stormwater management law, both administered by the DEP.

In addition to core law administration, the Maine Coastal Program has conducted a wide range of projects over the years to help balance conservation and development along the coast. These activities demonstrate the flexibility inherit in CZM's federal–state–local partnership. The program's activities, in helping communities manage growth, planning public access, assisting with sustainable coastal economic development, and developing innovative ways to manage marine resources respond to high-priority state issues and the differing regional needs of Maine's varied coastline and its population.

WATERSHED MANAGEMENT

The State Planning Office partners with other state agencies, municipalities, and nonprofit organizations to launch watershed management programs in coastal areas most threatened by nonpoint sources of pollution. In the Damariscotta River estuary (a high-quality resource that supports a thriving shellfish aquaculture industry), the Maine Coastal Program helped local officials from seven towns prepare a regional management plan and helped create a new nonprofit organization to implement the plan. In 1998, the Maine legislature created a Comprehensive Watershed Protection Program. The Coastal Program's priority watershed protection program now targets activities such as watershed surveys, educational programs, and capacity building for watershed groups in 17 priority estuaries identified as being at risk by agencies working together under the Comprehensive Watershed Protection Program.

AQUACULTURE DEVELOPMENT STRATEGY

To help foster sound coastal economic development, the Maine Coastal Program assisted the DMR in creating an aquaculture development strategy, helped to streamline laws for experimental leases, and created resource materials to educate municipal officials and citizens about the aquaculture leasing process. Increased demand for leases, lack of comprehensive scientific information on Maine's embayments, increased restrictions on the finfish industry as the result of the listing of Atlantic salmon as an endangered species, user conflicts at coastal access sites, and concerns about visual impacts of aquaculture development are current issues that cause aquaculture policy development to remain a high priority for the Maine Coastal Program.

MARINE FISHERY MANAGEMENT

The Maine CMP is also helping the state DMR implement a program for more effective management of traditional marine fisheries. Comanagement involves representatives from the fishing community, marine scientists, state agencies, and public interest groups in developing management plans. In recognition of their stewardship and local knowledge, the state shares some decision-making authority with lobster fishers through regional lobster zone management councils.

RIGHT-OF-WAY DISCOVER GRANTS

Most of the Maine coast is privately owned. Private property rights extend to the low-water mark in Maine, and the public interest in the intertidal area is limited to fishing, fowling, and navigation. For the most part, the public enjoys a tradition of free and easy passage over private land, but new ownership patterns and increasing use conflicts jeopardize this tradition. The Maine CMP has worked to confirm access rights to tidal waters by awarding Right-of-Way Discovery Grants that towns have used to research and inventory public access sites on the coast. The state's Land for Maine's Future program has appropriated $88 million for land acquisition since its inception in 1987. In the 1970s and 1980s the Coastal Program's Waterfront Action Grant Program made funds available for infrastructure improvements along Maine's working waterfronts. Demonstrated need for financial assistance for working waterfronts led to the Small Harbor Improvement Program, administered by the Maine Department of Transportation and funded by two successful bond issues.

ECOTOURISM

The chronically low income levels and persistent high unemployment in Maine's easternmost coastal county, Washington County, provided the impetus for an innovative partnership between the Maine Coastal Program and a nonprofit organization to promote ecotourism and employment in natural resource industries.

SMART GROWTH

Although Maine's population growth rate is low compared with that of most coastal states, Maine's population is becoming more suburban. Formerly thriving urban centers are experiencing population loss, whereas rural lands are developing at a rapid pace, a pace that exceeds existing municipal capacity to manage and serve this new growth. In the 20-year period from 1970 to 1990, as much land was developed in Maine as had been developed over the entire previous history of the state, and land consumption occurred at four times the rate of population growth (Maine SPO, 2000). Because the coastal zone has been fastest-growing region of the state, the Maine Coastal Program has placed a major emphasis on supporting smart growth techniques, beginning with research on the cumulative impacts of development on coastal systems and support for the development and implementation of Maine's Comprehensive Planning and Land Use Regulation Act in the late 1980s. A more recent multiyear effort of the Maine State Planning Office recently resulted in almost $2 million in state funds for smart growth initiatives, focusing on nonregulatory incentives and disincentives. These include prohibiting state investments (for roads, schools, and other public infrastructure) outside designated growth areas, providing grants to communities to evaluate and redevelop growth plans, developing a marketing campaign for homebuyers, creating a smart growth toolbox for towns, and sponsoring a Smart Growth Institute for the state's planning community. Although Maine's work on smart growth is ongoing, recent efforts place Maine among the leaders of states working to influence development patterns.

North Carolina

The North Carolina Coastal Area Management Act (CAMA) was adopted in 1974, evoking the most intense debate of any environmental bill in the state's history (Heath, 1974). CAMA established a coastal resource management program for the state's 20 coastal counties (Figure 6.2) that are influenced by tidal waters. The state CMP was approved by OCRM in September 1978. CAMA created the framework the program would follow by establishing a Coastal Resource Commission (CRC)

Figure 6.2. There are 20 CAMA counties in North Carolina. (From North Carolina Division of Coastal Management.)

that sets policy by which the program operates. The CRC consists of 15 members, appointed by the governor. Thirteen members of the CRC must be residents of the coastal area. A Coastal Resources Advisory Council advises the CRC on policy options and rulemaking and acts as the CRC's liaison with local governments in the coastal zone. The state DCM is the lead agency for the program. DCM administers coastal development (CAMA) permits and the public beach and waterfront access program, provides financial and technical assistance for local land use planning, and manages coastal reserves.

Two distinctive components of the North Carolina CMP are its local land use planning requirements and AEC permitting. The CRC sets standards that coastal counties must meet in adopting land use plans (Owens, 1985). Municipalities are allowed to adopt their own plans, and 72 have done so. All 20 CAMA counties have adopted their plans and consistently update them every 5 years. Before CAMA required local land use planning in 1974, coastal North Carolina had very little experience with planning and with zoning and subdivision ordinances. Political opposition to CAMA centered around a notion that coastal local governments were "being singled out unfairly" and were being forced to infringe on private property rights (Owens, 1985). The state legislature felt that the regulatory program could protect sensitive areas, but planning at the local level was the proper method for meeting long-term regional challenges such as growth, urban form, and community character (Owens, 1985). Although local governments are required to adopt land use plans that meet the CAMA standard, they are not required to adopt ordinances or policies that implement these plans. A majority of the more rapidly developing jurisdictions have adopted implementing ordinances because they believed that it was the appropriate thing to do. The Local Planning and Management Grant Program provides financial assistance to local governments to help pay for the preparation of land use plans and for other planning projects. All development must be consistent with the CRC-approved land use plan for CAMA permits to be granted.

The land use planning program has been criticized because implementing ordinances are not required and because in many cases the land use plans have adopted a laissez-faire policy that changed little from the days before the planning requirement was adopted by the General Assembly in 1974. The original regulations adopted by the CRC that set the standards used to review the local land use plans were largely procedural—that is, they listed the sorts of issues that the plans should consider but left the substance of the policy completely open. The regulations were amended from time to time, but this gap was not dealt with until 1999, when the CRC created a team to review the regulations and recommended changes. The team recommended that the CRC adopt a set of substantive standards that would protect the state interests in the coastal zone but still leave the local governments with a great deal of discretion as to how they would accomplish the standards. The CRC approved these recommendations in the spring of 2001 and held hearings on the proposed regulations in the summer and fall of 2001.

CAMA designates AECs in the coastal zone. There are four broad categories of AECs: estuarine and ocean, ocean hazard, public water supplies, and natural and cultural resource areas. All navigable waters in the CAMA counties and 3% of the land area are designated as AECs. The program sometimes is criticized because its permitting jurisdiction is limited to such a small portion of the entire coastal area. Defenders of the program point out that although the area is small, it is terribly important. Once an area has been designated as an AEC, all developers in that area must obtain permits and in doing so must show that the proposed development will meet the state requirements for the area. Minor permits may be obtained from a local permitting officer, but permits for major development must be obtained from the state. Most permits issued each year are considered general or minor and are issued within a few days of application by DCM staff or, in the case of minor permits, delegated to a local government representative. Major developments are those that require another state or federal permit, involve more than 20 acres of land disturbance, or include structures larger than 60,000 square feet.

The North Carolina CMP has placed a high priority on policy development related to coastal hazards, wetlands, and the cumulative and secondary impacts of development. As mentioned previously, the CRC established a 30-year setback for small structures and a 60-year setback for large structures, each measured from the "first line of stable vegetation," and has established a ban on shore-hardening devices. The mandatory local land use planning program was strengthened in the early years of the coastal program when a requirement was added to include a poststorm reconstruction policy section (McElyea et al., 1982). In the summer of 2000, the CRC established a 30-foot buffer along estuarine and public trust shorelines for the dual purpose of risk reduction and water quality protection. The cumulative and secondary impacts of development manifest themselves on the North Carolina coast in groundwater declines, seasonal fish kills caused by nutrient loading, and wetland degradation. The DCM will use a permit tracking system to follow the impacts of growth.

Early in the North Carolina CMP, the state inventoried all existing public accessways and identified them with signs. As part of the Public Beach and Waterfront Access Program, in 1981 North Carolina acquired public access sites along the coast and, in 1983, in inland areas including estuary beaches and waterways. The program gives local governments matching grants to fund improvements to existing coastal sites. Such improvements include the construction of dune crossovers, boardwalks, parking areas, and, in the case of regional accessways, toilets, changing areas, and showers. A current priority of the program is to identify and acquire unbuildable lots that have the potential to be used as accessways.

Oregon

The Oregon CMP is an important component of the statewide planning program that includes the 19 Statewide Planning Goals (Table 6.2) that were adopted by the rulemaking authority of the Oregon Land Conservation and Development Commission (LCDC). Cities and counties

Table 6.2. Oregon's 19 Statewide Planning Goals

Goal 1	Citizen Involvement
Goal 2	Land Use Planning
Goal 3	Agricultural Lands
Goal 4	Forest Lands
Goal 5	Open Spaces, Scenic and Historic Areas, and Natural Resources
Goal 6	Air, Water, and Land Resource Quality
Goal 7	Areas Subject to Natural Disasters and Hazards
Goal 8	Recreational Needs
Goal 9	Economic Development
Goal 10	Housing
Goal 11	Public Facilities and Services
Goal 12	Transportation
Goal 13	Energy Conservation
Goal 14	Urbanization
Goal 15	Willamette River Greenway
Goal 16	Estuarine Resources
Goal 17	Coastal Shorelands
Goal 18	Beaches and Dunes
Goal 19	Ocean Resources

Source: Oregon Department of Land Conservation and Development.

Photo 6.4. Coastal management in Oregon has been folded into its comprehensive statewide planning system. In recent years Oregon has expanded its coastal management area to include the ocean and continental shelf. (Photo by Tim Beatley.)

within the state are required to prepare comprehensive plans in accordance with the Statewide Planning Goals and LCDC rules. The local comprehensive plans are approved by the LCDC in a process known as acknowledgment. Once in place, the local comprehensive plans guide all local ordinances and are periodically reviewed by the LCDC, which allows the state to remain connected to the plans, any amendments, and their implementation. In addition, the state legislature adopted several laws to shape coastal and inland development, including the Oregon Beach Bill, Removal-Fill Law, and Senate Bill 100, which mandates the state's land use planning program (Oregon DLCD, 1997).

The Oregon LCDC is a seven-person panel appointed by the governor. The Department of Land Conservation and Development serves as the commission's staff; the department carries out commission decisions and is the state's lead agency for the CMP. Other state players in coastal management include the Division of State Lands (DSL), the Park and Recreation Department (PRD), the Department of Environmental Quality (DEQ), the Department of Geology and Mineral Industries

(DOGAMI), and the Department of Fish and Wildlife (DFW). The DSL regulates Oregon's territorial sea, including removal and filling of the seabed and estuaries, dredged material, and seabed minerals. The PRD has authority over the Ocean-Shore Recreation Area. This area includes all submerged lands and the adjacent dry sand beach up to a beach zone line set by the legislature (approximately 16 feet above high tide). The DEQ monitors air and water quality throughout the state and is the state's lead agency on oil spill prevention and response. DOGAMI assists with information and research on geology, coastal geologic hazards, and marine minerals. It is also the state permitter for offshore oil and gas drilling in state waters. Oregon's DFW regulates marine fisheries and protects marine life and habitat in state ocean waters and rocky shores.

Among the Statewide Planning Goals are strategies such as Goal 14 (Urbanization), which requires cities to establish urban growth boundaries and separate urban and rural lands by zoning. Rural lands are planned for resource use or for limited rural development. More than 80% of the Oregon coast is zoned for forest use. Goal 18 (Beaches and Dunes) prohibits residential development on beaches and foredunes. Goal 17 (Coastal Shorelands) defines the state coastal planning area boundary and sets management rules for different coastal lands such as marshes. The local coastal plans must contain a coastal shoreland boundary. Within this boundary area are zones for water-dependent uses, wetland mitigation and restoration sites, dredged material disposal, riparian vegetation, coastal hazard areas, significant habitat, public access, and "exceptional aesthetic resources." The Oregon Goal 16 (Estuarine Resources) requires local governments to classify Oregon's 22 major estuaries into four categories and describes types of land uses and activities that are permissible within these management units.

The Oregon CMP, approved in 1977, was the second approved program under the CZMA. Oregon's coastal zone includes all lands between the Washington border to the north, the California border to the south, seaward to the territorial sea, and inland to the crest of the coastal range (Figure 6.3). The public owns the wet sand beach, up to the ordinary high-tide line. The Oregon Beach Bill afforded the public a perpetual easement to use the dry sand beach up to the surveyed beach zone line. The Oregon PRD protects public rights to unobstructed use of the dry sand beach, and the state is a major landowner in its own coastal zone. More than 75,000 acres is owned by the state. As a result, 90% of the Oregon coastline is open and accessible to the

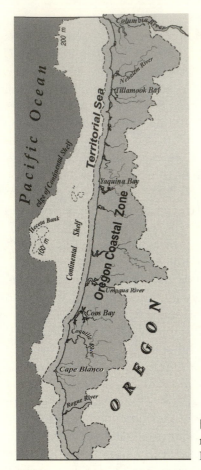

Figure 6.3. Oregon coastal boundary
map. (From Oregon Coastal Management
Program.)

public (NOAA, 1999d). An impediment to increased access is the effect
of public use on natural resources. In 1994, the state developed a
Rocky Shores Management Strategy to protect rocky shore habitat that
is viewed as particularly vulnerable to access users.

Oregon has been a model for other coastal states in ocean management. The LCDC adopted Goal 19 (Ocean Resources), which aims to
"conserve the long-term benefits, and natural resources of the
nearshore ocean and the continental shelf." The Oregon legislature
enacted its Ocean Resources Management Act in 1987 (SB630), initiat-
ing an ocean planning process and creating a 21-member Ocean
Resources Management Task Force. The task force oversees the development of the Ocean Resources Management Plan. This plan resulted
in extensive analyses of ocean uses, resources, and conditions and is

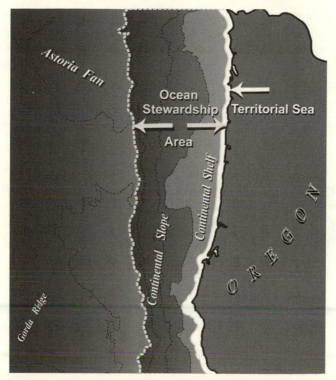

Figure 6.4. Oregon ocean stewardship area map. (From Oregon Coastal Management Program.)

intended to provide an overall management framework to guide activities and decisions within the Exclusive Economic Zone; a more detailed Territorial Sea Management Plan has also been prepared. The Oregon program has broken new ground in a number of respects, such as proposing the establishment of an Ocean Stewardship Area (Figure 6.4), which would extend to the seaward edge of the continental shelf (with a width varying from 35 to 80 miles) and in which management activities would be focused.

The Oregon CMP has prioritized a state natural hazard strategy for several years. A number of jurisdictions have amended their plans to improve their permit and siting standards for hazardous shoreline areas. Oregon is also moving toward area-wide hazard management through a CMP-sponsored Littoral Cell Management Program. Littoral cells are land between headlands along the Oregon coast. The management plans contain an inventory of the physical, biological, and cultural characteristics within each cell and a chronic hazard management strategy focused on avoidance and beach and shore protection. Each management plan also contains implementing mechanisms such as ordinances, memoranda of agreements, and other coordinating documents that adopt policies and procedures prescribed in the management strategy.

Through the formation of the Oregon coastal management and land use planning program, state officials have been aided by 1000 Friends of Oregon, a citizens' group devoted to land use planning throughout the state. Although challenged on several occasions, Senate Bill 100, which mandates state and local planning in Oregon, has not been overturned by judicial or political processes.

These three cases—Maine, North Carolina, and Oregon—demonstrate the flexibility of the CZMA and how this can play out in state coastal resource management. Maine is an example of a completely networked program, with a diverse cadre of state agencies, regional and local governments, and private sector interests. North Carolina is guided by a legislative act, CAMA, an example of coastal management through coastal-specific legislation and local planning mandates. Oregon also integrates local planning requirements but does so through a broader state planning strategy.

The Success of the CZMA

There are several different ways in which the success and effectiveness of the CZMA might be evaluated. First, the program authorized by CZMA is completely voluntary: The states may participate if they wish, but in no way are they compelled to do so. Therefore, it is fair to say the extent to which the states have opted to participate in the program is some indication of the program's success. Based on participation rates, then, the program has been quite successful. Of the 35 coastal states and territories eligible for funding, 33 now have federally approved programs.

Another, perhaps more relevant gauge of success is the extent to which state and local management capacity has increased in response to the CZMA. There is little doubt that the CZMA has served as a catalyst for the development of more extensive and more effective CMPs. Compared with the state management framework existing before the CZMA, it is clear that coastal development patterns and practices are more respectful of protecting coastal resources and reducing exposure of people and property to coastal risks. As Godschalk and Cousins

(1985) conclude, "When the plans, policies, regulations, and personnel of these individual programs are added up, the result is a quantum leap over 1972 institutional capacity for coastal planning and management" (p. 264).

The CZMA has not been without its problems and limitations, however. One concern stems from the very flexibility of the program, heralded by many as a virtue. Although state programs must include certain basic provisions and address certain issues, coastal states need not adopt very stringent or aggressive coastal management requirements. Whereas states such as North Carolina have adopted fairly extensive erosion-based setback requirements, other states enforce no shoreline setback at all. Some coastal states have adopted aggressive wetland protection and habitat acquisition programs, whereas other states have taken no action in these areas. It is generally up to each coastal state to determine the extent to which it wants to manage coastal resources. Some states, such as South Carolina, have severely curtailed their management programs with no federal repercussions. Despite the CZMA's strong statement of goals and findings, the program has had difficulty articulating clear substantive standards of state performance. Understandably, this has made NOAA's (OCRM) efforts to evaluate state program performance and compliance, required under the CZMA, difficult. In response to this perceived limitation, some have argued the need for clear substantive standards of review and a stronger system for monitoring and evaluating state programs. This situation has been exacerbated over time by the change in administrations and the ensuing change in attitude toward environmental management in general and the coast in particular. The program began with an exciting period during which the states explored a variety of ways to achieve the national goals along with the state goals, with the federal staff acting as both coaches and cheerleaders. This changed as interest ebbed and flowed with the changing attitude of the changing administrations, but many believe that the program now more resembles a block grant program than the original challenging program it was at the outset.

Conclusions

The U.S. approach to coastal management has been one of collaboration and partnership between the federal government and state governments. Under the CZMA, Congress created positive incentives (e.g., financial, consistency) for states to develop and implement CMPs. Most states have taken advantage of these opportunities, and the CZMA appears to have been a major catalyst for expanded state coastal management. Before the CZMA many states had little or no coastal management or planning capability.

Although state coastal programs must meet certain minimum criteria, the CZMA has provided states with much flexibility in devising programs that meet their unique physical and political circumstances. Certain common components of state programs have been identified and discussed, including local planning requirements, shoreline management and retreat provisions (e.g., shoreline setbacks), restrictions on shore-hardening structures, coastal wetland restrictions, provisions to guide and manage reconstruction, beach access and land acquisition, building codes and construction standards, and ocean management. The stringency of coastal management varies substantially from state to state, but there is little doubt that the coastal zone of the United States is in better shape today than if Congress had not passed and funded the CZMA, however minimally. But as the population of the coastal zone continues to grow, that population will push even harder at the boundaries of the remaining fragile areas, those that have not been developed because they are protected (at least for now) or because they have been too difficult to develop. If the national values expressed by Congress in the CZMA are to be honored, the much-heralded federal–state partnership must be reinvigorated with imagination, creativity, and, of course, more money.

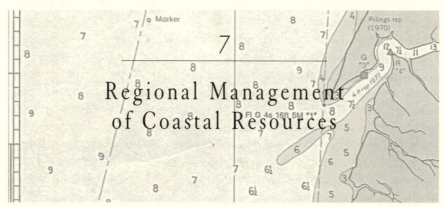

7

Regional Management
of Coastal Resources

Managing complex areas such as the coastal zone does not lend itself to traditional planning and management mechanisms, which tend to segment concerns and deal with problems on an isolated, ad hoc basis. However, as discussed in Chapter 2, the coastal zone is a process-driven, integrated system of interacting components in which one action, whether initiated from within or external to the system, has ramifications far beyond the initial impact. Further compounding these difficulties is the fact that natural resources often transcend political boundaries and do not conform to our artificial and arbitrary political and administrative jurisdictions.

One solution posed to address this dilemma is management of natural resources at the regional level. Although it can be variously defined and takes on many different characteristics throughout the United States, regionalism can be an effective means of ensuring the continued viability of our coastal areas.

What Is Regional Management?

Regions are geographic areas that share common issues of public policy, administration, resource management, pollution control, economic development, or other social, political, or environmental concerns and for which no government body exists. The organization of a regional management institution provides an entity that focuses on the region's needs, studies them, and tries to meet them or move others to do so (So et al., 1986).

There are many different approaches to implementing management on a regional scale. In some areas, management is undertaken by a regulatory agency. This may take the form of a free-standing body spanning state or national borders, or it may operate within a state government, either as a separate entity or as a division of an existing state department or agency. Such regulatory agencies usually are created by the legislators of the states and may be given both regulatory and enforcement powers. Other regional management bodies are more administrative in nature and may perform coordinating functions or act as advisory boards to state or local governments. Communication, education, and consensus building are typical roles of these types of regional organizations. In many regional institutions, planning is the principal activity and often is the only activity authorized. Planning bodies inform and advise decision-makers within the region as to policies and actions that can address the region's issues.

This chapter introduces some of the major regional management endeavors in the United States and provides a brief overview of a few exemplary programs. Some of the federal programs discussed here, such as the National Estuary Program (NEP), the National Marine Sanctuaries Program (NMSP), and Special Area Management Plans (SAMPs), were introduced in Chapter 5 as important federal programs affecting the coastal zone. This chapter emphasizes the ecosystem basis for management that these and other programs use.

The Watershed Protection Approach

Collaborative management of water resources on the watershed scale provides a means of balancing the many, often competing demands we place on our coastal water resources. The watershed approach to management takes into account the relationships between uplands and downstream areas, between surface and groundwater, and the ecological and hydrologic complexities of an entire water system rather than focusing on an isolated segment.

Protecting Water Quality from Nonpoint Source Pollution

All states and the federal government have water protection programs designed to reverse or prevent water quality degradation. Most of these programs include regulations on industrial and municipal point source discharges. However, one of the greatest dangers to the nation's water supply emanates from nonpoint sources of pollution, such as runoff into waterways and seepage into groundwater. Wetland degradation and habitat destruction are also threatened by these nonpoint sources of pollution.

Some federal programs are aimed at nonpoint source pollution, and the Environmental Protection Agency (EPA) has initiated activities to control nonpoint source pollutants on a watershed basis. However, absolute uniform regulation of nonpoint sources at the federal level would be prohibitively expensive. Furthermore, such federally imposed control probably would be politically unfeasible in our federalist system, where impingements on traditional state and local prerogatives such as land use regulation and economic development often are not tolerated. With the continuing devolution of authority from the federal government to state and local authorities, federally mandated regulation of water quality is less likely to be an effective management mechanism (National Research Council, 1999).

Fortunately, governments at all levels are broadening their outlook on water quality protection and refocusing existing water pollution control programs to operate in a more comprehensive and coordinated manner. International, national, state, regional, and local initiatives for collaborative watershed management are being developed and implemented. And although the holistic approach called for by watershed management has not been mandated, it has been endorsed by the federal government, as evidenced by President Clinton's 1998 Clean Water Action Plan (Michaels, 2001). There is a growing consensus that the pollution and habitat degradation problems now facing society can best be solved by following a basinwide approach that takes into account the dynamic relationships that sustain natural resources and their beneficial uses. The term *watershed protection approach* often is used to encompass these ideas (U.S. Environmental Protection Agency, 1991).

Defining the Watershed

Watersheds are defined by the waterscape, the combination of the hydrology and topography of the terrain. Although there are many ways to define the geographic unit that makes up a particular watershed, the term in its most basic sense refers to a geographic area in which water, sediments, and dissolved materials drain to a common outlet, which can be a point on a larger stream, a lake, an underlying aquifer, an estuary, or an ocean. This area is also called the drainage basin of the receiving water body.

Watersheds as geographic areas are optimal organizing units for dealing with the management of water and closely related resources, but the natural boundaries of watersheds rarely coincide with political jurisdictions (National Research Council, 1999). Therefore, when defining the boundaries of the watershed for institutional, political, regulatory, or funding purposes, a wide variety of factors may be considered. Decisions as to the scale of the watershed unit may involve analysis of underlying groundwater flow, channel morphology, natural habitats, economic uses, the type and scope of pollution problems, and the level of resources available for protection and restoration projects (U.S. Environmental Protection Agency, 1991).

Principles of the Watershed Protection Approach

Ideally, collaborative watershed management entails shared decision-making and implementation by public and private sector partners who share the common goal of conserving or enhancing hydrologic resources (Michaels, 2001). The watershed protection approach aims at targeted, cooperative, and integrated action.

The EPA sets forth three main principles for carrying out resource management under the watershed protection approach. First, the target watersheds should be those where pollution poses the greatest risk to human health, ecological resources, desirable uses of the water, or a combination of these. This risk-based geographic targeting may involve several different problems that pose health or ecological risks in the watershed. These problems include industrial wastewater discharges; municipal wastewater, stormwater, and combined sewer overflows; waste dumping and injection; nonpoint source runoff or seepage; accidental leaks and spills of toxic or hazardous substances; atmospheric deposition; habitat alteration, including wetlands loss; and flow variations. Based on evaluation of these and similar problems, the highest-risk watersheds are identified and one or more are selected for cooperative, integrated assessment and protection.

The second principle of the watershed protection approach entails stakeholder involvement; all parties with a stake in the specific local situation should participate in analyzing problems and creating solutions. Potential participants in watershed protection projects include state environmental, public health, agricultural, and natural resource agencies; local and regional boards, commissions, and agencies; EPA water and other programs; other federal agencies; Native American tribes;

public representatives; private wildlife and conservation organizations; industry sector representatives; and the academic community. Stakeholders should work as a task force, reaching consensus on goals and approaches for addressing a watershed's problems, the specific actions to be taken, and how they will be coordinated and evaluated. For too long, agencies at all levels, particularly at the federal level, have conducted programs and carried out activities in isolation. The U.S. Army Corps of Engineers (COE), the Bureau of Land Reclamation, the U.S. Department of Agriculture, the EPA, and the Federal Emergency Management Agency have not considered the basinwide ramifications of their policies and permitting procedures. Through the watershed protection approach there is greater opportunity for these and other stakeholders to consider the regional and downstream ecological, social, and economic consequences of their actions rather than focus merely on individual projects in an ad hoc manner (National Research Council, 1999).

The third principle in the watershed protection approach is that the actions undertaken should draw on the full range of methods and tools available, integrating them into a coordinated, multiorganization attack on the problems. Coordinated action may be taken in such areas as voluntary source reduction programs (e.g., waste minimization, best management practices), permit issuance and enforcement programs, standard setting and enforcement programs (nonpermitting), direct financing, economic incentives, education and information dissemination, technical assistance, remediation of contaminated soil or water, and emergency response to accidental leaks or spills. The selected tools are then applied to the watershed's problems, according to the plans and roles established through stakeholder consensus. Progress is evaluated periodically via ecological indicators and other measures (U.S. Environmental Protection Agency, 1991).

A fourth principle often is cited as critical to a successful watershed approach: Scientific understanding and research should be the underpinning of water resource management. However, watershed science is far from the stage at which data and analysis can be fully relied on to be accurate and informative. It is imperative that adequate funding for watershed research, monitoring, and planning be allocated to bolster management activities. "Watershed science in general has yet to develop an effective interface between what we know and how we use that knowledge. Good science is not enough; we need useful science.

Watershed management without significant input of new scientific understanding, especially understanding of watershed processes and of the human dimensions, is doomed to inefficiency and eventual loss of credibility; research without input from involved stakeholders and those with real management acumen will always prove less than useful" (National Research Council, 1999, p. 3).

Watershed Protection Projects

Numerous projects using the watershed protection approach have been implemented throughout the United States, and many more are in various planning stages. These activities were not mandated by the EPA or any other central agency; they have arisen spontaneously as the most effective way to address pressing local or regional problems (U.S. Environmental Protection Agency, 1991).

In general, these projects differ from conventional water quality initiatives in that they encompass all or most of the landscape in a well-defined watershed or other ecological, physiographic, or hydrologic unit, such as an embayment, an aquifer, or a mountain valley. Most such projects are more comprehensive than traditional water regulations and establish goals and objectives dealing with a vast array of watershed issues such as chemical water quality (conventional pollutants and toxics), physical water quality (e.g., temperature, flow, and circulation), habitat quality (e.g., channel morphology, composition, and health of biotic communities), and biodiversity (e.g., species number and range) (U.S. Environmental Protection Agency, 1991).

THE STILLAGUAMISH WATERSHED PROTECTION PROJECT

One watershed project that has had some success is the Stillaguamish Watershed Protection Project in Washington State. The Stillaguamish Watershed is a significant source of nonpoint source pollution to Puget Sound. Bacteria from livestock wastes and onsite sewage disposal systems are the main pollutants, as well as runoff of sediment from forests, farms, and development sites. In large part because of these pollutants, shellfish beds in Port Susan have been declared unsafe for commercial harvest.

A Watershed Management Committee (WMC) was formed in 1988 with a grant from the Washington Department of Ecology. The WMC was made up of representatives from the Tulalip and Stillaguamish tribes, county and city governments, environmental and business interests, and homeowners' and citizens' organizations. State and federal environmental regulators participated via a technical advisory committee.

The Stillaguamish Watershed Action Plan, completed in 1989, consists of five source control programs, a public education program, and a monitoring program. WMC recommendations include developing farm conservation plans, reducing improper disposal of human waste, preventing urban runoff, and sampling on a regular basis to track water quality trends (U.S. Environmental Protection Agency, 1991).

WATERSHED PROTECTION IN THE U.S. VIRGIN ISLANDS

The U.S. Virgin Islands is a place of great beauty, with varied terrain on the three islands of St. Thomas, St. John, and St. Croix. Steep volcanic slopes covered in dark green forests, sandy beaches, Caribbean blue waters, coral reefs, mangrove swamps, coastal plains, and numerous sites of cultural and historical significance support the islands' main industry of tourism and contribute to the quality of life for island residents. Unfortunately, the Virgin Islands also face serious issues of resource depletion, impaired water quality, and a high degree of vulnerability to flooding. Many of these problems are caused by poor land use decisions on the part of both the government and the private sector—decisions that have resulted in much development taking place without regard to the suitability of the site or the hydrology of the larger watershed.

Many of the Virgin Islands' problems are being tackled with a managerial and administrative system that is based on the watersheds of the islands. Various government programs are being integrated into the Islands' Unified Watershed Assessment and Restoration Priority Planning Process. Though initially generated as a response to water quality issues, the Watershed Assessment and Restoration Program provides a framework for addressing other pressing concerns in the Virgin Islands, including natural resource management and hazard mitigation.

The Virgin Islands Department of Planning and Natural Resources, in conjunction with the Natural Resources Conservation Service of the U.S. Department of Agriculture, has developed a Unified Watershed Assessment Report pursuant to the Clean Water Action Plan. A key objective of the action plan is to provide a new, cooperative process for restoring and protecting water quality on a watershed basis. The action plan calls on the territorial government to assess the condition of water resources and identify:

- watersheds not meeting or facing imminent threat of not meeting clean water or other natural resource goals

- watersheds meeting goals but needing action to sustain water quality
- watersheds with pristine or sensitive aquatic system conditions on federal, state, or tribal lands
- watersheds for which more information is needed to assess conditions

The watershed approach used in the U.S. Virgin Islands emphasizes the use of smaller hydrologic management units that are better equipped to handle the localized geographic focus of a watershed. The U.S. Virgin Islands has been divided into two hydrologic units: St. Croix and St. Thomas/St. John. This is a critical distinction because the topography and hydrologic characteristics of St. John and St. Thomas are very different from the conditions on St. Croix. These watersheds can be further subdivided into smaller sub-watersheds that fall within larger watersheds to target specific activities. There are no large freshwater lakes or ponds and no perennial streams on any of the islands; only intermittent streams can be seen after heavy rainfall. The absence of large freshwater resources and perennial streams means that guts (watercourses) form the basis for watershed management in the territory.

The sub-watersheds of the Virgin Islands are currently being drawn. These are being highlighted according to water quality parameters as areas of particular concern for management purposes under the Unified Watershed Assessment and Restoration Priorities Program. Using these sub-watersheds as the basis of a managerial approach could change the way the government of the Virgin Islands manages its water resources. It is now recognized that the critical environmental issues facing the Virgin Islands are so intertwined that a comprehensive, ecosystem-based approach is needed. Because the Virgin Islands have firmly embraced watershed management as the principal strategy for controlling pollutant discharges in the territory, other activities undertaken by the government are also being organized by watersheds, including flood control, wastewater treatment, nonpoint source pollution, and stormwater management.

Special Area Management Plans

SAMPs are a coordinated approach that addresses complex and often far-reaching environmental problems through regional management. The Federal Coastal Zone Management Act (CZMA) defines a SAMP as a "comprehensive plan providing for natural resource protection and reasonable coastal-dependent economic growth containing a detailed and comprehensive statement of policies; standards and criteria to guide public and private uses of lands and waters; and mechanisms for timely implementation in specific geographic areas within the coastal zone" (16 U.S.C. §1453(17)).

As a planning mechanism, special area management has been used with varying degrees of success throughout the United States. Although specific applications of SAMPs vary widely, the basic tenets of the technique are designed to accomplish similar broad goals, including the following:

- address environmental problems that are best solved through a multijurisdictional and integrated policy approach
- coordinate existing policies to adequately and comprehensively address environmental problems
- establish a balanced management framework to protect public or socially important resources while allowing for appropriate continued use of these resources

There are several scenarios in which SAMPs may be appropriate. First, environmental problems that warrant this approach typically involve natural systems lying within multiple political jurisdictions. Conflicts over the multiple use of resources, including numerous human and natural forces that may threaten the vitality of the resource, may make management by a single entity problematic. Second, high resource values (economic, recreational, social, or biological) often create conflicting interests regarding preservation or development, and in these cases an integrated special area approach allows for more flexible, tailored management. A publicly or socially important natural resource area (characterized as a public good) may also be targeted for special area management. Finally, particularly severe environmental problems ranging over a large geographic area may warrant the use of this management technique.

Special area management is founded on specific management goals and objectives pertaining to an explicit, well-defined problem area. Typically, this area is delineated spatially, according to resource-area boundaries that include the environmental system targeted by management goals and the human systems that affect it. Natural, political, and social systems within this area must also be identified. The planning area must also encompass a broad enough area to include the entire relevant environmental system in addition to the human systems that affect it.

In its best form, SAMP participants typically work together through consensus and negotiation to create an agreed-upon management text. Various interest groups can be involved in the SAMP process, including state and federal agencies, local officials, environmentalists, landowners, developers, citizens' groups, and others with a stake in the management of a particular area.

The final outcome of the special area management process can take several forms. Some SAMPs end as a loose, nonenforceable coalition of interests who confer with one another concerning policy goals. Other plans operate by means of an advisory committee that counsels relevant government units on how to deal with specific problems. Still other SAMPs become a formal part of state or local government and often are given some degree of regulatory control.

The Chesapeake Bay Program

The Chesapeake Bay is protected under its own federally mandated program, separate from but related to the NEP. The Chesapeake Bay Program raised awareness of the need to establish collaborative management institutions to protect estuaries threatened by pollution, development, and overuse, thus serving as a prototype for the NEP and providing a model for estuarine research and restoration programs worldwide.

Natural Features of the Chesapeake Bay

The Chesapeake Bay is 195 miles long and 4 to 30 miles wide and is the largest estuary in the United States. Approximately 50 major rivers and more than 100 smaller tributaries provide freshwater to the bay. The drainage basin includes an area of roughly 64,000 square miles, thus accounting for one-sixth of the Atlantic seaboard (Figure 7.1). The estuary is one of the most productive in the world and provides habitat to many species of aquatic life and wildlife including finfish, shellfish, bay grasses, bald eagles, and waterfowl.

A Working Partnership

The Chesapeake Bay Program is a unique regional partnership that has been directing and conducting the restoration of the Chesapeake Bay

Photo 7.1. Chesapeake Bay estuary. (Photo by NOAA.)

since the 1980s. Responding to public concern about declining water quality and diminishing fish and shellfish landings, in 1975 the EPA conducted a comprehensive study of the Chesapeake Bay. The findings of the 5-year study prompted the governors of Maryland, Virginia, and Pennsylvania, the mayor of the District of Columbia, the chair of the Chesapeake Bay Commission, and the administrator of the EPA to sign the 1983 Chesapeake Bay Agreement. Goals, priorities, and objectives under the agreement are established by consensus among all the partners in the program. The Chesapeake Bay Agreement relies entirely on individual state implementation of the goal and policy statements, and each state has approached watershed management differently. This flexibility has resulted in development of a management program that is politically acceptable to each state. Of the states within the watershed, only Delaware, New York, and West Virginia have not signed the Chesapeake Bay Agreement, but the 1992 amendments state that members should "explore cooperative working relationships" with these states.

Chesapeake 2000 Agreement

In June 2000, the Chesapeake Bay Program partners signed the Chesapeake 2000 Agreement to guide management efforts in the estuary for the next decade. Built on the foundation of the 1983 and 1987 agreements, the Chesapeake 2000 Agreement commits the members to pro-

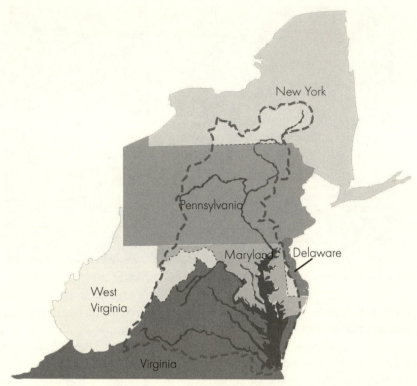

Figure 7.1. The Chesapeake Bay watershed crosses many jurisdictional lines, falling within New York, Pennsylvania, Delaware, Maryland, Virginia, and West Virginia. (From EPA Chesapeake Bay Program.)

tect and restore living resources, vital habitats, and water quality and is the most comprehensive and far-reaching agreement to date. The new plan emphasizes strategies to combat nutrient overenrichment, dwindling underwater bay grasses, and toxic pollution.

Toxics 2000 Strategy

The Toxics 2000 Strategy was formally adopted as an action plan by the Chesapeake Bay Program to prevent the release of chemical contaminants into the Chesapeake Bay and its tributaries. Voluntary goals exceed current regulations, committing partners to achieve zero release of toxics. Goals have been established to phase out chemical mixing zones, reduce point source loads, and ensure that finfish and shellfish are safe for human consumption. The Toxics 2000 Strategy also sets specific numerical goals to reduce toxics from nonpoint sources, including stormwater runoff and agricultural runoff.

Nutrient Reduction in the Bay

The 1987 Chesapeake Bay Agreement set a goal to reduce controllable loads of nitrogen and phosphorus entering the bay by 40% by the year 2000. Achieving a 40% nutrient reduction would ultimately improve the oxygen levels in bay waters and encourage aquatic life to flourish. In 1992, the Chesapeake Bay Program partners agreed to continue the 40% reduction goal beyond 2000 and to attack nutrients at their source: upstream in the bay's tributaries. As a result, Pennsylvania, Maryland, Virginia, and the District of Columbia began developing tributary strategies to achieve nutrient reduction targets. Models have indicated that phosphorus loads flowing into the bay from all of its tributaries were reduced by 6.8 million pounds per year between 1985 and 2000. Data show that nitrogen loads declined by 48 million pounds per year. In the areas most affected by excessive nutrient loads, the Potomac River and points north, phosphorus reduction goals were achieved, and nitrogen goals for those areas are expected to be met once tributary strategies are fully implemented. Despite this encouraging finding, baywide reductions of phosphorus and nitrogen fell short of the goal set for 2000, and efforts to meet the attainment goals must be strengthened.

The Great Lakes Program

The Great Lakes are the most important natural resource shared by Canada and the United States. The joint responsibility for this shared resource has produced large-scale cooperative arrangements such as the St. Lawrence Seaway, the Niagara Falls Treaty, the Great Lakes Water Quality Agreements (GLWQA), the Great Lakes Fishery Commission, and three Lake Levels Boards of Control. The institutional setting within which these management activities occur is complex and diverse. The responsibility for governance is shared by the two federal governments, eight American states, the province of Ontario, and numerous regional, local, and special-purpose districts of government.

With few exceptions, the lakes themselves are not directly managed. Of course, there are specific instances of direct management such as the regulation of water levels or the manipulation of biota (for exam-

ple, species of fish). But the major task of environmental protection for
the lakes involves managing certain human activities. The greater body
of law and policy is directed toward human activities that affect the
lakes and their quality (Caldwell, 1985). One such management system
is the Great Lakes Program (GLP), which began in the early 1970s as a
cooperative effort between the United States and Canada to address the
environmental problems facing the Great Lakes ecosystem.

The GLP is a true interjurisdictional effort that encompasses the
entire watershed of the Great Lakes. The United States and Canada
base their respective management programs on a series of international
agreements, the GLWQA (Imperial et al., 1993). The first GLWQA was
signed in Ottawa by President Nixon and Prime Minister Trudeau. After
the first 5-year review, the GLWQA of 1978 was signed at Ottawa.

The International Joint Commission (IJC) plays an important role in
guiding the efforts of the two countries and monitoring implementation
of the GLP. The IJC has a history predating the GLWQA and was actually established in 1909 by the Boundary Waters Treaty between the
United States and Canada to oversee navigation, water withdrawal, and
water levels. Today the IJC is the most prominent public body shaping
policy with respect to the Great Lakes, and it is a testament to the commission's effectiveness that it continues to oversee management today.
The U.S. portion of the GLP is administered by the Great Lakes National
Program Office, a separate and distinct office within the EPA.

With careful study of biannual and 5-year progress reports, the GLP
has been able to evolve to deal with increasingly complex issues
involving the integrity of the Great Lakes environment. As scientific
data have been acquired and interpreted and as new understandings of
the ecosystem have been reached, the GLP has been able to update
and adapt its management programs to respond to the lakes' environmental needs.

The first GLWQA, signed in 1972, contained general objectives and
addressed conventional pollutants. The early years of the program
focused primarily on point sources of pollution to address the problems
of oxygen depletion and eutrophication. To achieve these goals, major
municipal treatment plants within the management area were required
to reduce phosphorus in effluents, and phosphate detergents were
banned in many states (Imperial et al., 1993).

The 1978 agreement added more specific and quantitative objectives, including physical, microbiological, and radiological parameters
(Imperial et al., 1993). Specific objectives of the agreement include a

nondegradation clause, a policy that flow augmentation is not a substitute for adequate treatment, exclusion of inshore areas where natural phenomena prevent achievement of objectives, and designation of limited-use zones.

The 1978 GLWQA is most notable for being the first major international treaty or agreement to embrace the ecosystem approach for the management of large regional resources (National Research Council of the U.S. and the Royal Society of Canada, 1985). Thus, by formal agreement between Canada and the United States, policies directed toward water quality restoration and enhancement in the Great Lakes were to be based on a basinwide ecosystem view (Caldwell, 1985).

The 1978 GLWQA took a long-term perspective in managing pollutant threats, recognizing the need for both reactive and preventive measures to control the buildup of substances and the transport of materials from the land to the water and from the air to the water. In the agreement, the water resources transcend political boundaries within the basin and are treated as a single hydrologic system (National Research Council of the U.S. and the Royal Society of Canada, 1985).

The GLP has evolved substantially since the 1972 GLWQA. The adoption of a basinwide ecosystem approach to management of the lakes is a decision of major international importance (Caldwell, 1985). Aside from this more general achievement, progress in specific areas has also been notable. For instance, phosphorus loads from point sources have been reduced by an estimated 80 to 90% through regulation and financial assistance; all major dischargers as a group are currently meeting the 1 milligram per liter phosphorus goal; the GLP is now targeting the control of nonpoint sources of nutrients; support is being given to efforts to obtain information about sources, fates, and effects of pollutants to support a mass balance approach in remedial action programs; point source loads of almost all toxic substances have decreased in recent years; and the GLP is working to assess and address the problem of contaminated bottom sediments (Imperial et al., 1993).

There are also some lessons to be learned from the GLP that can be applied to other ecosystem-based management approaches. For instance, without clearly articulated goals and priorities to drive the decisions and actions of the GLP, its efforts often have lacked focus. This problem is exacerbated in a management system that is highly complex and involves many levels of government. Furthermore, it is clear that it is crucial to set risk-based goals and priorities and let the

Photo 7.2. Lake Superior in Houghton County, Michigan. (Photo by NOAA.)

priorities drive the management decisions and actions. The GLP will never have the authority or resources to address all the problems in the Great Lakes, and it is important that these resources be flexibly targeted and integrated in a manner that provides the greatest opportunity from the limited resources available (Imperial et al., 1993).

The National Estuary Program

The NEP was established in 1987 by amendments to the Clean Water Act and is administered by the EPA through the Office of Wetlands, Oceans and Watersheds. The act defines the NEP's primary goals to be the protection and improvement of water quality and the enhancement of living resources (33 U.S.C.S. §1330(a)(2)(A)). Before this formal declaration, however, the roots of the NEP had already been established through efforts to manage the coastal environment at both the federal and the state levels. In particular, the EPA's involvement in the GLP and the Chesapeake Bay Program supported the basic premise of the NEP: that management of hydrologic ecosystems must be approached holistically by recognizing the interconnections of all living resources within the estuarine environment. The NEP also relies on past experience, which demonstrates that a regional, cooperative approach to natural resource protection and management is both feasible and effective.

The NEP is a voluntary program operated at the state and local levels. Federal technical and financial assistance is available to the states to identify an estuary's problems and develop a management plan of action to address those problems. The management approach used by each program follows federal standards that are flexible enough to allow wide local variation in problem selection and managerial design. Although federal planning funds are provided through the NEP, state and local governments are responsible for funding implementation of the management plan.

The NEP encompasses estuaries that represent diverse ecosystems, including both heavily urbanized and rural watersheds, each of which has its own ecological, social, and economic issues. Furthermore, some estuaries of the NEP transcend both local and state boundaries, and many differ in their degree of jurisdictional complexity. To deal with these differences between estuaries, the structure of each NEP centers around its own Management Conference, made up of committees that oversee the various program activities undertaken by that particular NEP. The conference also acts as the primary decision-making unit. There is wide variation in the composition and size of the individual Management Conferences, depending on the specific conditions of each estuary program.

Although the EPA allows flexibility in composition, each Management Conference must contain several committees, headed by a policy committee, made up of EPA representatives, governors, and top agency officials. The conference also includes a management committee, which acts as the consensus builder for the group and whose members represent state water quality and natural resource agencies, state regulatory offices, and community and environmental groups. The management committee is responsible for developing the 5-year Management Conference Agreement between the state and the EPA, which identifies program activities and work products and sets major program milestones and work schedules. Other committees found in a Management Conference include a science and technical advisory committee, a citizens' advisory committee, a local government committee, and a financial planning committee.

The various committees of each NEP Management Conference work together to achieve seven basic federally mandated purposes, with the understanding that the ultimate goal of the NEP is to achieve basinwide planning to control pollution and manage living resources. The seven legislatively determined purposes of a Management Conference are as follows:

- assess trends in water quality, natural resources, and estuary uses
- collect data and assess toxins, nutrients, and natural resources within the estuarine zone to identify the causes of environmental problems
- develop the relationship between the point and nonpoint loads of pollutants to the estuarine zone and the potential uses of the zone, water quality, and natural resources
- develop a Comprehensive Conservation and Management Plan (CCMP) that includes recommendations for priority corrective actions and compliance schedules addressing sources of pollution and restoration of the biological, chemical, and physical integrity of the estuarine zone
- develop plans for the coordinated implementation of the CCMP by states and by the federal and local agencies participating in the conference
- monitor the effectiveness of actions taken pursuant to the plan
- review federal financial assistance programs and federal development programs for consistency with the CCMP (33 U.S.C.S. §1330(b))

The CCMPs are the heart of each NEP, but their implementability remains questionable. Federal assistance covers preparation and planning, but no federal money is available for implementation. Therefore, responsibility for putting the plans into action rests entirely with state and participating local governments. Furthermore, although the CCMP operates as a vehicle for problem identification, the plans do not automatically become state public policy. Further political action, along with budgetary and public support, is often needed before a CCMP gets on the state agenda. Despite the limitations in terms of policy execution and implementation financing, the structure of the NEP may prove to be flexible and adaptable enough to be successful in managing estuaries of national significance (Imperial et al., 1993).

Puget Sound: An NEP Success

Puget Sound often is cited as an example of an NEP success story. Established in 1987, the Puget Sound Estuary covers 42,791 square kilometers of watershed in Washington State. The sound is home to major habitat types including submerged aquatic vegetation such as sea grass and kelp; lagoon and shallow open water; rocky intertidal and subtidal areas; shellfish growing areas; cliffs and bluffs; sand, mud, and salt flats; tidal pools; salt and brackish marsh; freshwater tidal and nontidal marsh; forested wetland; freshwater lakes and ponds; scrub and shrub; nonwetland forest; and riparian and riverine habitat. Numerous federally endangered or threatened species make their home in Puget Sound, including several types of mammals, birds, reptiles, insects, and plants.

Puget Sound was one of the first estuaries to join the NEP. Protection of the sound's water quality and habitat for living resources is driven by 2-year work plans, which are based on the CCMP for the sound. Work plans also recognize other state and local water quality and resource protection programs, with the goals of coordinating programs better and reducing duplication. Efforts to protect water quality are enhanced by providing regional technical assistance to help local governments implement the work plans. Priority management issues for Puget Sound include toxics, conventional pollutants, pathogens, human population growth, habitat loss and alteration, introduced and pest species, sedimentation, and oil spills.

Nonpoint source pollution has contributed to declines in Puget Sound's water quality and has resulted in numerous shellfishing area closings. In particular, large amounts of fine sediment have been deposited in the sound from the Shell Creek watershed located in southwest Snohomish County near the City of Edmonds. The creek, which discharges into Puget Sound, is a spawning ground for cutthroat trout and coho and chum salmon. The creek receives stormwater runoff from 2 square miles of suburban neighborhoods.

The City of Edmonds and Snohomish County prepared a plan for the Shell Creek basin. The plan recommended comprehensive approaches to slow the resource degradation that was occurring in Shell Creek and affecting the sound. The plan addressed flooding, severe erosion of the stream bed, very heavy sedimentation, and increased pollutant loading. Secondary problems included reduced capacity in culverts and loss of fish habitat. Based on the plan's recommendations, the Shell Creek Stormwater Diversion Demonstration Project was initiated by the City of Edmonds with support from the Puget Sound NEP.

The primary objectives of the project were to manage stormwater flows and reduce sediment and pollutant loads into Puget Sound. This has been achieved by stream bed restoration and construction of a stormwater diversion and sediment entrapment system. The diversion structure has a vertical slot entrance that includes a fish ladder to help fish migrate. To reestablish trout and salmon populations and to restore stream bed and bank stability, the demonstration project included a restoration component focusing on a mile of Shell Creek upstream from the diversion structure. In addition, with the help of a local Boy Scout troop, the banks of the stream were planted with stabilizing vegetation.

Through the restoration and diversion, sediment loading to Puget Sound from Shell Creek was reduced by 5.7 tons in the first year and is estimated to have reduced stream bed erosion by 65%. Citizens now report that clear water runs through the creek where muddy water used to be prevalent. In addition, flooding and erosion have been eliminated, which in turn has reduced pollutant loads downstream. Trout and salmon have returned to Shell Creek, and vegetation has flourished on the banks.

The National
Marine Sanctuary Program

In response to growing public concern for the environmental and cultural value of our coastal waters, Congress passed the Marine Protection, Research and Sanctuaries Act of 1972 (now known as the National Marine Sanctuaries Act). The act authorizes the secretary of commerce to identify, designate, and manage marine and Great Lakes areas of national significance as National Marine Sanctuaries. The National Oceanic and Atmospheric Administration (NOAA) in the U.S. Department of Commerce administers the National Marine Sanctuary Program (NMSP).

The mission of the NMSP is to identify, designate, and manage areas of the marine environment of special national significance because of their conservation, recreational, ecological, historical, research, educational, or aesthetic qualities. Management of these areas is guided by the overriding goal of resource protection. Sanctuary stewardship, education, and research programs help meet this goal.

Since 1972, thirteen national marine sanctuaries have been designated. They include nearshore coral reefs and open ocean and range in size from less than 1 to more than 5,300 square miles. National marine sanctuaries are designated based on differing resources and management needs at individual sites. The latest designation and first in the Great Lakes is the Thunder Bay National Marine Sanctuary and Underwater Preserve, located on Lake Huron.

Thunder Bay National Marine Sanctuary

In partnership with the State of Michigan, NOAA designated the waters encompassing and surrounding Thunder Bay on Lake Huron as a national marine sanctuary. The sanctuary boundary extends from Presque Isle Lighthouse, south to Sturgeon Point Lighthouse, and lakeward to longitude 83 degrees west. In total, the sanctuary encompasses 808 square miles.

The Thunder Bay region contains a wide array of underwater cultural resources including shipwrecks, historical remnants of docks and piers, and materials from historic and prehistoric Native Americans. In particular, the area contains a collection of approximately 160 shipwrecks that spans more than a century of Great Lakes maritime history. National significance is attached to the entire collection of shipwrecks in the Thunder Bay region as well as to individual vessels. Although many of the wrecks have been identified, many more are thought to be in the area and have yet to be located. Collectively, Thunder Bay's shipwrecks represent a microcosm of the Great Lakes commercial shipping industry as it developed over the last 200 years. The sunken vessels reflect transitions in ship architecture and construction methods, from wooden sailboats to early steel-hulled steamers.

In 1981, Thunder Bay was established as the first State of Michigan Great Lakes Bottomland Preserve (commonly called an underwater preserve). The designation of Thunder Bay as a national marine sanctuary complements and supplements the comprehensive management of underwater cultural resources already undertaken by the State of Michigan. The limited financial support available for management efforts at both state and local levels strengthens the need for partnerships between the state, local communities, and the NMSP.

The purposes of the Thunder Bay National Marine Sanctuary are to work cooperatively with businesses and local, state, federal, and tribal agencies and organizations to:

- complement existing management and enforcement authorities protecting underwater cultural resources
- provide educational opportunities that promote understanding, appreciation, and involvement in the protection and stewardship of underwater cultural resources
- develop scientific knowledge and enhance management practices related to underwater cultural resources by encouraging research and monitoring programs
- encourage the exchange of knowledge and expertise to enhance sustainable uses of the Great Lakes and other underwater cultural resources

Regulations adopted by NOAA to protect the underwater cultural resources of Thunder Bay prohibit recovering, altering, destroying, possessing, or attempting to recover, alter, destroy, or possess an underwater cultural resource. The regulations prohibit the alteration of the lake bottom if such an activity causes an adverse impact on underwater cultural resources. Sanctuary regulations also prohibit the use of grappling hooks or other anchoring devices on underwater cultural resource sites that are marked with a mooring buoy.

Sanctuary regulations expand coverage to all underwater cultural resources, not just "abandoned" resources. Therefore, the sanctuary regulations serve as a federal safety net for underwater cultural resources that the State of Michigan may be unable to protect under state law or the federal Abandoned Shipwreck Act.

The well-established Michigan state permitting system provides the basis of many of the permits issued in the sanctuary. A separate sanctuary permit is not necessary if sanctuary concerns can be addressed through issuance of a state permit and through Section 106 of the National Historic Preservation Act. For federal permits, sanctuary concerns are addressed through the review and authorization by NOAA of the issuance of federal permits (e.g., from the COE).

The Cape Cod Commission

In the wake of an unprecedented growth boom in the 1980s, the Cape Cod Commission Act found that the region known as Cape Cod (Barnstable County) has unique natural, coastal, historical, cultural, and other values that are threatened by uncoordinated or inappropriate uses of the region's land and water resources. In response, the Cape Cod Commission was created in 1990 by an act of the Massachusetts General Court and confirmed by a majority of Barnstable County voters. The commission is a department of Barnstable County and is funded by the Cape Cod Environmental Protection Fund.

The commission was established as a regional planning and regulatory agency whose work is divided into three major areas: planning, technical assistance, and regulation. The commission is charged with preparing and implementing a regional land use policy plan for all of Cape Cod. The commission also reviews and regulates Developments of Regional Impact and recommends designation of certain areas as Districts of Critical Planning Concern. The commission is made up of

Photo 7.3. Cape Cod ship canal. (Photo by NOAA.)

19 members representing each of Barnstable County's 15 towns as well as the county commissioners, minorities, Native Americans, and a governor's appointee. They are citizen volunteers who guide a professional staff to plan for Cape Cod's future growth, provide technical assistance to towns, review and vote on major developments, and act as the commission's liaison to their communities.

The commission addresses a wide variety of regional issues and concerns through regional policy plans. Topics of these plans include land use planning, growth management, economic development, affordable housing, historic preservation, wetlands, open space, habitat and wildlife resources, water resources, coastal resources, solid and hazardous waste management, transportation planning, capital facilities and infrastructure, energy and telecommunication infrastructure, and heritage preservation and community character.

In addition to the broader concerns addressed by the commission, specialists on staff focus on certain issues. In particular, the commission's coastal and marine resources specialist works to facilitate municipal planning efforts to deal with coastal issues on the cape such as increasing development pressure, erosion of the shoreline, vulnerability of flood hazard areas, and stewardship for resources held in public trust. The specialist also monitors issues in the fishing industry and their bearing on local fishers, fishery stocks, and other aspects of the marine environment. With the collapse of the New England groundfish stocks and the strict conservation measures necessary to protect other species, many local fishers have been dealing with serious economic hardship, and the commission seeks to address their concerns.

Conclusions

This chapter has introduced the regional perspective in coastal management and discussed the primary benefits and advantages of a regional approach. Clearly, many coastal problems and the coastal ecosystem itself extend beyond local (and often state) jurisdictional boundaries. Regional planning approaches can help overcome these difficulties. Several key federal and state initiatives have been undertaken and promote regional coastal management. These include the watershed protection approach of the EPA, SAMPs under the CZMA, the Chesapeake Bay Program, the GLP, the NEP, the NMSP, and the Cape Cod Commission. These and other examples illustrate the potential importance and utility of regional coastal management approaches. Increasingly, regional, ecosystem-oriented strategies will be an integral element of effective coastal management in the United States and elsewhere.

8

Local Coastal Management

Many of the day-to-day planning and management decisions that occur in the coastal zone are made at the local level by hundreds of counties, cities, and towns. In the U.S. management framework, local governments have had primary responsibility for managing land use and development. Moreover, it is at the local level, it can be argued, that land use and comprehensive planning can be most responsive to the interests and needs of the constituents and to the special management issues and concerns of the locality.

In this chapter we examine in detail coastal planning and management at the local level—its potential and existing patterns. As the following discussion reveals, there is much management activity at the local level, and many local jurisdictions are implementing creative and effective management programs. Localities have important roles in shaping the pattern and nature of growth and development and, as we will argue, opportunities to promote broader sustainability in the management and operation of government itself.

Toward Sustainable
Coastal Communities

We believe that coastal localities—located in every state and in every region of the country—have the potential to become sustainable coastal communities. By *sustainable coastal communities* we mean communities (including a variety of local government units—counties, cities, towns, villages) that seek to minimize their destructive impact on natural systems and the natural environment, create highly livable and enduring places, and build communities that are socially just and in which the needs of all groups in the community are addressed.

As we have seen earlier, sustainability and sustainable development have become common goals of many in the environmental movement and those believing that a practical balance between development and conservation is needed. The 1987 report of the Brundtland Commission did much to popularize the concept of sustainable development, defining it as "development that meets the needs of the present without compromising the ability of future generations to meet their own needs" (World Commission on Environment and Development, 1987, p. 8).

In more recent years the concept of sustainable communities has received increasing attention among urban planners, architects, and others in the design field who want to apply these ideas to how cities and towns are designed, planned, and operated.

What precisely is a sustainable coastal community? We hesitate to identify a hard and fast template or a definitive list of characteristics, but there are certain features that we believe help to define these localities. What follows is a tentative list of these characteristics (adapted from Beatley and Brower, 1993).

- Sustainable coastal communities minimize disruption of natural systems and avoid consumption and destruction of ecologically sensitive lands (e.g., coastal wetlands, maritime forests, species habitat, and areas rich in biodiversity).
- They minimize their ecological footprints and reduce the wasteful consumption of land; they promote compact, contiguous development patterns and the separation of urban or urbanizable lands from rural and natural lands.
- They avoid environmental hazards and reduce the exposure of people and property to coastal hazards by keeping people and property out of coastal floodplains, high-erosion zones, and inlet hazard areas.
- They reduce the generation of waste (e.g., air pollution, water pollution) and the consumption of nonrenewable resources and promote the recycling and reuse of waste products; they respect the earth's ecological capital, using only the ecological interest; and they understand and live within the natural ecological carrying capacities of the area.
- They reduce dependence on the automobile and promote a more balanced and integrated transportation system; encourage and facilitate the use of a variety of alternative and more sustainable modes of transportation, including mass transit, bicycles, and walking; and integrate transportation and land use decisions.

- They promote and develop a sense of place and an understanding and appreciation of the bioregional context in which they are situated.
- They have a high degree of livability; they are aesthetically pleasing and visually stimulating communities whose architecture, streetscapes, and urban spaces inspire and uplift the human spirit.
- They incorporate a strong public and civic dimension, which is reflected in the community's spatial and physical form; they place importance on public spaces and buildings (e.g., squares, pedestrian plazas, and courthouses) as locations for social and public interaction that help to shape a sense of shared identity.
- They achieve a human scale and encourage integration of uses and activities (e.g., commercial and residential) and enhance livability in numerous ways, including reducing auto dependence, reducing crime, and providing more active and vibrant urban spaces.
- They seek to eradicate poverty and ensure a dignified life for all residents; provide affordable housing, health care, meaningful employment, and other basic conditions of a dignified life; reduce the physical and social separation between income and racial groups; and achieve a fair and equitable distribution of environmental and other risks.
- They value the participation of all citizens and provide opportunities for citizens to be actively involved in their governance.

The relationship between the concept of sustainable communities and several key functions in which local governments typically are involved is central to coastal zone management. Land use planning is one such activity and involves the allocation and distribution of different allowable uses throughout the community. Certain areas typically are designated for development (e.g., residential, commercial, industrial), whereas others may be identified as conservation or protected areas. Where some development is allowed, the type density and other characteristics of the development typically are specified. These activities are contained in the community's comprehensive plan (sometimes called the general plan or master plan), which typically addresses a host of other local development issues, including the location of roads, sewer lines, schools, and other public improvements.

In this way, then, land use planning and growth management programs are central to promoting local sustainability and to bringing about sustainable coastal communities. We begin with a survey of tools, policies, and good practice in managing coastal growth pressures. However, the idea of sustainable communities expands the set of concerns even further. It is concerned not only with how and where land development occurs but also how the city or community functions once land use decisions are made: the type and amount of energy it consumes, the products it buys, the ways it manages parks and public lands, and so on. The second half of the chapter examines these broader ideas of sustainable community.

As the following discussion illustrates, there are few coastal communities that could be described as sustainable in the sense that they have all (or even most) of the characteristics we have identified. What is true, however, is that a number of coastal localities are moving in the direction of greater sustainability, doing one or more interesting or innovative things that promote increased sustainability.

Overview of Local Coastal Planning and Management

Managing Coastal Growth

Guiding and managing growth may be the single most challenging issue for coastal localities today. A number of different tools, techniques, and strategies are possible, and a number of good examples of coastal jurisdictions tackling growth patterns are available. A coherent and integrative vision of future growth is essential, and we begin by describing several coastal examples, with more detailed discussion of specific growth management tools to follow.

It is increasingly recognized around the United States that low-density, scattered development patterns called sprawl—highly dependent on the automobile and very destructive of landscapes and environment—cannot be sustained. The last decade has seen a resounding call for smart growth. More compact land-conserving growth patterns, development through infill and reuse of brownfield sites, pedestrian-friendly and transit-oriented development, and protection of green spaces all characterize smart growth. A number of state and local governments, many coastal, have adopted smart growth initiatives. Maryland led the way, in 1997, under the leadership of Governor Paris Glendening. Under the Maryland Smart Growth Initiative, state agencies were no longer to provide funding for schools, highways, and other investments outside designated preferred growth areas. Though not without limitations, the experience of Maryland has been a positive example for other state and local governments wrestling with severe growth pressures.

Coastal localities can and should develop a clear sense of where they are going, what their community will look and feel like, and how inevitable growth and change can be guided to achieve these visions.

Overcoming sprawl, promoting more compact land-efficient growth patterns, and preserving greenspace are increasingly common goals along the coast. As discussed in Chapter 6, coastal localities in Oregon, for instance, delineate urban growth boundaries (UGBs)—indeed, they are required to do so under Oregon's land use planning system. The idea is that growth is directed to areas within the boundary, contiguous to existing development, and building onto and strengthening the existing cities and towns. Coastal communities such as Canon Beach, Oregon, have used the UGB and other planning tools to maintain a compact, walkable community with a high quality of life, preserving surrounding forest and resource lands and nurturing an image as an artistic colony and desired destination for tourists and coast-lovers. Strengthening town centers, discouraging growth and development of sensitive coastal resources, and working to reduce codependence are hallmarks of coastal smart growth.

The fast-growing city of Virginia Beach has sought to contain and guide growth in a similar way, through the designation of its so-called *Green Line*. This east-west boundary seeks to delimit or separate those areas to the north where urban services exist, or will exist in a reasonable timeframe, and where growth is to be encouraged, from those areas to the south where urban development is not to occur. The City's growth vision seeks to protect its most ecologically-sensitive watersheds and productive farmland, located south of the line. Growth is to be accommodated north of the line through infill development, redevelopment and investment in existing neighborhoods. Farmland and environmentally-sensitive land to the south will be protected through, among other tools, restrictive zoning and an agricultural reserve program where development rights are voluntarily purchased from farmers and landowners (see City of Virginia Beach, 1997). A transition zone serves as a buffer between these urban and resource/rural area in the city.

Coastal counties have developed similar strategies for managing growth. Palm Beach County, Florida, for example, guides development through its *Managed Growth Tier System,* adopted in 1999. Under the system, five distinct tiers are delineated, including urban/suburban, exurban, rural, agricultural reserve, and the Glades. The goals of this system are to:

• protect and enhance each tier's unique characteristics and quality of life
• promote job opportunities and a healthy economy

- prioritize and coordinate the delivery of public services at appropriate levels for each tier
- protect and preserve open space and natural resources and encourage their connectivity
- prevent suburban sprawl by guiding development's location, mix, and form
- improve the connections between home, work, and shopping
- create livable and sustainable cities, towns, suburbs, and rural communities

Within Palm Beach County's urban/suburban tier, a Revitalization and Redevelopment Overlay has been created to facilitate growth and development in already urbanized areas. Under the county tier system, growth is encouraged in the urban/suburban tier. Some degree of development is permitted in exurban and rural tiers but at very low densities, and development in the agricultural preserve and Glades tiers is essentially prohibited. A variety of local tools are used in implementing the tiered growth system, including transfer of development rights (TDR, from environmentally sensitive lands to urban suburban sites), integrated cooperation, land acquisition, and traditional neighborhood development (TND).

Areas designed under the redevelopment overlay will be targeted for a variety of incentives and initiatives to improve the conditions and attractiveness of these areas. Infrastructure investments and economic development will be given priority here, and these areas will be receiving zones under the county's TDR program. Infill projects and more compact TND will be encouraged in the urban/suburban tiers.

It is important as well to remember that effective growth management and bringing about more sustainable patterns of land use will ideally require coordinated action and policy at a broader regional level. One such regional vision is the Eastward Ho! Initiative, in south Florida. Resulting from recommendations of The Governor's Commission for a Sustainable South Florida, the initiative seeks to guide future growth into a one- to two-mile wide urban corridor. Such a growth pattern would both steer growth away from the sensitive Everglades ecosystem and serve to revitalize and reinvigorate this historic eastern corridor. One study comparing the cost and impacts associated with different growth patterns in the region concludes that by guiding new growth into the Eastward Ho! Corridor almost 70,000 acres of developable land will be saved, including prime farmland and fragile environmental land (Center for Urban Policy Research, 1998). Substantial reductions in the number of lane miles of roads needed, and the fiscal costs of growth, are also predicted from the more compact growth alternative.

While a voluntary program, a number of local governments in the region (including Palm Beach County) are participating and have initiated projects aimed at achieving the Eastward Ho! vision. These have included downtown redevelopment plans, design charrettes, and new subsidies for affordable housing on infill locations. The Florida legislature committed some $3 million in grants during the first 4 years of the initiative, providing substantial planning and startup grant money for a variety of such projects. The Earthward Ho! Brownfields Partnership, for instance, has focused on inventorying, rehabilitation, and redevelopment of contaminated sites in the corridor.

Managing growth in ways that respect the natural carrying capacities and ecological limits is another important vision of coastal communities. Sanibel Island, Florida, is a notable case in point (Figure 8.1). Its growth plan is based on an extensive ecological analysis of the island and the capacity of its ecological systems (e.g., wetlands) and infrastructure (e.g., roads) to accommodate future growth. As part of this analysis, the island was divided into a series of ecological zones. Growth decisions were guided in important ways by natural and physical limits. The most limiting factor in Sanibel turned out to be hurricane evacuation and the ultimate limit of 6,000 dwelling units (the addition of 2,000 more), based on what would ensure a 12-hour evacuation of the island (the amount of evacuation time the National Hurricane Center believes it can provide).

A second stage in the Sanibel plan involved allocating and distributing these new units, based again on the ecological qualities and capacities of the island. Permitted densities ranged from one unit per 33 acres in especially sensitive areas to five dwelling units per acre where infrastructure (e.g., sewer and water line, fire service) already existed and where the island's environment could accommodate more intense growth. For the most part, the Sanibel approach has been a success, and although zoning changes over the years have permitted more development than anticipated, the established limits have largely been honored.

Some coastal communities have sought to use these and other techniques to support and sustain traditional village growth patterns. The island of Nantucket is an example of such an effort (Figure 8.2). Nantucket, only 50 square miles in size, 13 by 10 miles, has continued to experience growth over the last decade. Year-round population has more than doubled since 1970, and the town experiences a surge in population during the summer. A new comprehensive plan was prepared in 2001 which seeks to control sprawl and address the sense that the qualities of place are being lost in Nantucket as a result of these

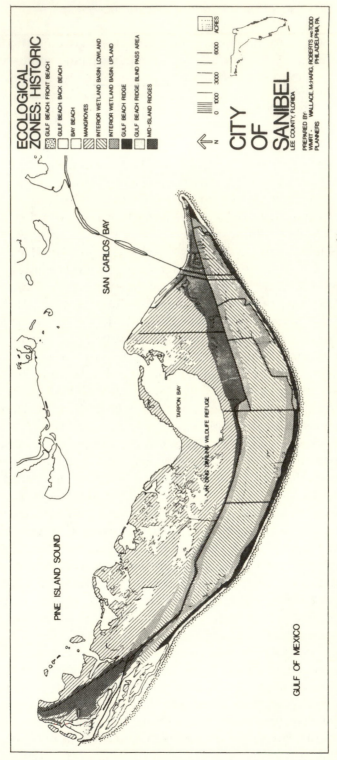

Figure 8.1. Sanibel Island, Florida, ecological zones. (From the Conservation Foundation, 1976.)

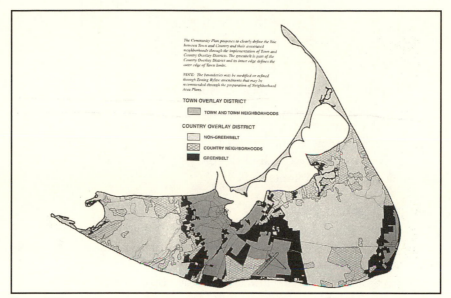

The Community Plan proposes to clearly define the line
between Town and Country and their associated
neighborhoods through the implementation of Town and
Country Overlay Districts. The greenbelt is part of the
Country Overlay District and its inner edge defines the
outer edge of Town limits.

NOTE: The boundaries may be modified or refined
through Zoning Bylaw amendments that may be
recommended through the preparation of Neighborhood
Area Plans.

TOWN OVERLAY DISTRICT

[ ] TOWN AND TOWN NEIGHBORHOODS

COUNTRY OVERLAY DISTRICT

[ ] NON-GREENBELT

[ ] COUNTRY NEIGHBORHOODS

[ ] GREENBELT

Figure 8.2. Nantucket Comprehensive Plan. (From Town of Nantucket, Massa-chusetts.)

growth pressures. Among other things, the plan calls for a greenbelt overlay zoning district to create a clearer separation and distinction between town and countryside. New growth is to be focused in towns and neighborhoods, and an emphasis is to be placed on acquiring open space and undeveloped lands in the countryside and greenbelt designations.

Other important aspirations of the new Nantucket plan include expanding the extent of public ownership of the island's shoreline (a goal of 25% public ownership by 2025) and gaining better control over the increasing number of autos on the island (and including the possibility of a seasonally based permit system to cap the number of cars). The plan also calls for reductions in allowable development in countryside or greenbelt locations and the creation of Neighborhood Center Zones (to provide basic services in countryside locations).

Already substantial progress has been made in Nantucket in preserving open space and natural lands. Some 42% of the island has been protected through acquisition. A 2% real estate transfer tax provides the Nantucket Land Bank with $8 to $9 million per year in acquisition funds (discussed further later).

Growth Management:
Tools and Techniques

As these examples illustrate, local jurisdictions have tremendous opportunities to shape the quality of coastal living environments in the future. A coherent vision and strategy are essential, although there are many specific planning and management tools available to implement them. What follows is a more detailed discussion of a number of these tools and their benefits and limitations.

Comprehensive Plans

Many coastal jurisdictions have adopted comprehensive plans and are using them effectively to guide growth and development. A comprehensive plan (or master plan, or general plan as they're called in California) is an essential tool—indeed, it is the cornerstone for any coastal community's effort to shape its future. A comprehensive plan is in many ways the orchestrating document, providing guidance for the myriad decisions a community makes and the land use and growth management tools discussed in this section. More specific land use tools—such as zoning and TDR—are intended to implement and be consistent with a community's comprehensive plan. And in some coastal states, such as Oregon, compliance with the plan is required by law.

The comprehensive plan establishes the overall vision for where the community wants to go. Plans have various timeframes but are commonly for 15- or 20-year periods, with updates and revisions every 5 years or so. They typically lay out goals and objectives, analyze current development patterns and community conditions, and identify issues and problems. An extensive inventory and description of the physical environment and the natural resources and conditions of the community is an essential component. The plan commonly includes important maps of sensitive environmental features, such as wetlands and important habitat areas, as well as sites with significant development constraints, such as floodplains. Other important community features and resources, such as historic buildings and sites and productive farmland, are also mapped and inventoried.

Other typical elements of the plan include sections on implementation, monitoring, and evaluation of the plan over time. One of the most important functions of the comprehensive plan is to put forth a con-

cept for what the community will look like in the future. This is typically expressed in a plan diagram or future land use map for the community.

In addition to the comprehensive plan, coastal communities may
also develop more specialized *functional* plans, such as a local transportation plan or hazard mitigation plan, to set direction and policy in
these more specific areas (and in ways consistent with the comprehensive plan). More detailed plans are also commonly prepared for
smaller geographic scales and areas in a community, such as neighborhood plans or focused-area plans.

Conventional Zoning

Conventional zoning ordinances control the type of land uses allowed
in particular parts of a community (e.g., residential, commercial, industrial) and their intensity (e.g., bulk, height, floor-area ratio, setback provisions). Zoning ordinances can be very useful in accomplishing a variety of local goals, such as prohibiting or reducing development in
environmentally sensitive coastal lands (e.g., coastal wetlands, aquifer
recharge zones, wellhead protection zones, maritime forests). These
ordinances can be used to prohibit or restrict development in high-risk
hazard zones, thus reducing exposure of people and property to hurricanes, riverine flooding, and other coastal hazards.

In addition to identifying permissible land uses, zoning ordinances
often stipulate a variety of performance controls or standards. These
include setback standards (e.g., side yard and front yard setbacks),
height restrictions, restrictions on the extent of impervious surfaces,
and stormwater management requirements. In many ways, there has
been a substantial greening of traditional zoning ordinances in recent
years, with greater attention paid to managing development in ways
that minimize environmental degradation. For instance, open space and
recreational uses may be the most appropriate activities to permit in
high-risk areas such as ocean erodible zones and National Flood Insurance Program V zones. Restricting such areas to commercial or public
recreational activities would substantially reduce the amount of property at risk and thereby reduce the property losses from future hurricanes and storms.

With its emphasis on separation of uses, predictability of land development, and regulation of building height, bulk, and land area, zoning
is the most common regulatory device for guiding coastal development.
Zoning has been upheld as constitutional and a legitimate exercise of

police power since the U.S. Supreme Court decision in *City of Euclid v. Ambler Realty Co.,* 272 U.S. 365 (1926), but the application of specific provisions is still subject to challenge. In North Carolina, for instance, the Supreme Court has held that a zoning ordinance is valid unless "it has no foundation in reason and is a merely arbitrary or irrational exercise of power having no substantial relation to the public health, the public morals, the public safety, or the public welfare in its proper sense."

Zoning can and has been very useful to many oceanfront communities in reducing or keeping density down in high-risk shorefront locations. The town of Nags Head, North Carolina, has changed beachfront zoning to reduce the extent of high-density development, thereby reducing the risk to lives and the tax base.

Setback Requirements

The concept of a development setback has long been a part of zoning and is an especially important regulatory element in many coastal communities. Setbacks are used in urban settings to ensure that sufficient land is available for future roads and other public improvements and to ensure adequate light, access, and separation of structures. Setbacks in coastal hazard areas are an extension of this zoning technique and have become common as a means of minimizing the impact of development on beach and dune systems and reducing exposure to storm hazards (Kusler et al., 1982; University of North Carolina, 1984). Such setbacks may be state mandated or local option. As we have seen, North Carolina's Coastal Area Management Act requires small structures to be located landward of the first line of vegetation by a distance of 30 times the annual rate of erosion for that segment of coast. In the case of structures more than 5,000 square feet in size, the setback is 60 times the annual rate of erosion.

The city of Myrtle Beach, South Carolina, is a good example of such an oceanfront setback. It has adopted a retreat policy and has delineated a 50-year erosion line to implement the policy. Only certain limited uses are allowed seaward of the line (e.g., sundecks, patios, gazebos, and walkways).

Community Character and Sense of Place

Zoning ordinances are also used by many coastal localities to protect community character. The town of Canon Beach, Oregon, for example, has included in its zoning ordinance several provisions intended to preserve the community's image as an artist colony and to protect the small-town coastal feeling that attracts tourists each year. Among other things, the town's zoning code specifically prohibits drive-in and "formula food" restaurants. The latter are defined in the code as any restaurant "required by contractual or other arrangements to offer standardized menus, ingredients, food preparation, interior or exterior design or uniforms" (Beatley et al., 1988, p. 66), excluding the likes of McDonald's and Pizza Hut. The town has also created a special design review board that imposes certain design standards on new development. (Hilton Head, South Carolina, imposes similar design standards.) The town of Nantucket, Massachusetts, is another example of a coastal community imposing architectural design standards in an effort to protect the integrity of the town's historic architecture.

Subdivision Ordinances

Subdivision regulations govern the conversion of raw land into building sites and the type and extent of improvements made in this conversion. Subdivision regulations can control the configuration and layout of development. They can also establish effective requirements and standards for public improvements, including streets, drainage pipes, and sewer outlets. The requirement of minimum lot size, although usually done in the zoning ordinance, can reduce the amount of new development exposed to storm hazards. Site plan review and other requirements for subdivision approval can provide the opportunity to encourage the location of development sites in ways that minimize storm risks. For instance, subdivision regulations may require that new single-family dwellings on lots in hazard areas be sited so as to maximize the distance from high-hazard oceanfront areas.

Dedication or reservation of recreation areas adequate to serve the residents of the immediate neighborhood within the subdivision often is required. Dedications of a specified amount of land (usually for parks or schools) or money in lieu of land force the subdivision developer to provide for needs generated by the subdivision. When the developer is allowed to pay in cash instead of land, the community is given additional flexibility in meeting the needs of the subdivision. For example, if a good park site is not available on the land owned by a developer, the cash contribution can allow the local government to purchase a nearby park site for the neighborhood.

Subdivision approval might also be made contingent on mitigation actions such as the protection of dunes, wetlands, or natural vegetation.

Table 8.1. Development Management Measures in Order of Frequency Used[a]

Type of measure	Survey communities using measure	
	Number	Percentage
1. Zoning ordinance	354	87.8
2. Subdivision ordinance	347	86.1
3. Comprehensive land use plan	340	84.4
4. Evacuation plan	272	67.5
5. Shoreline setback regulation	218	54.1
6. Capital improvement program	216	53.6
7. Location of public structures and buildings to reduce storm risks	185	45.9
8. Dune protection regulations	152	37.7
9. Location of capital facilities to reduce or discourage development in high-hazard areas	126	31.3
10. Acquisition of undeveloped land in hazardous areas	118	29.3
11. Special hazard area ordinance	109	27.0
12. Hazard disclosure requirements in real estate transactions	103	25.6
13. Recovery/reconstruction plan or policies	87	21.6
14. Transfer of development potential from hazardous to nonhazardous sites	84	20.8
15. Hurricane or storm component of comprehensive plan	80	19.9
16. Construction practice seminars	62	15.4
17. Acquisition of development rights or scenic easements	56	13.9
18. Reduced or below-market taxation	44	10.9
19. Acquisition of damaged buildings in hazardous areas	12	3.0
20. Building relocation program	9	2.2
21. Impact taxes or special assessments	7	1.7

Source: Godschalk et al. (1989).

[a]N = 403.

For instance, subdivision provisions may require that structures be located a sufficient distance from protective dunes. Subdivision approvals may also be made contingent on the planting of certain vegetation and the restoration and repair of existing dunes. Another promising alternative is to preserve the option of moving a structure back from the ocean by requiring lots that are sufficiently deep for this purpose. The additional depth could be considered analogous to the repair areas often required for septic tank use. If necessary, a structure could then be moved to the landward portion of the lot, in a safer location.

Although traditional zoning and subdivision controls are common in coastal areas, as Table 8.1 indicates, there are major concerns about their ability to promote local sustainability. In the following sections we describe some of the limitations of traditional land use controls and more recent trends and innovations that address these concerns.

CRITIQUE OF CONVENTIONAL ZONING AND SUBDIVISION CONTROL

Traditional zoning and subdivision controls have come under increasing criticism in recent years. "Euclidean zoning," in its traditional effort at classifying and separating different uses, is increasingly seen as inflexible and rigid, promoting inefficient and undesirable land use patterns. Fixed in early thinking that certain noxious commercial and industrial uses (e.g., the tannery or noisy factory) must be isolated from residential uses, conventional zoning has created land use patterns that virtually require automobile use, work against pedestrian orientation, and reduce social interaction and the integration of uses and activities viewed today as important ingredients in the livability of cities and towns. Moreover, such rigid land use controls discourage creative land development and design.

Conventional zoning and subdivision controls are also criticized for how they function in newly urbanized and suburbanizing locations. In many coastal localities it is common to require 5- or 10-acre minimum lot sizes. The objective is to protect the coastal character and to minimize the need for public facilities and other public investments. However, what often results is a wasteful consumption of coastal land, allowing or requiring that such areas be carved up that much faster because of the minimum lot size.

In many coastal areas, however, larger lots may be legitimately mandated for environmental protection reasons—for instance, to reduce the amount of nonpoint source runoff and the number of on-site septic tanks.

It is paradoxical that in such sensitive environmental locations keeping density down through such large-lot requirements may lead to a pattern of unsightly development, wasteful land consumption, and loss of coastal open space. This is a trade-off that local coastal officials must grapple with. However, it is important to recognize that even where density must, for environmental or ecological reasons, be kept to a minimum, there may well be other land use control techniques available that do not create such development patterns, such as development clustering, acquisition of sensitive lands, and TDR (all discussed later in this chapter). It is also important to understand that it is not the tool per se that produces desired or undesired results; it is how that tool is used.

URBAN GROWTH BOUNDARIES

A common criticism of American urban growth patterns is that there is usually no clear separation between urban and rural areas. Urban development sprawls into the countryside and important agricultural and natural resource areas. Commercial development tends to follow highways and major roads, leading to the pejorative description *strip commercial*. As we have seen, conventional land use controls may not prevent coastal sprawl and may facilitate it.

A number of cities and towns around the country are using UGBs, which limit the spatial extent of urban development and growth and seek to promote a more compact and contiguous urban growth pattern. As noted earlier, the State of Oregon mandates the adoption of UGBs by all incorporated communities. Under Oregon's statewide growth management system (Senate Bill 100), cities must delineate a UGB (through negotiation with counties) that includes a sufficient supply of land to accommodate approximately 20 years of growth. Major public facility expenditures (e.g., for sewers and water) can occur only within the UGB, and major residential development projects are not permitted outside UGBs. And as mentioned, coastal communities such as Canon Beach have used the tool successfully.

The UGB concept can be an important tool for coastal localities seeking to promote more efficient, less land-consumptive development patterns. In redirecting growth and activity inward, such a technique may also help to reinvigorate existing towns and communities and provide a critical mix of people and development to support a variety of cultural amenities, businesses, and vibrant and active public spaces.

Coastal localities may need to consider a host of other related changes in policy to help bring about growth containment if this is a desired goal. Sufficient and necessary public services, facilities, and other public investments must occur in designated growth areas, and restrictions on building outside of these areas must also be enacted.

Other policies might include eliminating the prohibition (which is quite common) on accessory units (or "granny flats") in residential areas, identifying existing vacant infill development sites and promoting new development in these areas, permitting and encouraging adaptive reuse of sites and buildings in existing towns and communities, and allowing and promoting the integration of different land uses (e.g., commercial and residential).

Redirecting growth back toward existing city and town centers has many potential payoffs, including increased economic vitality, a greater supply of affordable housing, more efficient provision of services and facilities, creation of more vital and livable urban spaces, and protection of coastal open space and sensitive lands. Efforts of older port communities to revitalize their waterfronts and rejuvenate their downtowns represent positive moves toward coastal sustainability. Baltimore's Harborplace is one of the most successful examples of such an effort.

CLUSTERED DEVELOPMENT

Another increasingly mandated requirement is the clustering of development. Clustering may either be required generally or be presented to developers as an option. Applied either way, these provisions do not affect the overall density permitted on a particular site but instead seek to concentrate or cluster a higher density of structures on portions of the site. By directing density to a particular portion of a site, clustering can both permit and encourage development on the less hazardous portions of a site while keeping hazard-prone or more sensitive areas undeveloped.

A prime opportunity for accomplishing such a reorientation of development could occur during reconstruction after a damaging storm. For instance, poststorm development regulations could encourage clustering of new development on the landward side of ocean highways, with parking and recreational open space areas on the seaward side. Undeveloped beachfront areas may include features such as wetlands or vegetation, which in themselves protect against storm forces. Clustering may encourage the construction of buildings that are more structurally resistant to storm forces. Clustering can also economize on public facilities, such as sewer, water, and roads, which must accompany development, in turn reducing the amount of property at risk.

TRADITIONAL NEIGHBORHOOD DEVELOPMENT

Much attention has been paid in recent years to revisiting the qualities and characteristics of the traditional American town and attempting to encourage new development that embodies and reflects these characteristics. Among these qualities are an orientation toward walking (and less emphasis on the automobile), a mixing of different uses (i.e., residential and commercial), incorporation of a public or civic realm (e.g., public squares and open space, civic buildings), and clustering of development around town centers (see Chapter 9). Architects Andres Duany and Elizabeth Plater-Zyberk are often credited with popularizing the notion of neotraditional planning and have been instrumental in designing a number of neotraditional communities. The best known among these is Seaside, Florida.

Proponents of neotraditionalism (recently relabeled by some as new urbanism) are critical of traditional American zoning and development codes, which often impose rigid and inflexible development standards. Such codes typically require the sharp separation of uses (so-called Euclidean zoning), mandate minimum street and parking requirements favoring auto use, and encourage large-lot conventional (cul-de-sac) style development patterns. Increasingly, to overcome such rigidity, localities are adopting TND ordinances, which allow greater flexibility in the layout and design of projects.

Neotraditional town design also has great potential to protect the natural environment and minimize the consumption of land during the development process. In the design of Seaside, for instance (discussed more extensively in Chapter 9), most of the town is set well back from the Gulf of Mexico, with a wide strip along the beach preserved in an undeveloped state as open space. The pedestrian orientation and mixing of uses can substantially reduce auto usage, with accompanying reductions in air pollution and energy consumption. In scaling back on the width and extent of roads and parking lots, such development patterns can be much less costly.

BONUS OR INCENTIVE ZONING

Bonus or incentive zoning allows developers to exceed limitations, usually height or density limitations, imposed by the zoning ordinance in exchange for developer-supplied amenities or concessions. For example, a builder may be permitted to exceed a height restriction if he or she provides open space adjacent to the proposed building. Incentive zoning has been used for some time in large urban developments. In New York, for example, a developer may obtain a 20% increase in permissible floor area for projects that incorporate cultural amenities such as theaters. Density bonuses have been given to encourage the incorporation of low- and moderate-income housing into development projects (Fox and Davis, 1978). In the case of coastal hazard areas, developers may be granted additional development units if projects incorporate hazard-reduction features. These features may include the dedication of sensitive coastal lands, for example, or the provision of design features that increase the ability of structures to withstand storm forces.

Hilton Head, South Carolina, has used density bonuses for several years in exchange for dune restoration, beach access, and improvements in neighborhood drainage (Beatley et al., 1988).

Critics of density bonuses sometimes express concern that the traded mitigation and design amenities do not make up for the negatives of increased density. For instance, although an oceanfront development project may provide additional drainage improvements, it can be argued that the increased number of people and property placed at risk to a coastal storm make the outcome questionable. Density bonuses tend to be the most successful where the added density occurs in especially desirable locations (e.g., an existing town center where additional density may even be seen as a positive contribution).

Performance Zoning

Performance zoning sets standards for each zone based on permissible effects of a development rather than specifically enumerating the types of uses, dimensions, or densities permitted. If the prescribed standards are met, any development is allowed in the zone. This technique has been used extensively in industrial zoning to set limits on noise, dust, noxious emissions, and glare. More recently, the technique has been used in broader applications, with standards keyed to demands on public services such as water supply, wastewater treatment, and roads. Standards may be established to protect the environment by specifying maximum levels of permissible stress on natural systems. For example, a community may specify the amount of permissible disturbance of vegetation in a given zone, and any use would have to meet that standard before development could take place. Performance controls for sensitive lands may work as a system to protect natural processes in environmentally sensitive areas such as wetlands, floodplains, and dune systems.

PLANNED UNIT DEVELOPMENTS

A number of coastal jurisdictions have adopted special provisions to allow planned unit developments (PUDs). PUDs combine elements of zoning and subdivision regulation in permitting flexible design of large- and small-scale developments that are planned and built as a unit. Specific plans for the development are required in advance and must be approved by the administrative body. This concept eliminates the lot-by-lot approach common to zoning and subdivision regulation and can be used as an incentive for better development by enabling complete development proposals to be planned and approved.

In its simplest form, PUD takes the shape of cluster development. An example might involve a developer with 100 acres of land, which he could divide into 400 quarter-acre lots as a matter of right according to existing local ordinances. Cluster zoning would give the developer the alternative of clustering units closer together in one part of the site, provided that the overall number of units does not exceed 400. The open space saved by clustering is left for the common use of the residents. From this simple "density transfer," PUD builds into complex forms. In its most advanced stage, PUD allows a variety of housing types as well as commercial, agricultural, and industrial uses. Typically, developers are permitted to develop under PUD provisions when the proposed development exceeds a minimum specified number of acres or housing units. PUDs usually are subject to zoning ordinances, although they are not actually mapped, and must therefore comply with the use restrictions within the zones where they occur. Increasingly, however, some mixing of uses and expansion of density are permitted.

The PUD technique provides flexibility because the final design is a matter of negotiation between the developers and the planning authorities. PUDs generally are attractive to developers of large tracts of land. These projects often can be provided with urban services and facilities more economically than conventional development. They also allow environmental protection of sensitive areas while providing for residential and commercial development. PUD project design can enhance storm hazard reduction when the developer's plans incorporate features such as protective land and vegetation buffers and the provision of on-site storm shelters.

Carrying Capacity

The possibility of tying permitted new growth to the ability of a coastal locality and its residents to respond to a storm hazard is a well-known use of carrying capacity. Such an approach has been used in the growth management system adopted by Sanibel Island, Florida, described earlier, where future growth was limited according to the evacuation capacity of the island's bridge and causeway. Of course, there are other ways in which growth can be pegged to the carrying capacities of the coastal environment, and this is another important critique of conventional zoning and land use controls that typically fail to acknowledge such limits.

Carrying capacity is a measure of the natural and artificial limits to development beyond which significant harm will occur. Carrying capacity can be used to assess the effects of development on such natural factors as groundwater supply and wetland productivity and artificial factors such as sewage treatment and roadway capacity. This concept has been applied in practice to a number of coastal localities. Several implications for storm hazard reduction arise from the application of carrying capacity analysis. The first is that, as in Sanibel, carrying capacity is particularly relevant to assessing evacuation capacity. Second, natural and artificial limitations on coastal development may provide a rational way to regulate the location and quantity of new growth, which in turn may reduce storm hazards. In other words, carrying capacity objectives may be used to reinforce and complement efforts to reduce storm hazards.

Land and Property Acquisition

The acquisition of land and property, or interests therein, can be a very effective approach to achieving a variety of coastal objectives, from hazard reduction to reduction of nonpoint sources to conservation of coastal open space. Several acquisition approaches are discussed here: fee-simple acquisition of undeveloped land, acquisition of less-than-fee-simple interests in undeveloped land, and fee-simple acquisition or relocation of existing development.

FEE-SIMPLE ACQUISITION OF UNDEVELOPED LAND

Fee-simple acquisition involves obtaining the full bundle of rights associated with a parcel. With respect to local sustainability, land acquisition may have several functions. The first is to secure for the public certain lands, especially those that are sensitive, vulnerable, or hazardous and should not be developed. A large-scale acquisition of land can influence the direction and timing of development in a locality. Urban land banking programs, particularly popular in Europe, have attempted to regulate growth by preventing development in some locations while strategically releasing other land more desirable for development. Land acquisition can also be used to secure, in advance and typically at lower prices, land that will be needed at some point in the future for public facilities and services.

The use of fee-simple acquisition as a coastal management tool poses a number of practical questions. Perhaps the most significant problem is the cost and means of financing acquisitions. Outright purchase of land in coastal areas experiencing moderate or high levels of market demand tends to be very expensive—prohibitively so for many localities.

There are several examples of coastal communities that have successfully used fee-simple acquisition. Nantucket's Land Bank is one of the best examples. Created in 1984 in response to a growth boom and the attendant loss of open space, the bank is funded through a 2% real estate transfer tax (paid at closing by the buyer). This funding source has proven to be an effective way to generate a sizable level of funding and is probably much more politically feasible than many other possible sources (e.g., raising local property taxes).

The Nantucket Land Bank is independent of the town and is governed by a commission. In addition to its power to impose the land transfer tax, the bank also has the power to float bonds, which it has done recently, to acquire as much land as possible before it is lost to development. The acquisition program will do much to help the island preserve its natural environment (e.g., the moors and hearth lands) and may prove to be one of the most effective growth management tools for promoting more traditional village-oriented growth patterns.

Based on these experiences, Cape Cod Land Bank was created by the 15 towns that make up the cape in 1998. Unlike Nantucket, the Cape Cod Land Bank is funded through a 3% surcharge on property taxes. An original proposal failed by referendum a year earlier as a result of stiff opposition by the local real estate lobby. The conflict over that proposal, which would have imposed a 1% real estate transfer tax (paid by the seller), is instructive about the equity arguments and political issues that may emerge in such cases. Opponents were able to cast the real estate transfer tax as an unfair financial burden placed on a small proportion of the residents to pay for a collective benefit (Merchant, 1998). A coalition of development, environmental, and local efforts was able to overcome this objection by shifting to a surcharge. Already some 800 acres have been purchased, with a special eye toward protecting land serving as recharge areas for the cape's aquifer.

Other coastal localities have also followed Nantucket's lead in the area of land banking. For instance, Block Island, Rhode Island, uses a 3% land transfer tax, and about one-third of that island is now in protected open space. Hilton Head, South Carolina, has pursued a similar acquisition strategy, also using real estate transfer taxes.

PURCHASE OF DEVELOPMENT RIGHTS

Where the fee-simple purchase of hazardous lands is not feasible, the purchase of less-than-fee-simple interests in land may work. One such approach is to acquire only certain rights to develop environmentally sensitive, high-hazard, or other lands that should not be developed. Under this arrangement, rather than fee-simple title, a local government would pay the landowner the fair market value of just those rights in exchange for agreeing to leave the land in an undeveloped state for a specified period of time (but often in perpetuity). The transaction usually is accomplished through a restrictive covenant attached to the property.

As with fee-simple acquisition, a number of practical questions arise. First, in what manner are development rights acquired? Does the jurisdiction use its powers of eminent domain, or does it simply negotiate with willing sellers on the open market for the development rights? This question may have significant implications for the ability of the purchase of development rights (PDR) to protect large blocks of sensitive coastal land. For instance, relying on voluntary sales may permit, even encourage, substantial development in an adjacent undeveloped sensitive area, merely shifting new development from some parcels to other parcels in the area. Through the use of eminent domain over the entire area, this potential "checkerboard effect" can be prevented.

There is also the question of exactly which development rights are being purchased by a locality. The greater the economic use that stays with the property owner, the greater will be the parcel's remaining fair market value and therefore the less costly the development rights will be. Exactly which uses are permitted after development rights have been purchased may also influence overall property at risk in other areas. For instance, if private recreational activities are permitted, this may in turn induce further residential and other development in adjacent areas where rights have not been purchased. These types of development influences and side effects should be considered when defining the rights to be purchased and the types of uses and activities that will be permitted.

PDR can be used effectively in combination with development regulation. On one hand, restricting development in a particularly sensitive area of the jurisdiction may prevent the checkerboard effect that sometimes results from a voluntary PDR. In turn, PDR may soften the economic effects of development regulations and reduce the political opposition typically engendered by regulatory programs.

There are now a number of creative uses of PDR in the coastal zone. Virginia Beach has one of the most active programs along the east coast. Since 1995, development rights to some 4,900 acres of farmland in the city's southern watershed have been secured. Eventually, the city hopes to protect 20,000 acres through the program, which is funded in part through a new tax on cellular phones. Development rights are secured through a 25-year installment purchase agreement (with the city paying a lump sum payment at the end of the 25 years and semi-annual interest payments). An important preservation element in implementing Virginia Beach's growth containment vision, it illustrates the importance of cooperation between agricultural and environmental interests (Heinricht, 1996).

In the Midwest, few coastal communities have adopted PDR pro-

Photo 8.1. Peninsula Township, Michigan, shown here, has been implementing an extensive program for purchasing development rights. Focused on protecting important agricultural land, the program has already protected more than 1,700 acres. (Photo by Peninsula Township, Michigan.)

grams. One of the few that has is Peninsula Township in Michigan. The township comprises the old Mission Peninsula that juts into a bay in northern Lake Michigan. The peninsula is about 17 miles long and about 3 miles across, with a small population of about 6,000.

This program purchased its first easements in 1996 and has now secured some 1,736 acres of prime and unique farmland (Figure 8.3).

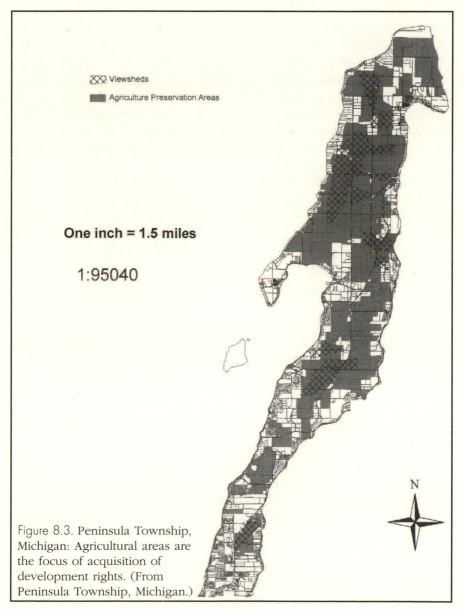

Viewsheds

Agriculture Preservation Areas

One inch = 1.5 miles

1:95040

N

Figure 8.3. Peninsula Township, Michigan: Agricultural areas are the focus of acquisition of development rights. (From Peninsula Township, Michigan.)

Some of these easements have been purchased using matching funds from state agencies and the federal government, and 11 of the 27 individual easements are being purchased using installment contracts (Peninsula Township, 2001). The township has imposed a 1.25 mill levy ($1.25 per $1000 of assessed property value) on itself to pay for its share.

Much of the township has been designated agricultural preserve, where PDR is to be encouraged. The township hopes to eventually preserve as much as one-third of the jurisdiction's 10,000 acres of agricultural land. The township has also designated key viewsheds—important views of lake and shoreline visible from roadway locations—and hopes these will be protected as well. In addition to PDR, the township has created other options for protecting land, including TDR and a cluster option under the township's zoning ordinance.

Opposition to the PDR program arose early, mostly around concerns about the costs of the program. Township planners worked hard to educate residents about it—a key lesson—and to demonstrate that protecting the land in an undeveloped state was the least expensive option.

As an alternative to PDR, a coastal locality could encourage the donation of scenic or conservation easements. Landowners can be encouraged to make such donations in large part because of the income tax deductions permissible under the Internal Revenue Code.

TRANSFER OF DEVELOPMENT RIGHTS

One potentially effective approach to managing coastal development is TDR. TDR is an innovative approach to development management that is being used in only a few places in the country (Carmichael, 1974; Costonis, 1973; Rose, 1975; Merriam, 1978). The basic concept underlying TDR is that ownership of land includes a right to develop the land, a right that may be separated from other ownership rights and transferred to someone else. For example, an owner may sell this development right to another property owner, who under the TDR system must collect a specified number of development rights before developing his or her property at the desired density.

Transfer of development rights is no longer a novel and untested management tool, and there are now a number of coastal examples. These include the use of TDR to protect coastal farmland, as in Calvert County, Maryland, and its use in protecting coastal wetlands, as in Collier County, Florida, among other coastal localities.

TDR has a number of potential advantages. TDR can substantially eliminate the value shifts and inequities of zoning by allowing the market to compensate owners for whom the development potential of their land is severely restricted (Rose, 1975; Merriam, 1978). A TDR system can be either voluntary or mandatory. Under the latter, a locality would simply zone open space or sensitive coastal lands so that development would not be allowed, and the owner of land within this zone would then be permitted to transfer all or some of this unused development density to parcels in designated development areas or to sell the development rights on the open market to others who own land in areas designated for development. The locality would then permit increased levels of development in the receiving zone as a result of possessing extra development rights, thus creating a natural market for the transferable development rights. A voluntary approach would simply present the transfer as an additional option for the landowner—a way of maintaining the land in its undeveloped state if the landowner wishes. The landowner in this case would still have the option of developing his or her land or selling it for development purchases.

The TDR approach raises a number of practical issues. First, there are several alternative institutional arrangements for operating a TDR program. On one hand, the transfer of development rights can be left entirely to market dynamics, with the locality involved only in designating sending and receiving zones and determining the number of rights to be transferred. Whether a selling landowner receives a fair price for his or her rights depends simply on what the market will provide. An alternative institutional structure would have the jurisdiction play a more direct and active role in the development rights transaction itself, perhaps serving as a broker, buying and selling rights as needed. This in turn helps to ensure that an adequate price is obtained, thereby overcoming short-term market fluctuations.

Another important issue involves the method for assigning development rights. They might be allocated strictly according to acreage (e.g., one right per acre) or to the market value of the property. Eventually the question will arise as to whether additional rights should be allocated. If new supplies of development rights are needed, a practical and fair procedure for allocating additional TDRs must be devised.

The locality must also decide how rights transferred from sending zones can be used. If a developer purchases 10 development rights from land in a sensitive area and seeks to apply them in a receiving zone, what rights is he or she entitled to? For example, each additional TDR might translate into a certain amount of additional floor space or square footage allowed in the receiving zone. In the case of residential development, these additions may be measured in terms of additional dwelling units or bedrooms.

GREENWAYS, TRAILS, AND OPEN SPACE

A number of coastal communities and regions have rediscovered their waterfronts and bayfronts and have begun developing greenways and trail systems to more effectively allow coastal residents to enjoy these immense coastal resources. A number of recent, successful coastal greenway initiatives merit special mention.

In Georgia, a plan laying out a comprehensive coastal greenways network has been developed. The Coastal Georgia Greenway plan, as it is more formally known, has been adopted by all six coastal counties, and each will incorporate this network into updates of its comprehensive plan. In total, the greenway will include 450 miles of new trails, including a 125-mile continuous north–south greenway that will connect the neighboring states of South Carolina and Florida. The network of trails will include bicycle and pedestrian trails, equestrian trails, and even water routes, for canoeing and kayaking. Twenty-three new water access points (for nonmotorized craft) will also be provided under the plan. Funding for the project has come from two main sources: Intermodal Surface Transportation Efficiency Act funding (through the Georgia Department of Transportation) and an Environmental Protection Agency Sustainable Development Challenges Grant.

Unique and special landscape qualities will exist in every coastal region and can be merged with abundant opportunities to regenerate community and economy. Efforts to restore and re-envision the Lake Ontario waterfront on the Canadian side are exemplary in this regard. The catalyst here has been an unusual and highly productive group: the Waterfront Regeneration Trust, a nonprofit registered charity created in 1992 by the province of Ontario. The trust has been an important force in helping communities rediscover the waterfront and see its potential economic, social, and recreational benefits. The obstacles have been substantial, including dealing with a contaminated industrial landscape and a recent history of development that has largely ignored the unique connections to the lake. A number of regeneration projects have been undertaken, but the most important of these has been the creation of a 350-kilometer-long Ontario Waterfront Trail. The trail winds through and connects some 22 different communities and hundreds of parks, natural areas, and historic sites along the waterfront. The trail passes through industrial sites and is both an excellent example of reuse and an important catalyst for reconnecting these communities and residents back to their waterfront. A common trail logo has been created and used along the trail: a stylized logo of a bird, leaf, and fish, intended to symbolized the interface of air, land, and water. The trail, which eventually will be extended to 650 kilometers, has the potential to stimulate pride in place and reconnection to the physical environment and serve as an important stimulus for economic development in the area. As Beth Benson, the executive director of the trust, notes, investments in the open space, environment, and green infrastructure are effective precursors to private investment (Rivers West, 2000).

Taxation and Fiscal Incentives

The specific management provisions included in this broad category are designed primarily to affect indirectly the quantity and type of development to occur in sensitive coastal lands. In contrast to the public acquisition of land, a taxation policy might seek to reduce development in certain areas by decreasing the holding costs of open space and vacant land, in turn reducing the opportunity costs of not developing such lands for more intensive uses. Although taxation and fiscal policy can encompass numerous specific tools and mechanisms, attention is focused primarily on differential property taxation and special assessments and impact fees.

DIFFERENTIAL TAXATION

The use of differential taxation is based on the theory that by reducing the property tax burden on undeveloped parcels of land, pressures to convert the parcels to more intensive uses will be reduced by decreasing holding costs and increasing the profitability of current uses. Almost every state now has provisions for some form of preferential assessment (Coughlin and Keene, 1981; Keene et al., 1976). The uses that are typically eligible for property tax relief are farm and forestland, open space, and recreational uses.

Three basic variations of differential assessment are currently in use: pure preferential assessment, deferred taxation, and restrictive agreements (Keene et al., 1976). Under the first type of program, preferred land uses are assessed for local property tax purposes not at their fair market value (i.e., the potential development value) but rather at their value in their current uses. If the land is in farmland, for instance, it is assessed according to its agricultural use value, usually based on a state-determined capitalization formula. If after several years of receiving the lower assessment the benefited landowner decides to develop the land, he or she is permitted to do so without having to repay the property taxes forgone as a result of the use value assessment. In contrast to this pure approach is that of deferred taxation. The difference here is that the landowner changing the use of his or her land is required to repay a portion of the tax benefits received. However, the recapture period typically is not very long, with 5 years perhaps the average. In addition, most states using this approach require the landowner to pay interest on the recaptured fund, usually at a below-market rate. A third approach, the use of restrictive agreements, is best exemplified by California's Williamson Act (Gustafson and Wallace, 1975). Here, to obtain lower tax assessments, qualifying landowners must be willing to enter into written agreements to keep their land in its current use for at least 10 years. This contract is a "rolling-front" agreement that is self-renewing each year unless the landowner explicitly notifies the locality of an intention to change the use. There are also provisions that permit the landowner to break the contract subject to certain penalties.

Although differential taxation has been used in most states as a technique to preserve farmland, its effectiveness at retaining land in undeveloped uses is moderate to low. Preferential assessment may reduce holding costs somewhat or even substantially, but in the face of high market prices and thus high opportunity costs of maintaining land in open space, the pressures to develop generally far outweigh the tax incentives (Dressler, 1979). Consequently, differential assessment is likely to be most successful in situations where development pressures are slight to moderate and where landowners are actively interested in maintaining the present undeveloped use of the land.

Differential assessment is also a more effective tool when used in collaboration with other approaches, such as the regulation of new development, the fee-simple purchase of land, and the transfer of development rights. For instance, reducing the permissible development density in a hazardous location, together with preferential assessment, may reduce opportunity costs to the landowner enough to reduce conversion of lands subject to hazards to developed uses.

IMPACT FEES AND SPECIAL ASSESSMENTS

People who build in and inhabit sensitive coastal areas (e.g., high-risk hazard zones) often impose substantially greater costs on the public than those who dwell elsewhere. These costs are realized when a hurricane or coastal storm strikes or threatens to strike a locality. Such public costs include evacuation, search and rescue, temporary housing, debris clearance, and the reconstruction of public facilities such as roads, utilities, and water and sewer lines. One public policy approach is to acknowledge that additional public expenses will be entailed by permitting development in certain hazardous areas and to assess those who will ultimately benefit from the expenditures. This approach can be accomplished through several means.

One technique is to attempt to tie more closely benefits received and costs incurred through the use of special benefit assessments. A special assessment, technically not a tax, is a method of raising revenue in which all or part of the cost of a facility (such as a road improvement, sewer, or water system) is charged to a property owner who is so situated in relation to the facility as to derive a special benefit from the improvement. The amount charged each property owner usually is proportionate to the frontage along which the facility abuts his or her property, the area of the land served by the improvement, or the value added to the land served by the project. Special assessments typically are confined to a geographic district in which property owners are determined to receive a direct and substantial benefit beyond the general benefits received by the public at large (Hagman and Misczynski, 1979).

A variation on the theme of requiring private parties who impose public costs to pay for them is the impact fee, which is increasingly popular with local governments around the country. In theory, the impact fee levy is designed to recoup and mitigate the overall impacts of a project or development on the community at large—impacts that may extend beyond the immediate environs and requirements of a discrete project or development. For instance, whereas a special assessment may be levied to cover the immediate costs associated with the floodproofing of sewer and water service, an impact fee would cover broader and more diffuse consequences of development in a hazardous area that are less clearly related to services or benefits received directly by a specific site or development. An impact fee is designed not to cover the costs of a specific improvement by which a particular development will reap a special benefit but to require the developer (and future residents who purchase these properties) to compensate the public for the additional costs of these consequences.

The impact fee may be instituted as a separate instrument or, more typically, attached to the exactions process during development review and approval (Hagman and Misczynski, 1979). In some states, the impact fee may also be a way of getting around legislative and court-imposed limitations on the extent of exactions permissible (e.g., restricted to the installation of roads, sewers, and other facilities or the donation of open space, school sites, and other land). The impact fee holds promise as a formal procedure for calculating and assessing impacts that may present a greater level of certainty for developers than currently exists under the highly negotiated exaction process. Adjusting the expectations of the development community and creating a clear and consistent set of public safety and environmental management obligations may well be an important local objective.

Capital Facilities and Public Infrastructure Policy

Coastal development—its type, location, density, and timing—is highly influenced by capital facilities such as roads, sewers, and water services. Such public investments have been aptly called growth shapers. In this section we briefly review the potential role to be played by the location, type, and timing of capital facilities in managing coastal development. Issues relating to the financing of these facilities have been discussed in a general way in the earlier section on taxation and financial incentives. The use of particular pricing policies may also significantly affect patterns of development, but this strategy is not discussed here.

Policies to Prevent Location of Public Facilities in Sensitive or High-Risk Areas

There are two primary dimensions of public investment in capital facilities that have implications for local management; one is geographic (where capital facilities are placed) and the other is temporal (when they are put in place). With respect to the first dimension, a locality can develop an explicit set of capital facilities extension policies designed, for instance, to avoid high-hazard areas, thus reducing the amount of development and property attracted to the area and the potential threats to lives and property. However, this approach can become an effective deterrent only if development in such areas is dependent on (or deems highly attractive) the existence of public facilities. If, as is often the case in resort areas, coastal development is able to obtain water through individual site wells and dispose of wastewater through septic tanks, a reorienting of sewer and water facilities by the locality will do little to impede growth in undesirable locations. It may then be necessary for the locality to foreclose other service or facility options available to developers by, for example, restricting the issuance of septic tank permits. But without valid health reasons, foreclosing such alternative options for development may be legally problematic.

The use of public infrastructure policy to restrict or direct the growth of a city may be subject to a variety of legal challenges. Within the city limits, a city may be required to provide equal service to all its residents once it provides a service to any of them. The city may extend utility services beyond the city limits, but only within reasonable limits and for the public benefit. When considering the extension of services beyond its limits, the city must consider the amount of territory to be serviced, its distance from the city, and the effect the extension will have on customers' rates and the city's capital debt structure. If the city extends services beyond the city limits, it has some discretionary power to condition the provision of the services. The agreement to provide extraterritorial services is contractual in nature, subject to the usual rules of bargain and contract. Rates may be higher for extraterritorial customers.

Redirecting capital facilities and the development that accompanies them into safer or more desirable areas of the locality can be facilitated by several means. One is the clear delineation of an urban service area in which the jurisdiction agrees to provide certain facilities or services. The service district might also entail a temporal dimension, including sufficient land to accommodate 10 or 20 years of future growth under various assumptions (as discussed in earlier sections on UGBs).

The urban service area technique has several advantages. It provides a long-term perspective on growth and development and permits developers, residents, and the local government to visualize where and when public facilities will become available in the future and where they cannot be expected. This, in effect, modifies long-term expectations about where future development will and will not be acceptable to the community.

In more intermediate terms, the locality needs a policy instrument by which to systematically identify, finance, and sequence specific capital improvements. This is generally the function of a capital improvement program (CIP). Ideally, the CIP follows closely designated service boundaries as well as the comprehensive plan, zoning, and other regulatory and planning provisions. The CIP provides a specific framework for making short-term (annual) decisions about which improvements to make and where. Storm hazard avoidance areas can easily be incorporated into this instrument and decision framework as a specific CIP policy.

A close connection between the designation of service areas, the CIP, and the overall planning process (including the local comprehensive plan) in a jurisdiction is essential. Such a close linkage will tend to enhance the combined effectiveness of each policy or technique in advancing overall local objectives and will emphasize their authority.

It should be remembered that public investments encompass more than sewers and roads and include numerous structures and buildings from town halls to schools to police and fire stations. Again, it may be possible to locate these investments away from sensitive coastal lands or in areas less susceptible to storm forces, in turn reducing the quantity of actual public property at risk and discouraging the location of other private development, and in ways that achieve other local objectives.

Relocating or Strengthening Capital Investments after Disaster Events

Special opportunities may exist after a hurricane or coastal storm to implement a community's capital facility objectives. If the facilities are sufficiently damaged, it may be possible to rebuild roads and sewers in areas less susceptible to damage from the next storm. Even if the facilities are not relocated, they may be repaired and reconstructed in ways that make them stronger or less susceptible to storm forces. Roads and sewers can be elevated, for instance, and sewer and water lines can be floodproofed. Also, placing power and telephone lines underground after the storm will help ensure safer evacuation when the next storm threatens.

It also may be possible to reconstruct public facilities in ways that not only reduce the possibility of their own damage but also reduce other storm-related hazards. As before, the presence of certain public facilities will influence development patterns. If certain facility repairs are not permitted to occur after a storm has hit, this may preclude or discourage the private redevelopment of the area. This technique was used subtly in Baytown, Texas. The option of selling out and leaving the Brownwood subdivision was made much more attractive to homeowners because they were uncertain that sewers and roads would be restored or maintained.

A similar approach might be taken with the rebuilding or reconstruction of damaged public buildings such as town halls and fire stations. If they are sufficiently damaged, it may be logical to move these structures to safer sites in the community. After Hurricane Camille, for instance, the Pass Christian Town Hall was rebuilt on higher ground and consequently was much more protected from future storm damage than if it had been rebuilt in the same location. When structures are not relocated, it may be possible to repair or rebuild them in ways that reduce their susceptibility to future storm damage, such as through elevation. It also may be desirable to rebuild public structures in ways that permit their usage as storm shelters.

Information Dissemination and Community Awareness

Classical economic theory supposes that the more informed consumers are, the more rational and efficient their market decisions will be. This implies an additional set of local management strategies that aim primarily at supplementing and enlightening individual market decisions regarding the hurricane and storm threat. Several approaches can be taken in this vein.

The first approach is to seek mechanisms and processes that effectively inform potential buyers of the risks and physical characteristics associated with a particular area. Hazard information and the information about the coastal physical environment can be provided in several ways. Legislation might require that real estate agents inform prospective buyers about the potential dangers or risks. Prospective owners might be required to sign disclosure forms as a condition of receiving a development permit.

Whether such real estate disclosure provisions have any influence on the decisions of coastal developers or homeowners is questionable, however. This disclosure technique has been used in California in an attempt to inform prospective homebuyers of the risks of living near earthquake fault lines, and some evidence about effectiveness is available here. Under the Alquist–Priolo Special Studies Zones Act, a real estate agent or individual selling property must disclose to the prospective buyer the fact that the property lies in a "special studies zone" (earthquake fault zone). However, a study by Palm (1981) indicates that this requirement has had little measurable effect on the market behavior of housing consumers. Among the problems identified are a tendency for homeowners to assign the earthquake threat a low priority, the issuance of the disclosure in the latter stages of a home purchase, a downplaying of the importance of the earthquake hazard zones, and a disclosure technique (a single line that says simply "in Alquist–Priolo zone") that conveys little or no real information about the earthquake risk. As Palm (1981, p. 102) observes, "At present, real estate agents are disclosing at the least sensitive time in the sales transaction, and are using methods which convey the least amount of information about special studies zones."

Consequently, if similar disclosure requirements are to be applied in coastal areas, the disclosure must be provided early in the sales transaction, preferably during the initial agent–purchaser meeting, and the disclosure must convey real and accurate information about the location and nature of coastal hazards. Not only should the disclosure form or process be labeled in a meaningful way (i.e., the home is in a "storm hazard zone" or "high-risk erosion zone," as opposed to an ambiguous "special studies zone"), it must provide a full description of the nature of the coastal risks. More passive types of hazard disclosure might also be useful. Included in this category are requirements that coastal hazard zone designations be recorded on deeds and subdivision plats and that public signs be erected indicating the boundaries of erosion or flood hazard areas (and perhaps the location of past storm damage). A number of coastal states and localities have used such passive approaches (indeed, they are required under the National Flood Insurance Program).

A locality might also attempt to disseminate coastal hazard information on the supply side. This technique might take the form of construction practice seminars for coastal builders and developers, introducing both conventional and innovative approaches to building and designing structures and to siting and planning the orientation of buildings in vulnerable locations. However, the success of such a strategy depends on the integrity of builders and developers, and those who are conscious and conscientious about storm threats probably are already planning their projects accordingly.

Efforts can also be made to directly educate the housing consumer about coastal hazards and the coastal environment more generally. These programs might take the form of brochures and other materials distributed to new and prospective residents of the community, informing them of the nature and location of hazard zones, for instance, and information about what to look for in a new home or business structure (such as elevation and floodproofing). For existing residents, this approach may be one of educating them about actions they can take to enhance the integrity of their existing structures (such as installing "hurricane clips") and reducing future property damages.

Beyond Growth Management: Broader Community Sustainability

Although the pattern of land use and development in any coastal community has tremendous implications for its level of sustainability, there are many other ways in which coastal jurisdictions can reduce their ecological footprints. A number of these ideas and practices are described briefly here in the hopes that local coastal managers and officials will begin to think in broader, more visionary ways about the future of their communities.

Towards Ecological Cities on the Coast

There are many ways in which coastal localities can become more fundamentally green and ecological in their operation and management and there are increasingly good examples of cities and towns that have developed bold initiatives to make this happen.

Few coastal cities have gone as far as Santa Monica in embracing the concept of sustainability and adopting programs and initiatives to give the concept practical meaning. In 1991, the city began its Sustainable City Program, which has included the adoption of a set of guiding principles (Box 8.1), a set of sustainability indicators and targets, green building standards and guidelines, and adoption of the Natural Step principles to guide the preparation of the new conservation element of their General (Comprehensive) Plan. The text of the National Step—a Swedish effort to give practical definition to sustainability—is a set of basic principles or "system conditions" that should be satisfied, including that concentrations of substances from the earth's crust (e.g., carbon) and substances produced by society (e.g., chemicals, volatile organic compounds) should not be allowed to increase (Box 8.2).

This commitment to sustainability has led Santa Monica to adopt some exemplary policies and programs, including the decision to purchase 100% of its municipal power from green energy sources (i.e., renewable energy), even though the choice is more expensive. Assuming responsibility for the ecological impacts and effects of such decisions, and looking at every local decision or action as one having environmental implications, is a hallmark of such coastal sustainable communities.

Box 8.1. Santa Monica Sustainable City Program: Guiding Principles

The Concept of Sustainability Guides City Policy

Santa Monica is committed to meeting its existing needs without compromising the ability of future generations to meet their own needs. The long-term impacts of policy choices will be considered to ensure a sustainable legacy.

Protection, Preservation and Restoration of the Natural Environment Is a High Priority of the City

Santa Monica is committed to protecting, preserving and restoring the natural environment. City decision-making will be guided by a mandate to maximize environmental benefits and reduce or eliminate negative environmental impacts.

Environmental Quality and Economic Health Are Mutually Dependent

A healthy environment is integral to the long-term economic interests of the City. In achieving a healthy environment, we must ensure that inequitable burdens are not placed on any one geographic or socioeconomic sector of the population.

All Decisions Have Environmental Implications

The City will ensure that . . . its policy decisions and programs are interconnected through the common bond of sustainability as expressed in these guiding principles. The policy and decision-making processes of the City will reflect our environmental objectives.

Community Awareness, Responsibility, Involvement and Education Are Key Elements of Successful Programs/Policies

Individual citizens, community-based groups and businesses must be aware of their impacts on the environment, must take responsibility for reducing or eliminating those impacts, and must take an active part in community efforts to address environmental concerns. The City will therefore be a leader in the creation and sponsorship of environmental education opportunities in cooperation with schools, colleges and other organizations in the community.

Santa Monica Recognizes Its Linkage with the Regional, National, and Global Community

Local environmental problems and ameliorative actions cannot be separated from their broader context. This relationship between local issues and regional, national and global issues will be recognized and acted upon in the City's programs and policies. The City's environmental programs and policies should therefore be developed as models which can be emulated by other communities. The City must also act as a strong advocate for the development and implementation of model programs and innovative approaches by state and federal government which embody the goals of sustainability.

Those Environmental Issues Most Important to the Community Should Be Addressed First, and the Most Cost-Effective Programs and Policies Should Be Selected

The financial and human resources which are available to the City are limited. The City and the community should reevaluate its environmental priorities and implemented programs and policies annually to ensure that the best possible investments in the future are being made. The evaluation of a program's cost-effectiveness should be based on a complete analysis of the associated costs and benefits, including environmental and social costs and benefits.

The City Is Committed to Procurement Decisions Which Minimize Negative Environmental and Social Impacts

The procurement of products and services by the City results in environmental and social impacts both in this country and in other areas of the world. The City must develop and abide by an environmentally and socially responsible procurement policy which emphasizes long-term values and will become a model for other public as well as private organizations. The adopted procurement policy will be applicable to City programs and services in all areas.

Source: City of Santa Monica, CA.

Green Governance

Other coastal cities have taken similar steps in the direction of green governance. The City of San Francisco has embarked on an impressive sustainability agenda, led by the city's Department of the Environment. Elements of this city's program include a Resource Efficiency Building Ordinance that mandates that the city develop 10 green building pilot projects to demonstrate how green ideas might be incorporated (and

---

Box 8.2. System Conditions of the Natural Step

In order for a society to be sustainable, Nature's functions and diversity are not systematically:

- subject to increasing concentrations of substances extracted from the earth's crust;
- subject to increasing concentrations of substances produced by society;
- impoverished by physical displacement, overharvesting or other forms of ecosystem manipulation; and resources are used fairly and efficiently in order to meet basic human needs globally.

Source: The Natural Step.

---

later to be followed by code changes). These pilot projects include a hospital, a convention center, a municipal office tower, a community center, and the city's new EcoCenter, completed in September 2000 (San Francisco Department of the Environment, 2000).

The EcoCenter is itself an important initiative, a place where citizens can learn about green products and ideas and see firsthand some of the ways this 1906 building was renovated ecologically (e.g., use of nontoxic paint, recycled carpet, salvaged wood).

Another unique element is the city's integrated pest management (IPM) ordinance, applied to all city and county parks and open spaces. Pesticide and herbicide use have been reduced by more than 50% since the program began in 1996. The city now shares these ideas through an annual IPM conference.

Other elements of San Francisco's initiative include a clean air program, which includes a mandate that new city and county vehicles must run on natural gas or electricity, help for employees with the cost of public transit, and use of bicycles by police officers and other city staff (San Francisco Department of the Environment, 2000).

Ecological Infrastructure

An increasing number of coastal localities have taken actions to reduce their ecological impacts in some dramatic ways and through some creative strategies that extend beyond the typical land use or growth management techniques. The progressive coastal community of Arcata, California, is one such place. A small community of about 15,000 in population, Arcata has become a leader in progressive coastal sustainability.

Arcata has a sustainably managed community forest, which makes it a unique place. About 600 acres, the forest was acquired in several purchases over a long period of time. The forest provides the community with a number of benefits, including recreation. It is also intended to serve as a model for forest stewardship. In the year 2000, timber was harvested on about 8.5 acres of the forest using an individual tree selection method. The harvesting is well within sustainable levels, estimated to account for about 30% of that year's growth increment. The forest received a sustainably managed certification under the Forest Stewardship Council in 1998 (under its Smart Wood label), and the harvested woods are sent to a sawmill that has been certified as a sustainable chain of custody sawmill. The proceeds of the harvest go into a Forest Trust Fund to be used for forest management, trail improvement, and possible expansion of forest land base (Town of Arcata, 2001).

The town has also taken a unique approach to combining conservation of coastal resources with municipal sewage treatment. Confronted with a controversial and expensive regional plan for treating wastewater, Arcata chose a different path: to restore a coastal wetland (a former dump) into a natural wastewater treatment system. Completed in 1986, the Arcata Marsh and Wildlife Sanctuary naturally treats the city's wastewater and has become a popular natural area. Some 200 bird species visit the marsh, and the marsh has become a popular bird-watching site. An interpretive center was constructed in 1987, using a $100,000 prize awarded by the Ford Foundation for innovation in local government.

Sustainable Economy

There are many positive examples of efforts around the country to promote economic activities that are more sustainable and compatible with coastal ecosystems. Key strategies include supporting the development and marketing of locally unique agricultural or aquacultural products, supporting local producers though community-supported agriculture and farmers' markets, and promoting various forms of coastal ecotourism, from waterfront festivals to bird-watching events.

Many of these ideas have been applied successfully on Virginia's eastern shore (Box 8.3). Under the leadership of The Nature Conservancy (TNC), for instance, a Conservation Business Alliance has been formed to support the development of a more sustainable economy

---

Box 8.3. Sustainable Coastal Development: Some Examples from the Eastern Shore of Virginia

Compatible Development

Gradually, a new vision of economic development has been emerging that could hold the promise of economic prosperity and protection of the natural treasures and way of life of the Eastern Shore. Here are a few examples that already have proven their value:

- Clam aquaculture began on the Eastern Shore in a small way more than 20 years ago. It has since grown to become a multi–million dollar industry, and the future of aquaculture depends upon a healthy seaside ecosystem. Protection of the ecosystem, then, means a profitable aquaculture industry.
- While aquaculture represents a pragmatic use of the resource, the more aesthetic values of the islands are equally important. People enjoy the wilderness aspects of the islands, and they visit the Eastern Shore to enjoy these special places, just as people enjoy the wilderness areas of the American West. In turn, these visitors have a need for supporting goods and services that can benefit many local businesses as well.
- The Eastern Shore has become well known worldwide for the incredible number of birds that use the islands and the forested mainland during spring and fall migrations. Local festivals draw thousands of birders, who return time and again. Protecting the resource means protecting a valuable aspect of our economic base.
- Farming on the Eastern Shore has always been a mainstay of the local economy. Some exciting new enterprises on the Shore show promise for adding value to agriculture while protecting the marshes and waters that border the area's seaside farms. Current projects range from Hayman sweet potato growing to flower-drying operations. These projects demonstrate sustainable farming practices, preserving rural ways of life as well as a real potential for compatible economic development.

- Nature oriented tourism has become one of the fastest growing aspects of the hospitality industry. Local businesses conduct birdwatching tours, bicycle outings, and canoeing and kayaking adventures. These businesses, when conducted responsibly, make use of the resource, yet do not compromise it. Indeed, when done right, they reinforce the fact that the island ecosystem is special and requires long term protection.

  Businesses and industries such as these are redefining the traditional roles of business and conservation. They serve as working examples of "Compatible Development." In their visionary attitude to their human and natural context, they serve as examples for other businesses to follow and for other communities across rural America to seek out and attract.

  Source: Excerpted from the Nature Conservancy (undated, pp. 5–6).

there (The Nature Conservancy, undated). A two-step process is involved. The first step is inclusion in a registry of businesses representing compatible development, with businesses asked to sign a Statement of Principles. A second step is the entering into specific business contracts, through which the TNC assists these companies in marketing and selling their products and in other ways that help the companies flourish.

In Northampton County, also on Virginia's eastern shore, the Cape Charles Sustainable Technology Park is another interesting alternative model for economic and industrial growth. Selected as one of 12 Brownfield Showcase Communities, the park aspires to achieve a different model of industrial growth and development, one where industries achieve a symbiosis in which the waste from one serves as productive input to others and where all industries reflect high environmental standards of responsibility. Of the 200 acres in the park, 90 have been set aside as a natural area (including a new Coastal Dune Preserve) that connects the park to the Chesapeake Bay. Design for the park grew out of a community design charrette coordinated by William McDonough and Partners. Long-term plans also include providing more direct pedestrian connection to the Town of Cape Charles (the park is adjacent to the town but hard to reach at the moment). So far, the first building has been completed: a 31,000-square-foot structure with photovoltaic cells covering much of its rooftop. Companies in the park include a manufacturer of desalinization plants and a local cookie company.

Most recently the park has been actively exploring the incorporation of wind energy. The park is in discussions with a German company that could lead to the building of the Cape Charles Wind Farm, consisting of six turbines that together could generate energy sufficient for about half the county's population. In addition to generating power, the park would become the U.S. headquarters and showcase for this important technology.

Sustainable Mobility in Coastal Communities

Traffic congestion is a problem in many coastal localities. Especially during the summer tourist season, when populations balloon, moving people from place to place becomes a daunting challenge. A number of actions and strategies are being pursued by coastal localities to promote less environmentally damaging, more sustainable forms of mobility. These strategies include efforts to get visitors out of their cars, promote use of public transit, and encourage walking and bicycle riding wherever possible. Cities such as Ocean City, Maryland, offer frequent bus service along the major roadway running north–south along the island. The route is simple and the system easy to use. A boardwalk shuttle also moves visitors up and down the beach.

A number of examples exist of efforts to facilitate bicycle use. Along the northern Outer Banks of North Carolina, many visitors are able to move by bicycles along a paved north–south bikeway that follows the main beach road. Communities such as Hilton Head and Kiawah have extensive networks of bike paths. Indeed, coastal communities generally have special opportunities to promote and enhance bicycle use (e.g., generally flat areas, with good climate and weather conditions and recreation-based economies).

Older, historic coastal towns offer excellent pedestrian environments, and these pedestrian qualities can be strengthened and enhanced in many ways. Ensuring compact development that ties into the existing town, village, or city street patterns with adequate sidewalks and pedestrian crossings would be a good start. Mixed-use development incorporating office, commercial, and residential uses together in a single location is an important ingredient.

Some coastal communities, such as Dewees Island, South Carolina, have banned automobiles entirely, and some historic coastal towns, such as St. Augustine (Florida), have significant pedestrian areas in their core.

Coastal towns with a square or pedestrian plaza at the center find that these are important areas for public and civic functions. In Arcata the square is the site of festivals, concerts, and the weekly farmers' market. New residential areas can be designed in ways that calm auto traffic, build onto the existing network of streets and bicycle paths, and provide a mix of uses and activities. Coastal towns and cities can and should strive to create places and environments in which residents and visitors have viable alternatives to the automobile.

Many other innovative mobility options exist for coastal communities. The City of San Francisco has just begun a car-sharing initiative, and a new public bike initiative was started recently in the Presidio, the former army base, also in San Francisco.

Educating the Public for a Sustainable Future

Public education is another potentially effective local (or regional) approach to long-term sustainable coastal management and planning. There are many impressive educational programs around the country, some aimed at citizens and homeowners, others at developers and realtors, and still others at businesses.

One of the most impressive and unique educational initiatives is Puget Sound's Public Involvement and Education (PIE) program. PIE is administered by the Puget Sound Water Quality Action Team, with an emphasis on water quality and watershed education and management. Created in 1987, the fund has taken the unique approach of making a large number of small grants to community groups, neighborhoods, nonprofits, local governments, and others to support a variety of grassroots educational and stewardship initiatives. A total of $5.2 million has gone to more than 300 projects that are solicited and funded on a biennial basis.

The PIE approach has many advantages. It reflects the stated belief that "community-based organizations, businesses, local and trial governments, and schools can involve and educate people about water quality in ways that government, by itself, cannot" (Puget Sound Water Quality Action Team, 1996, p. 1). It builds grassroots institutions and constituents educated about and supportive of water quality issues and overcomes the typical "us–them" distinctions that occur in traditional government-initiated programs (Puget Sound Water Quality Action Team, 2001, p. 1). A wide variety of educational projects and initiatives have received funding (in the form of service contracts, not grants): educational meetings and collaborative dialogues (e.g., watershed-

Photo 8.2. The Bremerton Rain Barrel Project, funded through Puget Sound's PIE program, has provided more than 100 rain barrels to homeowners for use in watering their gardens and lawns. Shown in photo: Jessica Wheeler. (Photo by Puget Sound Water Quality Action Team.)

based neighborhood meetings), training programs, production of educational booklets and other materials, demonstration projects, and environmentally oriented community service programs and school-based initiatives. A number of creative and nontraditional techniques have been used to get the message out, including public theater (Seattle Public Theater wrote and put on an interactive play about water quality and environmental issues in a watershed in Snohomish County).

Among the projects funded in the most recent round are a series of Fish-Friendly Construction Workshops, put on by the local Master Builders Association; a project to educate landowners about watershed restoration; a program called Horses for Clean Water aimed at educating horse owners about good horse keeping practices; the stream stewards program in the city of SeaTac, where students install special devices in storm drains to catch oil and other pollutants; and a 36-week water education curriculum in a local school.

The Bremerton Rain Barrel Project is giving 100 rain collection barrels to homeowners for use in collecting rooftop water and using it for gardens and lawns. "The barrels provide hands-on education about the quantities of stormwater coming off typical rooftops that must be handled by municipal stormwater systems, encourage residents to disconnect from the city's system, and is an effective way to promote water conservation" (Puget Sound Water Quality Action Team, 2001, p. 5).

Although the cumulative long-range effect of these efforts is hard to document, the extent and variety of the initiatives are impressive, and the educational benefits are considerable, especially given the generally modest level of funding.

Finding ways to educate public officials about serious coastal management problems and the relationships between land use decisions and policy and environmental quality is a major challenge. One successful example is Nonpoint Education for Municipal Officials (or NEMO). Started by the University of Connecticut Cooperative Extension Service, the idea is being applied in coastal communities in several states. In NEMO a variety of educational tools are used to educate about nonpoint pollution, but most effective is the application of geographic information system (GIS) technology. Specifically, extension officials simulate what would happen for a specific community if buildout were to occur, as allowed under the community's existing zoning and land use controls. The amount of impervious surface and runoff from conventional development is compared with a conservation alternative. Through the use of GIS, public officials can see graphically what the implications of their land use decisions and policies are (NRDC, 2001).

Of course, there are many other creative ideas for educating the public and public officials about coastal resources. They include signage and public exhibits about coastal resources and practices such as stenciling messages on storm drains ("drains to the Chesapeake Bay"). Stream cleanups or stream adoption programs are another approach. The City of Monterey, California, uses volunteers in its urban watch program to test and monitor stream quality and stormwater outfalls flowing into the Monterey Bay. These volunteers help to educate the public and work with polluters to reduce their effluents. An effective coastal education program will rely on many different ideas and initiatives and will target particular education messages to particular groups in the community; for example, mock wetland boards have been organized for secondary students in Virginia Beach, where students role-play about a wetland development proposal (Schillinger, 1997).

Impediments and Obstacles
to Local Sustainability

Although there is tremendous potential for effective coastal management at the local level, it is not always easy to develop, enact, and implement such programs. Table 8.2 presents the results from a National Science Foundation (NSF) funded study of local programs to mitigate coastal storms, specifically citing in rank order the perceived obstacles to the enactment of development management (or growth management) measures to address hazards in such high-risk localities. As the table indicates, coastal localities will confront a host of impediments, including conservative attitudes toward government control of private property rights, a feeling that the community can weather the storm, lack of financial resources, the existence of more pressing local problems and concerns, opposition of real estate and development interests, and lack of trained personnel. Similar problems of enforcement and implementation were highlighted in the survey results (Table 8.3).

Local officials probably will also confront several arguments against effectively managing growth and development management, including that such efforts will increase the costs of development, will dampen

Table 8.2. Arguments against Enactment of Development Management Measures in Order of Frequency

Arguments	Frequency	Percentage	Importance index[a]
1. Development management measures lead to increased developmental costs (N = 368)	315	85.6	3.18
2. Decisions about risks from coastal storms are best left to the individual (N = 346)	246	71.1	2.66
3. Development management measures dampen local economy (N = 355)	245	69.0	2.52
4. Particular development management measures are illegal or unconstitutional (N = 338)	225	66.6	2.42

Source: Godschalk et al. (1989).

[a]Based on a five-point scale.

Table 8.3. Problems in Enforcement and Implementation of Development Management Measures

Problem	Frequency	Percentage
1. Insufficient funds (N = 195)	116	59.5
2. Public opposition (N = 194)	89	45.9
3. Lack of support by public officials (N = 192)	83	43.2
4. Lack of qualified personnel (N = 195)	79	40.5
5. Insufficient database (N = 195)	63	32.3

Source: Godschalk et al. (1989).

the local economy, and are illegal or unconstitutional (see Table 8.2). Local officials may also confront the argument that decisions about such things as hurricane and coastal storm risks are best left to individuals. Although such arguments against planning and management generally are unfounded, supporters and proponents of management must be prepared to address them.

The attitudes of residents and property owners in coastal areas and the general attraction of coastal living might also be thought of as obstacles to more sensible and sustainable development patterns. Recent surveys of coastal property owners suggest that many of them have a solid appreciation for the danger and riskiness of building and living in coastal areas but see hurricanes and coastal storms as simply a necessary part of the trade-off for the benefits of coastal living (Beatley, 1992). Table 8.4 represents the results of a mail questionnaire administered to owners of beachfront property in South Carolina heavily damaged by Hurricane Hugo. As the results indicate, even those who have been devastated by such events generally do not have regrets or plan to move to safer locations. A related obstacle is the economic advantage of beachfront locations. A major reason why beachfront property owners are reluctant to relocate their structures (and are willing to wait until the structure has nearly collapsed in the surf) is that many rent their units, and rental incomes are substantially higher on the first-row beachfront than on more inland sites.

Thinking beyond more conventional growth management and embracing a broader sustainability agenda, as argued for here, is fraught with even more obstacles. Many would question whether it is a legitimate role of a community to own, manage, and sustainably harvest a community forest or promote green energy and green products through its purchasing decisions. Rethinking the ways in which a

Table 8.4. Results of Questionnaire Administered to Owners of
Beachfront Property Damaged by Hurricane Hugo[a]

Possible responses	Frequency	Percentage
1. Yes, would not buy beachfront property again	8	6.1
2. Yes, would like to sell my property and buy property in safer location	9	6.8
3. No, hurricanes are just a normal risk in beachfront property	52	39.3
4. No, the benefits and enjoyment of beachfront living outweigh the potential risks	55	41.7
5. Other	8	6.1

Source: Beatley (1992).

[a]The following question was asked of the property owners (N = 132): "Now that you have experienced the effects of a hurricane, has this had any influence on your feelings about owning beachfront property?" (circle all that apply).

coastal community tackles everything from economic development to transportation, and viewing these traditional sectors through the lens of sustainability, is essential but difficult.

Conclusions

This chapter has examined coastal management at the local level, including existing patterns and potential future directions. We have emphasized that coastal localities often are in the best position to formulate and implement coastal management programs and to move in the direction of sustainability. We offered some ideas about what constitutes a sustainable coastal community. We do not expect complete agreement on our proposed definition but see it as a starting point from which local planners, elected officials, citizens, and others should begin to discuss and debate.

In reviewing the existing patterns of local management, it is clear that coastal localities are more likely to adopt conventional planning measures such as basic zoning and subdivision ordinances. Although these measures can be useful in advancing a number of local objectives, many other tools, techniques, and strategies are available that coastal localities may want to add to their arsenal in promoting sustainability. Indeed, effective growth management will take a bold vision about how the community should look and function in the future and a cohesive, integrated package of management tools and strategies.

We have argued here that although growth management and land use issues are the building blocks of a sustainable coastal community, a broader view must also be taken. Sustainability in coastal communities entails thinking about such things as economic development, sustainable mobility, and the purchasing decisions that a community makes.

A number of obstacles to effective local management were identified. It will remain a real challenge for proponents of sustainable communities to overcome these obstacles, but we believe it is possible. There are enough impressive local efforts to illustrate the great potential of such local strategies.

9

Creative Coastal Development: Building Sustainably along the Coast

Although we argue in many places in this book that the best planning option is not to build at all—for instance, in wetlands, floodplains, and coastal high-hazard areas—growth in the coastal zone is unavoidable. The question then becomes how to encourage it in ways that reduce its impact on the natural environment and that are restorative rather than destructive. In this chapter we identify some principles for building in the coastal zone and describe a number of tangible examples of exemplary projects and buildings that illustrate what is possible. The buildings and projects could be labeled in many ways—*ecological design, green building,* or *sustainable design,* to name a few. They aim to reduce the ecological impact or footprint of the development, blend harmoniously with the site and surrounding community, and acknowledge responsibilities to broader publics than the rather immediate developer, property owner, or homeowner. For the most part these are private projects that seek to do well (i.e., make money) but also to do good (i.e., benefit the community).

The environmental (and social) benefits of these projects are substantial, and together they have the potential to shape a more sustainable coastal zone. Building and construction in this country account for approximately 30% of the raw material needs of our society and consume more than 40% of our energy. Moreover, coastal development in its form and physical footprint have a tremendous impact on the health of our coastal environments—from water quality to biodiversity to the condition of beaches and dunes. Therefore, building and developing sensitively have great potential to make a difference in the coastal zone.

What follows is a snapshot of leading practice at this time, and the specific cases undoubtedly will be eclipsed by the next round of innovative development. Subsequent editions of this book will update, expand, and add new examples and cases as they emerge.

Environmentally Sensitive Coastal Development Is Not New

We tend to think that ecological or sustainable building is a new trend, and to be sure, much cutting-edge practice has emerged in just the last decade or two. Yet it is important to acknowledge that many of our historical patterns of coastal building were by necessity quite sensitive to environment and place. Homes were designed to facilitate movement of air and to take advantage of prevailing wind patterns for summer cooling. Homes were built with local materials and by local builders. Homes were often elevated to guard against flooding and built in safer locations than is often the case today. Much of this building wisdom remains as relevant today in coastal areas as ever before.

Our modern ideas about building in closer harmony with the coastal environment date to the environmental movement and growing environmental awareness of the 1960s. *Sea Ranch,* a recreational development 100 miles north of San Francisco, is perhaps the first clear manifestation of these environmental values. Here, the master plan prepared by Lawrence Halprin and Associates creatively called for clusters of homes sited in ways to maximize coastal views and to minimize disruption of this spectacular 5,000-acre coastal site. Unlike most developments of the day, Sea Ranch was conceived as a place where the beaches, rocky coasts, and meadows were set aside for common use and where homes were designed and sited to take explicit account of the climatic and environmental conditions of place. Homes were sited along hedgerows, with maximum use of the sun, to shield against the steady wind from the northwest. Roads were located to reduce visual intrusiveness. The homes were built of wood, a distinctive Sea Ranch style, and in the words of one of the main architects, William Turnbill, Jr., "succinctly brought together and intermingled the man-made and natural landscapes" (Turnbill, 1970, p. 2). Although Sea Ranch reflects few of the more contemporary ideas and technologies of ecological building, it remains an important precedent in responsible coastal building.

Especially along the East coast, the 1970s saw notable examples of early master-planned communities such as Sea Pines on Hilton Head, or Kiawah Island, both in South Carolina, with significant land conservation elements and ecological planning ideas and standards that remain relevant today. Many of these examples could be described as conservation communities because they seek, in their physical design and layout, to conserve coastal land and habitat and to minimize the overall impact on the environment. The eventual residents of these projects may or may not have environment and sustainability as core values. A more cynical view of some of the projects is that conservation has become an important marketing ploy and tactic and that buyers are attracted to such places because of the open space and green amenities and less because of the environmental or conservation grounds being pursued. In reality, many of the coastal projects described here involve a mix of these goals, and a key premise is that developers can make money building some projects that both protect land and appeal to a certain quality of living.

Conservation Communities in the Coastal Zone

Kiawah is an especially positive early model of efforts to build on a barrier island in a very environmentally sensitive way. On this master-planned island, efforts were made in siting roads and buildings to minimize environmental disturbance and to protect existing wetlands, dunes, and other habitats of the island. Particularly impressive was the protection of the island's extensive natural dune system. Homes and condominium buildings were placed far landward, leaving largely intact primary and secondary dunes. Wooden walkover structures provide access to the beach without damaging dunes or dune vegetation. Other environmental elements of Kiawah include a system of interior lagoons designed to catch rainwater and to be emptied in advance of an oncoming storm, a program to protect sea turtles and other wildlife, and extensive efforts to protect trees and native vegetation. Also, architectural standards require that buildings use natural colors and earth tones and blend into the natural setting.

Bonita Bay, near Bonita Springs, Florida, is an example of a recent large master-planned coastal community designed around ecological principles. The master plan of this 2,400-acre development sets aside more than half of the land as protected open space, preserves natural

Photo 9.1. On Kiawah Island, South Carolina, homes and buildings are built well behind the secondary dunes. Access to the beach is provided by an extensive network of walkover structures. (Photo by Tim Beatley.)

wetlands, sites residential areas on upper ridges to protect vegetation and to encourage natural drainage, and promotes the use of native vegetation (ULI, 1999). All landscaping plans in the development must use at least 50% native vegetation. A dual water system is used in the development, with one line delivering potable water and another delivering treated effluent and well water for use in golf course irrigation and vegetation watering (ULI, 1999).

As in many other large coastal developments, golf courses are a central feature here and represent a difficult dilemma for coastal conservation. In Bonita Bay there are five of them, and efforts have been made to design and maintain them in more environmentally responsible ways. Specifically, all five are registered in Audubon International's environmental golf courses program, and one has received its highest designation.

Audubon International certifies ecological golf courses under its Signature Cooperative Sanctuary Program (or Audubon Signature Program). The stated goal of the program is to "merge wildlife conservation, habitat enhancement, resource conservation, and environmental improvement with the economic agenda associated with the development" (Audubon International, 2001). Specifically, developers must develop a Natural Resource Management Plan, addressing at least the following areas: site assessment, wildlife enhancement and management, waste management, energy efficiency, water quality and conservation, and integrated pest management (IPM). The plan is reviewed and must be approved by Audubon, and site visits and annual reports are required under the process. Three designations or rankings are possible, with "gold" reserved for golf courses achieving the highest environmental standards. The Bonita Bay course meets this top standard.

Numerous examples of projects, many in more urban contexts in and around the coastal zone, can be cited which seek to preserve trees and elements of the natural environment. *Magdalene Reserve,* a 15-acre subdivision in Tampa, Florida, is one such example (Figure 9.1). Here 39 homes (in the first phase) were built in an overall design intended to preserve much of the dense oak hammock that existed on the site. Through sensitive placement of the homes, reduced grading, use of common driveways, and a site plan guided by a comprehensive

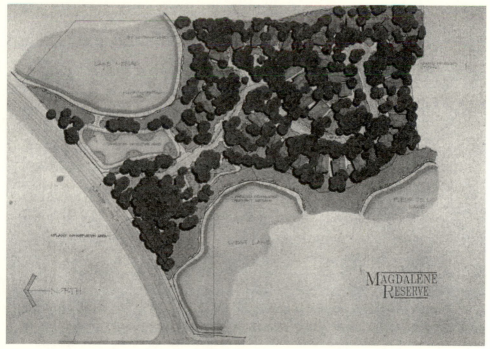

Figure 9.1. Magdalene Reserve master plan. (From Ekistics Design.)

Photo 9.2. The Magdalene Reserve development in Tampa, Florida, was able to preserve 1,000 oak trees with a sensitive site plan and careful placement of houses. (Photo by Ekistics Design.)

tree survey, the resulting loss of trees and vegetation was significantly lower than would have been the case under conventional development, and site clearance by heavy machinery. Homes in the development also incorporate xeriscaping and use of drought-resistant plants and emphasize natural drainage and on-site stormwater retention. The developer estimates that the project preserved 1,000 oak trees, some 800 more than a conventionally planned and built project would have protected. The county made this possible, in part by giving the developer important flexibility such as waiving the requirement for sidewalks on both sides of the street and not imposing sideyard requirements (ULI, 1994).

A development called *The Sanctuary,* along Lake Pontchartrain in Louisiana, near the town of Mandeville, demonstrates that trees and vegetation can be protected and impervious surfaces kept to a minimum. This 1,170-acre development sets aside 700 acres of cypress swamp and another 300 acres of adjacent savanna bottomlands where a network of nature trails can be found. Efforts were made to save and protect trees during construction. Building techniques included planning and building around trees, retaining wall foundations to minimize the amount of fill placed on trees, permeable limestone driveways rather than concrete in areas close to trees, and installation of utility lines through directional boring (rather than through open trenches). The development encourages natural stormwater drainage and generally keeps the extent of parking lots and paved surfaces to a minimum.

Ecological Site Design

Projects such as Magdalene Reserve and The Sanctuary demonstrate that much can be done in site design to respect the natural environment. Homes can be clustered to avoid wetlands, beaches, or other sensitive coastal resources, trees and vegetation can be preserved, impervious surfaces can be kept to a minimum, and parking lots and other traditional land surfaces can be significantly greened through the use of trees and creative stormwater management approaches.

There are many ways in which sensitive site planning can reduce the environmental impacts of development in the coastal zone. Homes and buildings can be sited in ways that protect trees and native vegetation, as we have seen, protect habitat movement corridors, and stay out of wetlands, floodplains, and other sensitive land. Every effort can be made to reduce the extent of impervious cover in a development by reducing the number of parking spaces and the size and extent of roadways and other paved surfaces and using permeable pavements and biofiltration strips for stormwater management. Parking lots should be designed with extensive tree coverage and vegetation.

Clustering of development—that is, maintaining the overall density of development but shifting its location to a particular portion of a site—is one especially effective strategy. This can reduce the amount of impermeable surface (by reducing the extent of road surface needed to serve the same number of units) and thus reduce stormwater runoff, resulting in fewer water quality problems (Arnold and Gibbons, 1996).

Maintaining more natural landscapes around homes and buildings in the coastal zone is also an important strategy. Conventional turfgrass lawns are highly polluting (causing runoff of fertilizer and pesticides) and resource intensive (because high amounts of energy and water are needed to maintain them). Developers and homeowners should be encouraged to use native vegetation and to preserve and protect the trees and other natural elements of the site. An example of a more natural approach to lawns and yards can be seen in Woodlands, north of Houston, Texas, where emphasis is placed on protecting existing trees in the development process, maintaining the critical hydrology of the site, and limiting the extent of turfgrass allowed for each home.

Programs such as *Florida Yards and Neighborhoods,* run by the University of Florida Extension Service, can also facilitate and encourage more natural coastal landscaping. Among the many educational and outreach activities of this initiative, a handbook has been produced that helps homeowners select suitable plants and create more ecological yards and provides tips on maintaining yards. Under the program, which is active in 21 Florida counties, if a yard meets certain minimum standards (Box 9.1), it can become a Certified Florida Yard and display a yard placard to celebrate this accomplishment.

Box 9.1. Yard Certification Checklist, Florida Yards and Neighborhoods

To be certified as Florida Yard, your landscape must:

- Collect at least 36 inches on this Yardstick Checklist
- Receive full points for practices marked with 2 asterisks
- Receive partial credit for practices marked with 1 asterisk
- Comply with all existing codes and laws

Water Efficiently

Mow lawns high to encourage a deeper, more drought and pest tolerant root system.**   2"

Irrigate lawn and landscape only when they wilt. Apply <3/4 inches water per application.   3"

For a yard that uses an irrigation system (in-ground or hose-end sprinklers):

Calibrate irrigation/sprinkler system to apply <3/4 inches of water.**   3"

Put a rain gauge in your yard to track irrigation amounts.**   2"

Install a rain shut-off device for in-ground irrigation systems.**   2"

Make sure irrigation system waters lawn areas separately from plant beds.   2"

Use drip or micro-irrigation in plant and flower beds.   2"

For a yard that does not use an irrigation system:

Design and maintain a landscape that exists predominantly on rainfall once plants are established.   6"

Mulch

Maintain a 2–3" layer of organic mulch over tree roots, shrubs and plant beds, leaving a 2 inch space between the plant base and the mulch.*   2"

Create self-mulching areas under trees where leaves can remain as they fall.   1"

Use by-product mulches such as pine bark, melaleuca or recycled mulches.   1"

Replenish mulch once or twice a year to maintain 2–3" depth.   1"

Recycle

Whenever possible, recycle grass clippings by allowing the to remain on the lawn.**   2"

Use leaves and pine needles found in your yard as mulch.   2"

Create and maintain a compost pile with yard clippings, leaves, kitchen scraps, etc.   3"

Wildlife

Plant vines, shrubs, and trees that provide cover, nesting areas or food source for birds, butterflies and other wildlife.   3"

Provide a water source, such as a bird bath or a small pond for wildlife.   1"

Provide wildlife shelters such as a bat house, bird house, brush pile, etc.   1"

Identify five kinds of wildlife (insects, reptile, birds, etc.) that live in your yard.   2"

Yard Pests

Treat only affected plants or lawn areas with pesticide applications. Avoid indiscriminate spraying.**   3"

Check your landscape every 1–2 weeks for signs of problems.   2"

Learn to identify 5 beneficial insects that provide natural control of harmful pests.   2"

Use environmentally friendly pesticides such as horticultural oils and insecticidal soaps.   2"

Use non-chemical approaches to pest control, such as pruning off affected areas, hand removing insects, etc., whenever possible.   3"

Right Plant, Right Place

Ensure that your landscape does not contain plants identified by legal code as invasive exotics, such as Brazilian pepper, melaleuca, Australian pine, and Chinese tallow.**   2"

Replace problem-prone plants with low maintenance native or non-native species.   2"

Group plants according to their water and maintenance needs.   2"

Determine how much grass you need for children, pets and recreation. Replace the rest with low maintenance ground covers, shrubs, mulch, or other porous surfaces.   3"

Use trees and shrubs to shade eastern and western walls of home and air conditioner compressor.   1"

continues

Box 9.1. *Continued*

Right Plant, Right Place (*Continued*)

Use deciduous trees on southern exposures to allow the sun to passively heat your home in winter.   1″

Reduce yard waste by choosing plants that will not require frequent pruning at maturity.   1″

Preserve native plants when building on a new site. Maintain a protective "do not disturb" barrier under the dripline of trees.   3″

Fertilizing

Fertilize as needed to maintain quality of lawns and landscape plants.*   2″

Use natural organic or other slow release fertilizers.*   2″

Use iron instead of nitrogen to make your lawn green during the summer.   1″

Stormwater Runoff

Direct downspouts and gutters to drain onto the lawn, plant beds, or containment areas.*   1″

Plant groundcovers or use mulch on thinly vegetated areas to decrease erosion.*   2″

Use mulch, bricks, flagstones, gravel, or other porous surfaces on walkways, patios or drives.   1″

Collect and use rainwater to irrigate plants.   2″

Create swales or terracing to catch and filter stormwater.   3″

Pick up after pets to reduce bacterial and nutrient pollution in storm drain systems.   1″

Clean up oil spills and leaks using cat litter on driveways.   2″

Sweep grass clippings, fertilizer, and soil from driveway onto lawn. Remove trash from street gutters.   2″

On the Waterfront

Remove invasive exotic aquatic plants by cutting, pulling, or raking. Remove dead plant material from water after using herbicides to reduce pollution.   2″

Protect your mangroves. All pruning must be in compliance with existing laws.**   2″

Establish a border of low maintenance plants between your lawn and shoreline/seawall to absorb nutrients and to provide wildlife habitat.   2″

Establish a 10–30 foot "no fertilizer" zone along your shoreline.   2″

Where feasible, plant native vegetation in the littoral zone in front of your seawall or along shoreline.   4″

Decrease wave action and increase habitat by placing clean, native limestone rock in front of your seawall.   3″

Total inches _____

Source: Florida Yards and Neighborhoods, Florida Cooperative Extension Service.

Photo 9.3. Through the Florida Yards and Neighborhoods Program, home-owners are encouraged to create more natural lawns and gardens. Once a home meets minimum standards, it can be certified as a natural yard and is entitled to display a sign, as shown here. (Photo by the Florida Yards and Neighborhoods Program.)

Building Ecologically but Profitably

The examples of creative coastal developments demonstrate that it is possible to conserve the coastal environment while also building profitably. Ecologically-responsible development is also likely to be economically successful.

Spring Island, South Carolina, is another impressive example of a successful coastal community with a conservation ethic (Figure 9.2). The brainchild of Jim Chapin (former president of the Urban Land Institute [ULI]) and Betsy Chapin, the island was developed with strong ecologi-

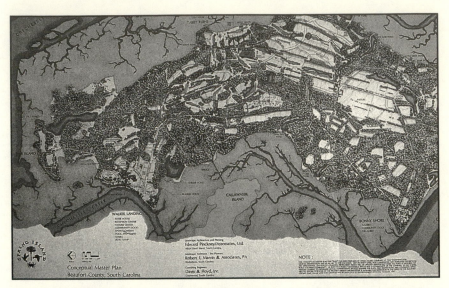

Figure 9.2. Spring Island, South Carolina, master plan. (From Spring Island Trust.)

cal and environmental principles at its core. Beginning with the overall plan for the island, not far from Hilton Head but not an oceanfront barrier, the plan accommodates a small number of development sites: about 500 on an island of 3,000 acres. Originally zoned to allow 5,500 units, the current approach is a substantial scaling back and a greater effort to protect and preserve the natural environment of the island. A key element in the plan is the setting aside of about one-third of the island, or about 1,300 acres, as conservation land and the creation of the Spring Island Land Trust to manage these lands. As Jim Chapin says, Spring Island is "a park with a community as opposed to a community with a park in it" (Environmental News Network, 2001, p. 1).

Spring Island Trust is funded through a set of property transfer fees—1.5% of the homesite sales price and 1% of the sale price of homes—to be applied in perpetuity. The trust is touted as a model of land stewardship and is active in both land management of the island and education of homeowners. The education programs are extensive and include habitat workshops, a variety of environmental publications, nature tours, and fireside chats by visiting artists and naturalists (Spring Island Trust, undated). A land management team representing different scientific disciplines has been assembled to advise on managing the natural areas, meeting four times a year.

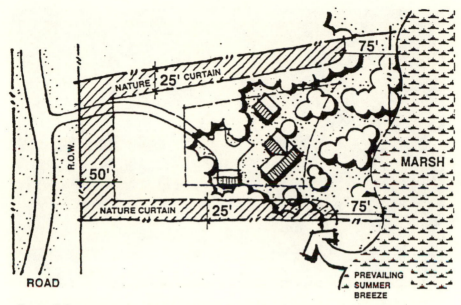

Figure 9.3. Vegetation standards for Spring Island, South Carolina. (From Spring Island Trust.)

Blending new homes with the natural environment of the island is a key objective. Prospective homeowners must work closely with staff naturalists to ensure that homes are sited to minimize environmental damage, and all plans must be submitted to the island's habitat review board. A set of vegetation standards apply to new development, including a requirement for a vegetative curtain to surround the home site. The curtain, intended to provide wildlife habitat and corridors and to reduce the visual impact of the house, must be 50 feet along the landward property line and 25 feet along the sides of one's property. A 75-foot setback from the marshes is also required (Figure 9.3). The Spring Island golf course has also been designed with ecology in mind, also certified under the Audubon Cooperative Sanctuary Program. Designed to follow the outline of existing cornfields, the course protects extensive trees, native grass, dunes, and marshes and uses a lagoon system that collects, filters, and reuses runoff water to irrigate the course.

Building coastal resorts in more ecologically sensitive ways is another important opportunity. The Caribbean is the site of several innovative examples. In particular, developer Stanley Selengut has made a name for himself by building several significant ecological and low-impact projects. Selengut's first project was *Maho Bay:* 114 tent

Photo 9.4. Homes built on Spring Island, South Carolina, must ensure minimum vegetated curtains. These vegetated buffers are intended to provide important wildlife habitat and to reduce the visual impact of the homes. (Photo by Tim Beatley.)

cabins located on 14 acres on St. John, U.S. Virgin Islands. Minimizing impact on the land is the key goal, and the tents sit on wooden platforms, laying lightly on the land, connected by a network of elevated wooden walkways. All utility and electrical lines are carried by these walkways, further minimizing land disturbance. The ULI reference file describes in more detail the design of the tent cabins:

> The tent cabins, designed by New York architect Jim Hadley, are made out of translucent, water repellent fabric, and are built upon a 256-square-foot (16-feet-by-16-feet) wooden platform supported by four-inch-by-four-inch beams that cantilever over the hillside. Surprisingly roomy and comfortable, the tents have a sleeping area with twin beds; a sitting area just large enough for a trundle couch that sleeps two; a small cooking unit with a propane stove, electrical outlet, cooler, dishes, utensils, and fan; and an outside deck equipped with lawn furniture. The cost to build and furnish each unit has varied throughout the resort's buildout (rang-

ing from $3400 in the 1970s to about $12,000 in the 1990s).
(ULI, 1995, p. 3)

Other ecological features of Maho Bay include the use of graywater, water conservation devices installed on bathroom fixtures, use of recycled materials, and composting toilets. These tent cabins are very popular and demonstrate the great potential of tapping into the expanding market in coastal ecotourism. Developers such as Selengut can make a profit while building with environmental care.

Few coastal developments have incorporated as many ecological features as Dewees Island, South Carolina. A former rice plantation, the island, located north of the Isle of Palms, has been designed to exemplify many principles of sustainability. John Knott, president of the Island Preservation Partnership, has been responsible for many of these ideas. The Dewees Island Guidelines, adopted in 1992 (and upon signing one's deed, adopted by each homeowner as well), strongly emphasize the importance of understanding and respecting the ecology and natural environment of the island (Knott 2001, p. 2):

> Living on Dewees Island means more than owning and occupying a dwelling. It is a responsibility that each owner, as part of the natural environment, assumes. You should view your existence on Dewees as nesting within the environment as other species of wildlife nest within their selected habitats. Each resident at Dewees Island should take no more from the Island environment than what is needed to enjoy the experience of this sanctuary. It is important that each owner be committed to learn from, and understand how, this environment works, so that the daily activities and decisions made while on the Island can be based on a thorough understanding of the potential impact of your actions on the environment. It is the goal of this community that knowledge of the Island and its environment be expanded and shared with others, and passed on to future inhabitants.

The sustainability dimensions of the island are many and begin with transportation. There is no bridge to the mainland, and all travel is by ferry, which runs from 6 A.M. to midnight. Cars are not allowed on the island; instead, residents ride electric golf carts, bicycle, or walk. There are no paved roads on the island, another important ecological decision made early on.

Much of the natural environment on the island has been protected. About 65% of the island's 1,200 acres have been set aside as conservation lands. Compared with earlier plans to develop the island, the amount of development is modest: Buildout will occur at 150 single family units. There is no minimum home size, but homes cannot be any larger than 5,000 square feet.

A number of provisions are designed to protect the island's natural qualities and features. Notably, total site disturbance (including driveways and footpaths) is limited to just 7,500 square feet (or about one-sixth of an acre). Other restrictions stipulated in the development's covenants include mandatory setbacks from marshlands and wildlife areas, maximum driveway width of 12 feet, and a requirement that only native vegetation can be planted. Several shared docks around the island take the place of private docks for each property. Extensive interior wetlands have been set aside, and a network of wooden walkover structures has been installed to allow pedestrian (and golf cart) access to the homes on the beachfront side of the island.

Sustainable design has been encouraged on the island. Some things, such as water-saving plumbing fixtures, are mandatory. All home designs must be approved by the island's architectural review board and must be sited and designed to fit into the island's natural setting. Trees must be protected and homes sited to take advantage of natural breezes and solar energy. The island's guest lodge, the Huyler House, is a showcase for green design ideas and an effort to lead by example.

The Huyler House is designed with windows and ceilings to allow natural cross-ventilation and to harvest natural light but minimize summer heat, with wood floors recycled from a Chicago warehouse and a pool that uses a nonchlorine water treatment system.

Environmental education is central to the development, and developer John Knott is fond of remarking that the environment is Dewees's golf course (because it does not have one). An impressive environmental education center has been built offering a host of programs and activities for adults and children. A full-time environmental program coordinator is on staff. The island has become a regional environmen-

Photo 9.5. No cars are permitted on Dewees Island, South Carolina. Instead, residents walk, bicycle, or use electric golf carts, as shown here. (Photo by Tim Beatley.)

tal education site and has been hosting bird-watching groups and visits from area schools.

Dewees also illustrates well the dovetailing of the goals of ecological development and hazard resilience. The island's hazard mitigation provisions include a required 1-foot additional elevation of buildings above expected flood levels, a 125-foot oceanfront setback line (more stringent than required by the state of South Carolina), and deeper piling depths for homes. On the beachfront side of the island a sand-fencing program has helped to promote dune accretion, and if the island ever needs to renourish its beaches, it will already have a contingency fund set aside for this purpose. Specifically, a special environmental assessment of 1.5% of the gross sales price of home lots has been collected and accumulated in a fund for renourishment (one-half paid for by the seller, one-half paid for by the buyer).

Dewees illustrates the common experience that ecological design and building can reduce environmental damages and impacts while reducing development costs (Figure 9.4). The decision not to pave any roads on the island, for instance, reduces runoff and minimizes damage to natural systems on the island; it also represents a significant cost savings for the developer.

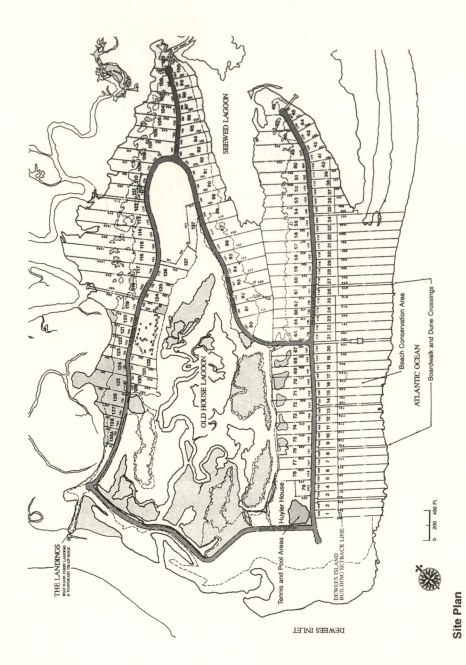

Site Plan

Figure 9.4. Dewees Island, South Carolina, master plan. (From Island Preservation Partnership.)

Green Buildings in the Coastal Zone

Some impressive new examples of green buildings in coastal areas can be cited. One especially promising model is the Chesapeake Bay Foundation's (CBF) new Philip Merrill Environmental Center. Its new headquarters, including a training and education center, accommodates 90 employees. The 32,000-square-foot building was designed from the beginning to demonstrate the possibilities of a low-impact office building and incorporates almost every imaginable ecological design feature.

Although the CBF had originally hoped to find a site within the City of Annapolis, the eventual location was in a smart growth priority funding area designated by the county under Maryland's smart growth system. A cradle-to-cradle approach was taken throughout its design, giving great emphasis to using recycled materials, beginning with the site itself. Built on the 31-acre site of the former Bay Ridge Inn, the new building occupies the footprint of the former inn, and most of the materials obtained during deconstruction have been recycled (e.g., the cement was crushed and used in road construction).

Photo 9.6. The new headquarters building of the Chesapeake Bay Foundation, near Annapolis, Maryland, incorporates many ecological design features, including the use of solar energy, recycled wood, wood from sustainably harvested forests, composting toilets, and rainwater collection. (Photo by Tim Beatley.)

The building was designed using the U.S. Green Building Council's *Leadership in Energy and Environmental Design* (LEED) rating system (described later). The LEED evaluates the greenness of buildings, and the Merrill Center obtained the platinum rating—the only building in the world to receive this highest score. Thus, the center is a positive model of how office buildings and other office and commercial structures in the coastal zone can be designed and built to reduce their footprints.

The building includes a number of innovative features, including building design that takes advantage of passive solar energy, natural bay breezes, photovoltaic (PV) cells, and a solar water-heating system. The south-facing front harvests daylight through a system of wooden louvers that block sunlight in summer and allow sunlight during the winter (the louvers are made from recycled barrel staves from an Eastern Shore pickle factory). PV cells are incorporated into the sunshades. A system of 48 closed-loop geothermal wells is also included. The daylighting and use of compact fluorescent lights, moderated automatically through light sensors, further reduce energy consumption. Together these features lead to a dramatic reduction in energy demand: The building is expected to use about one-third the energy of a conventional office building of this size.

Emphasis was also given to using renewable building materials, ideally from local or regional sources. At least 51% of the building materials had to come from within a 300-mile radius, and many other materials, such as cork for flooring, were derived from renewable sources (cork from cork oak trees in Portugal can be harvested without harming the trees and can be regrown within about 7 to 9 years). Bamboo, another fast-growing renewable resource, was also used.

Use of older-growth wood was avoided in some creative ways. Parallel structured lumber (trade name Parallam) was used for structural members, which involved gluing and pressing together shorter strands of second-growth timber. Other wood used in the structure is certified sustainably harvested through the Forest Stewardship Council. Chlorofluorocarbon-free structural insulated panels were used for ceilings and walls. The galvanized steel used for roofing and siding had a 75% recycled content (Gibson, 2001).

Creative water conservation is another important aspect of this building. The features here include a rainwater collection system (for such uses as handwashing and cleaning), composting toilets, and an effort to reduce the extent of impervious surfaces on the sites. Most parking is located under the building, and permeable pavement used for the limited parking available around the building. What runoff remains is guided to a bioretention stormwater system, which filters the stormwater through constructed wetlands. Estimates are that this building uses only about one-tenth the water of a conventional office structure.

A detailed transportation plan has also been prepared for the facility in an effort to reduce the energy and environmental costs of car dependence. Specifically, employees are given incentives to ride bicycles to work and to use electric or hybrid vehicles. Bicycles are also made available in the building for use by employees during the day (Chesapeake Bay Foundation, 2000a).

Ecological restoration of the site is also part of the scheme. Native grass will be planted and a nontidal wetland restored. Controlling invasive species and working to reestablish oyster reefs in Black Walnut Creek and Bay are also planned. A restoration center will be created, and the site will be used as a "hands-on training center for restoration volunteers, school students and teachers" (CBF, 2000a, p. 14).

Setting a positive example clearly was one of the main goals behind the structure. As Will Baker, CBF president, notes, "One of our goals for the Merrill Center is to promote environmentally sound building design throughout the Bay watershed and the nation" (CBF, 2000b, p. 1). The overall design is intended to "reflect our mission of Restoring the Bay and the nature of our organization" (CBF, 2000a, p. 3).

> The Center allows us to demonstrate our work as staff and volunteers restore the 33-acre site, and provides us a place to educate school students, their teachers, and the general public. It demonstrates to a broad audience, the values of a holistic, integrated approach to building design and construction that minimizes impacts on the Chesapeake ecosystem. (CBF, 2000a, p. 3)

The ecological features did add to the cost of the structure compared with a conventional office building. The structure (including parking, decking, landscaping) cost about $7.2 million—about $199 per square foot (of which it is estimated about $46 is for green features). Much of this cost, however, will be recouped through lower energy and operating costs.

New Urbanism in the Coastal Zone

In the planning and design fields, few movements have had as much influence on thinking and practice as neotraditional town planning, or what has come to be known as the *new urbanism*. The main idea is that new development should be designed around the principles of traditional American towns: a compact grid street pattern, with homes closer to one another and closer to the street. Traditional amenities such as sidewalks, street trees, picket fences and porches create more pleasant, livable places, new urbanists believe, and also provide a physical form in which neighbors know one another and a sense of community flourishes. Alleys behind homes, with garages in the rear, minimize the presence and impact of cars. It began slowly in the 1980s and was actively promoted by architects such as Andres Duany and Elizabeth Plater-Zyberk on the East Coast and Peter Calthorpe on the West Coast, and many projects have been completed. The Congress of New Urbanism was formed in 1993 and now has more than 2,000 members (see www.cnu.org).

Many new urbanist projects have already been built in the coastal zone, and many more are in the planning stages. Indeed, the first such project in the country was along the Florida Gulf Coast: Seaside, a new village. Located on 54 acres along the northwest Gulf Coast of Florida, Seaside, built in the early 1980s, exemplifies many new urbanist qualities and has emerged as a national model of neotraditional town design. The town's basic layout builds on traditional Florida towns, emphasizing connected streets, a network of paths and walkways, a compact walkable town form, and an urban code that stipulates elements such as front porches, picket fences, and pastel paint colors. A town center contains a post office, meeting hall, and town green (Mohney and Easterling, 1991). Admirably, and unlike conventional coastal developments, the town is set far back from the beachfront, with sandy beach reserved as an element of the public realm, open to all and a short walk from home and the town center. Gazebos and obelisks at the end of main streets serve as a visible gateways to this public resource and act as invitations "to share the beach—a stark contrast to the highrise condominiums that [typically] block the view and access to the sea" (Brooke, 1995, p.21). Preserving the beach and dunes as public park has also provided protection from storms. This was demonstrated in 1995, when Hurricane Opal struck. Whereas substantial oceanfront damages occurred in other communities, Seaside was left unscathed (*Tampa Tribune,* 1995).

Applications of new urbanist principles in the coastal zone are increasingly common. Small and large projects are being built to emulate the feel and pattern of historic coastal towns. As an example of a more recent project, Daniel Island in Charleston, South Carolina, shares many planning and design ideas in common with Seaside, but on a larger scale. This 1,000-unit project (on about 4,000 acres) organizes development around a series of compact neighborhoods, each with its own park, encouraging walkability, and with a town square to provide for the daily needs of residents. Neighborhoods and the town center are connected by foot and bicycle paths, making movement without an automobile possible. Sandwiched between the Cooper and Wando Rivers, the Daniel Island development scheme also emphasizes connections with the water (Hammatt, 2001).

A creative application of new urbanist principles on a smaller scale can be seen in the development *Newpoint* in Beaufort County, South Carolina. This 126-unit development is designed to emulate the qualities and architecture of low-country towns such as Savannah and Charleston. Designed in a connected grid street pattern, the streets are narrow and the homes close together, promoting a human scale and a highly walkable environment. The architecture is reminiscent of low-country buildings, with the Newpoint architectural code governing building materials, architectural styles, and dimensions. A wooded park sits in the center, directly accessible to adjoining property owners and a short walk for other residents. Called the *Rambles,* the green area contains a treehouse and play areas for neighborhood children. Trees along streets, sidewalks (which bend in interesting places), and traffic islands slow car movement and add to the visual flavor of the community.

Perhaps Newpoint's most creative feature is its waterfront green. In the Newpoint plan, the best waterfront locations, overlooking the Beaufort River, are reserved as a common area including a park and common dock. Two pedestrian access points are provided at the end of the two major streets in the community.

New urbanist projects are undoubtedly improvements over conventional coastal development and admirably seek to build on the impressive historic qualities and feel of coastal towns and cities. They are indeed more compact, more pedestrian-friendly and land-conserving. But there are reasons to be critical as well. Many such developments, including Newpoint, are located away from and unconnected to existing towns and are essentially car-dependent, pedestrian-friendly islands. Moreover, few new urbanist projects reflect a serious concern about the environment and tend to incorporate few ecological design features. Also, concerns exist about their affordability. In Newport, for instance, although some homes are modest in size, many are very large (and expensive), some homes up to 7,000 square feet. Despite the effort in many new urbanist projects to incorporate secondary housing units (carriage home houses, apartments over garages), most of these communities remain expensive places to live.

Equity and Affordability as Key Elements

Explicit in definitions of sustainable development is a concern about social justice and equity and the fair distribution of environmental benefits and quality of life. While many ecological projects are for higher-income residents, but it is important to search for ways to build more susutainably on the coast while improving the life prospects of the least advantaged in society. Indeed, arguably it is the poorest residents of our coast who are in most need of lower energy bills and access to nature.

Some creative examples of the overlap of social justice and affordable housing with sustainable coastal development are beginning to emerge. Along the eastern shore of Virginia, the impoverished community of Bayview is one such example. In this poor African American community, for many years residents have endured substandard housing conditions, including lack of indoor plumbing. Things began to change in 1994 when a group called Citizens for Social Justice was formed and started to tackle these terrible living conditions and to chart a new vision for this community. With funding from the Environmental Protection Agency, the Nature Conservancy, and other sources, and with architectural design assistance from the University of Virginia, a series of community assessments and workshops were undertaken.

So far, several homes have been demolished and a community bulletin board erected. Most important are long-range plans for a new Bayview Rural Village. Building onto the town's existing site and a layout, the new plan envisions a compact, pedestrian-oriented village with a village square, an agricultural cooperative, and community gardens interspersed between the residential streets. Existing substandard homes would gradually be demolished and replaced with new homes, and the village would grow to about 400 people (RBGC, undated).

Tremendous possibilities exist to find overlap between ecological and green buildings and affordable housing. A unique partnership in this area emerged in south Florida after Hurricane Andrew in 1992 between Habitat for Humanity and the Metro Dade Department of Environmental Resources Management. Specifically, a 200-unit project of affordable houses, called *Jordan Commons,* is being constructed through a collaboration, marrying the goals of low-cost housing with ecological sustainability. The homes are not being built one by one in isolation but as a compact, walkable neighborhood. The houses themselves incorporate a variety of energy efficiency provisions and other environmental elements. These include low-energy air conditioners and appliances, passive solar orientation, solar water heaters, low-flow faucets and toilets, a graywater recycling system, and highly reflective steel roofing and paving materials. Extensive tree planting (15 trees per home) will provide further cooling in the warm climate, and the homes will be landscaped with drought-resistant plants. The homes are being built with steel frame construction and, consequently, will be much better prepared to deal with hurricane winds typical for the region. A homeowner education program will teach residents about the environmental features of the homes and how residents can reduce these environmental impacts.

The homes will have many new urbanist features, including porches and street orientation and common spaces and facilities (e.g., playing fields, day care) (Adair, 1995). As in all Habitat for Humanity projects, much of the construction is done by volunteers, and the eventual owners of the homes are required to contribute a certain number of hours of sweat equity. Each home also has a corporate sponsor, which pays for approximately 80% of the construction cost (each costing about $50,000) (Center of Excellence for Sustainable Development, undated). The neighborhood represents an important model for collaboration on affordable ecological coastal homes.

In the spring of 2000, Habitat for Humanity entered into a formal agreement with Florida Power and Light (FPL) to build and certify low-energy homes for low-income families in that state. Under the agreement, low-energy homes are to be built by Habitat and inspected and certified by FPL under its *SmartBuild* Certification Program. (Sixteen of these homes will be in Jordan Commons.) To receive this certification, homes must use 30% less energy than required under State of Florida building standards. FPL is working with other affordable housing groups around the state, in addition to Habitat, in an initiative to build

Photo 9.7. Habitat for Humanity is building homes in south Florida, such as this one, that are affordable, sustainable, and safe. These homes are built with steel frames and are very energy efficient. (Photo by Tim Beatley.)

and certify some 1,000 SmartBuild homes (Florida Power and Light Company, 2000). Such partnerships demonstrate the potential and importance of linking ecological and sustainable building in the coastal zone with affordable and low-income housing.

Redevelopment and Rebuilding: Recycling Coastal Lands

One of the most important sustainable development strategies in the coastal zone is to reuse sites and parcels that have already been developed and already committed to the urban landscape. Good examples now exist of projects that recycle brownfield sites and former military bases and facilities and achieve urban and town infill.

Redevelopment of the Truman Annex in Key West—a naval facility that included President Harry Truman's so-called little White House, is one example. This 43-acre site has gone through an environmental remediation process and now accommodates a mix of residential, hotel, and museum space. A number of the original buildings have been preserved and adaptively reused, including the Old Surgeon's Quarters, the officers' quarters, and the Old Marine Hospital. The former naval administration building has been restored and is now an integral part of a multifamily housing complex, Harbor Place (ULI, 1996). An effort was made to design the new buildings in this project to fit into the historic fabric of Key West. Traditional architectural styles were used (e.g., alleyways, porches, balconies, and local architectural styles), and buildings were painted white to connect with the past of the site. The overall density of 23 units per acre is positive from a sustainable development point of view, and reuse of the buildings and building site is an example of good coastal development practice.

There are many other good examples of creative reuse. One of the most impressive in the coastal zone can be seen in the redevelopment of the *Presidio,* a former army base in San Francisco. Since it was turned over to the National Park Service (NPS) in 1994 (and is now part of the Golden Gate National Recreation area), almost all aspects of the Presidio's redevelopment have been guided by principles of sustainability. A "greening of the Presidio" charette convened in 1995 by the NPS generated a large number of ideas. The Presidio Trust was created in 1996 to manage the park with a goal of self-sufficiency by 2013.

Under the plan for the Presidio, many of the historic buildings on the base have been renovated and reused and have incorporated green building and rebuilding ideas. A recent specific example of green design is the renovation of the military police headquarters building. Among the green elements incorporated are renewable bamboo wood, recycled carpet materials, low-wattage electric bulbs, and water-saving bathroom fixtures.

One of the most creative pieces of this redevelopment scheme is the natural restoration of Crissy Field, a former army airfield and later fuel depot and dump. Here, an effort has been made to restore the ecological systems and habitat that existed before the base was built. The Crissy Field restoration, helped by the work of 2,000 volunteers, has restored meadows, dunes, and coastal wetlands. This volunteer group shows dramatically how coastal restoration can become an act of citizenship. In the end, some 100,000 plants were planted, 270,000 cubic yards of rubble and soil removed from the tidal marsh (it was used as a deposition site for debris from the 1906 earthquake), and more than 70 acres of pavement taken up.

The airfield has become a 28-acre natural meadow, an 18-acre tidal wetland, and a new park and nature site located in close proximity to a large metropolitan population. Extensive trails and walkways exist on the site, as well as an environmental education center.

Much of the funding for the restoration work came from donations by private individuals. About half of the cost of restoration is from 2,400 individual donations, most $100 or less. Other major sources of funding included a foundation, the City and County of San Francisco, and the California Coastal Conservancy.

In 1999, the tidal marsh was finally reconnected to the ocean in what became a major community event. Some 500 people watched breathlessly as a heavy equipment operator cleared a channel between the wetlands and the sea. The crowd whistled and cheered as the first water flowed. Returning this site to a use that probably existed for

a. Before

b. After

c. Before

d. After

Photo 9.8. Crissy Field, a former Army airfield at the Presidio near San Francisco, is an excellent example of how ecologically damaged and degraded coastal environments can be restored. These two sets of before-and-after photos show the miraculous results of such coastal restoration efforts. a) Before, a parking lot at Crissy Field; b) after, the parking lot has been taken out and tidal wetlands returned. c) Before, a polluted and degraded beach; d) after, the beach has been cleaned, cleared, and restored to a usable recreational resource. (Photos by Golden Gate National Park.)

thousands of years before the military field became a celebratory event demonstrating the power of community commitment and volunteer effort to restore the ecological values of the coast.

The Presidio has now become the center for experimentation on ideas of sustainability. These sustainability innovations include a planned combined heat and power plant, other green building demonstrations, restoration of native plants, promotion of composting, IPM, an extensive energy conservation program, and a compressed natural gas shuttle bus system, among others.

Innovative transportation initiatives at the Presidio include a planned electric car-sharing program (with a $100,000 clean air grant from the San Francisco County Transportation Authority) and a shared bicycle program (a joint effort with the nonprofit Bicycle Community Project). The shared bike initiative has placed 30 new mountain bikes (donated by a bike manufacturer) at the 24-hour disposal of visitors and residents. The bikes are stored at locked bike stations throughout the park, available to users who pay a small annual fee. Because most travel distances within and around the park are short, mobility by bicycle is an ideal option.

Strategies for Promoting Creative Coastal Development

Green coastal building can be promoted in a variety of ways. Some U.S. communities have adopted green building programs that certify that homes and buildings meet certain standards (e.g., up to five stars under the Austin, Texas, Green Builders Program) and provide education and certification for local builders interested in this market. Adopting mandatory minimum green building provisions is another approach, and some communities have enacted point systems that require builders to meet a certain minimum point total (e.g., Boulder's green points program) but allow flexibility about which ecological building measures to include. Financially (and in other ways) supporting and encouraging green building is yet another tactic, and some communities (e.g., Chicago) have recently sponsored competitions to design and build green homes.

The coastal city of Santa Monica, California, has adopted a set of Green Building Design and Construction Guidelines, which include both required and recommended provisions. The guidelines apply only to certain building types including commercial offices, light industrial buildings, retail buildings, multifamily residential buildings, and hotels and motels. Required elements include two sets of performance standards: one for energy conservation, the other for stormwater management. Under the latter, for instance, buildings and developments in the city must submit an Urban Runoff Mitigation Plan and must achieve a 20% reduction in stormwater runoff. Proposed developments must minimize the amount of impermeable surface but have the flexibility of adopting alternative methods to achieve the performance standard.

Coastal communities have other new tools to guide and evaluate green projects. One new tool is the LEED green building rating system (Leadership in Energy and Environmental Design), a program of the U.S. Green Building Council. Under the system, a building is evaluated or scored against five green building categories: Sustainable Sites, Water Efficiency, Energy and Atmosphere, Materials and Resources, and Indoor Environmental Quality. A building must achieve a minimum of 26 points to receive LEED certification. With more extensive green features come higher ratings: silver, gold, and the highest rating, platinum (at least 52 points necessary out of the maximum of 69 points) (Calkins, 2001). Though applied only to commercial buildings, this system is becoming more popular, with some local governments now considering it a minimum requirement and others rewarding LEED certification (e.g., though density bonuses).

Having model green buildings and projects in the community can be a powerful tool for encouraging more ambitious and creative building initiatives. A recent coastal example is the Center for Sustainable Living in Charleston, South Carolina, a renovated 125-year-old home in the heart of the historic district intended to demonstrate hazard resistance and sustainable building priorities. The center is a showcase for sustainable living ideas and ways of renovating buildings sustainably so they are less vulnerable to coastal storm damage. As an example of sustainable renovation, recycled wood products were used in rebuilding (e.g., to replace siding), a high-efficiency ground-sourced heat pump was installed, and the building was strengthened to better handle wind loads. Visitors can see and learn about a variety of ideas and technologies for sustainable living, including water-conserving landscaping, permeable paving materials, and more ecological methods for controlling pests (see the center's Web site at wwww.113calhoun.org). The building also makes a convincing case that a storm-resistant structure

Photo 9.9. This house in the heart of historic Charleston, South Carolina, has been renovated and converted to the Center for Sustainable Living. The center, a joint initiative of the City of Charleston, South Carolina, the South Carolina Sea Grant Consortium, and the Clemson University Extension Service, is intended to provide examples of ideas and technologies for building houses more sustainably and in ways that better resist the forces of storms and hurricanes. (Photo by South Carolina Sea Grant.)

is a more ecological structure: "The debris from [Hurricane] Hugo added the equivalent of ten years of normal fill to the area's landfill in just one year. That constitutes a highly significant, but little understood, public cost associated with hurricane damage. Making houses more resistant to wind, flood and earthquake damage makes them more environmentally friendly, or sustainable" (Center for Sustainable Living, 2000). Interestingly, the home is owned and managed by the 113 Calhoun Street Foundation, a nonprofit entity created by the City of Charleston, the South Carolina Sea Grant Consortium, and the Clemson University Extension Service.

In some cases local (and state) governments can encourage better, more creative development by loosening rigid standards that may represent undesirable obstacles. For instance, many localities have adopted traditional neighborhood development ordinances that allow developers to bypass the conventional development regulations (e.g., side yard and front yard setbacks, minimum street widths) in exchange for more desirable, compact, walkable neighborhoods. Advocates of new urbanism often argue that conventional development codes impede and obstruct more land-efficient, conventional neighborhood designs. Other examples of greater regulatory flexibility include so-called smart redevelopment codes (such as New Jersey's), which make adaptive reuse of older building easier, and greater flexibility in permitting such techniques as natural stormwater retention, graywater recycling, and ecological wastewater treatment, to name a few.

Forging alliances between different groups and organizations with an interest in ecological building is another important strategy. The creation of the 113 Calhoun Street Foundation, in Charleston, is one example. The joining together of Habitat for Humanity and FPL to build and certify low-energy homes is another example. There are many groups and organizations active in the coastal zone with common interests and concerns, with much potential for collaboration in promoting more creative, responsible growth.

Conclusions

As the project examples and cases discussed in this chapter demonstrate, it is possible to significantly reduce the overall environmental impact of development along the coast. Substantial reductions in the immediate and direct impacts (e.g., minimizing disruption of vegetation and ecological system functions) and more indirect effects (e.g., lower energy consumption and lower greenhouse gas emissions) are both possible. Coastal development also often presents important opportunities to restore or repair elements of the ecosystem.

These examples also show convincingly that ecological footprints can be reduced while achieving other important goals, including making a profit, increasing the safety of coastal residents, and creating places where quality of life is high and where people want to live and visit. Some key design and planning principles of building ecologically in the coastal zone are summarized in Box 9.2. Looking for ways to implement and give tangible meaning to these building values is a significant task for coastal planners and policymakers today.

The projects profiled here are not perfect, of course, and we have few ideal examples of coastal green development. One troubling paradox is the fact that some of the most impressive conservation communities are socially exclusive (as of 2001, home prices in the Sanctuary are averaging $500,000; building lots alone on Dewees Island are selling for more than $500,000). Projects such as Magdalene Reserve are exclusive enclaves, with an electronic gate at the entrance to this development. Homes on Spring Island are hardly modest in size, ranging from 3,500 to 12,000 square feet. This is a troubling paradox that

Box 9.2. Principles of Ecological Coastal Development

- Minimize the amount of water, energy, and other resources needed to build and operate the buildings; incorporate renewable energy, including solar energy, into the design and siting of buildings.
- Use local building materials and materials obtained from sustainably managed sources (e.g., a sustainably harvested forest, certified by the Forest Stewardship Council).
- Minimize waste during construction; recycle and use previously used building materials.
- Build compactly and conserve as much coastal land as possible; cluster away from wetlands, beaches, and other sensitive lands.
- Locate new development projects in close proximity to public transit and to town centers and in areas where residents and workers can walk and ride bicycles; discourage automobile use in the design of building projects.
- Choose in-town locations over rural or exurban sites; look for opportunities to strengthen and revitalize existing coastal cities and towns.
- Minimize the embodied energy of structures (i.e., the energy necessary to produce the materials of the building).
- Look for infill sites and opportunities to reuse the built environment before developing greenfield locations.
- Design and build to last; durability and quality should be favored over short-term profit.
- View every building project as an opportunity to restore and repair damaged coastal ecosystems.
- Protect trees, vegetation, and existing elements of the natural landscape; build within nature's ecological envelope.
- Reduce impervious surfaces and maintain the natural hydrology of the landscape.
- Avoid hazardous coastal locations, such as incipient inlet zones, floodplains, and high erosion zones.
- Strive to make projects affordable and create economically and ethnically diverse neighborhoods and communities.
- Design projects through an inclusive, participatory process; affected parties should be consulted and have the opportunity to influence designs.
- Incorporate features that educate future residents about ecological sustainability; make visible the natural processes on which we all rely.
- Search for designs that harmoniously blend projects into the natural and cultural landscape; design and build to strengthen sense of place.
- Incorporate design elements that strengthen connections for others and the broader community (e.g., connected streets, trails, common spaces); discourage developments that separate and isolate from the broader community.

coastal planners must keep in mind. The examples of Bayview and Jordan Commons illustrate that it is possible to build in ways that reduce environmental impacts and achieve sustainability but that also create inclusive and affordable communities.

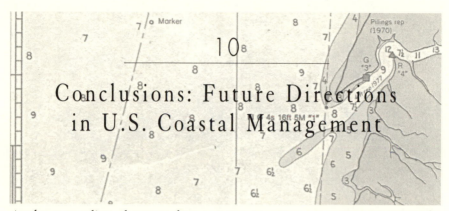

10

Conclusions: Future Directions in U.S. Coastal Management

As the preceding chapters demonstrate, we are as a nation increasingly drawn to live and recreate in close proximity to sea and shore, despite the hazards and costs of doing so. Alarm bells are ringing everywhere as our coastal environment endures unabated development pressures and environmental degradation. National Oceanic and Atmospheric Administration (NOAA) estimates that more than 750,000 new homes are constructed along the coast each year, with serious wetland and habitat destruction, diminishing water quality, and growing exposure to natural disasters. By 2025, nearly 75% of our nation's population may well be located in these ecologically fragile areas. Global climate change, and resulting sea level rise, will further increase the hazardousness of coastal areas at precisely the same time that the nation is rushing to the edge. Conflicts over use of coastal and marine resources are accelerating, including debates between advocates for oil and gas production and recreational beaches, marine protection and commercial fishing, and shoreline armoring and ecosystem protection. Now is the time for serious, concerted management. Our current planning and management systems are, unfortunately, not up to the challenge.

Although coastal growth and development in the United States probably are inevitable, the destructive and hazardous nature of these land use and development patterns need not be. This book has attempted to highlight some of the current and potential strategies and policies that can be used to minimize the impacts of such pressures. We have reviewed promising programs and strategies at each government level and can conclude that there already is in place a useful pol-

Photo 10.1. Protecting and sustaining our coastal environment must become a national priority: Cypress Point, California. (Photo by NOAA.)

icy and management framework. However, we believe that major improvements in this framework can and must occur in the years ahead if our fragile and irreplaceable coastal environments are to be protected.

Sustaining the Coast: Looking to the Future

We believe that in the future sustainability must be the centerpiece of coastal management efforts at federal, state, regional, and local levels. As we discussed previously, there are many definitions of sustainability and sustainable development, and many are fraught with subjectivity and ambiguity. However, we believe that, as much as anything, coastal management programs must imbue a *philosophy* or *perspective* of sustainability, even though its precise meaning may be open to discussion. This would be a major positive step in the future.

As the Brundtland Report says, sustainable development is development that "meets the needs of the present without compromising the ability of future generations to meet their own needs" (World Commission on Environment and Development, 1987, p. 2). In a more recent report, the National Commission on the Environment, using more words but saying essentially the same thing, defined sustainable development as:

A strategy for improving the quality of life while preserving the environmental potential for the future, of living off interest rather than consuming natural capital. Sustainable development mandates that the present generation must not narrow the choices of future generations but must strive to expand them by passing on an environment and an accumulation of resources that will allow its children to live at least as well as, and preferably better than, people today. Sustainable development is premised on living within the earth's means. (1993, p. 2)

Sustainable coastal development, then, implies new respect for environmental and ecological limits, a goal of living off the ecological interest while protecting the principal, a new orientation toward the future and toward adopting a long-term planning and management timeframe. Indeed, protecting coastal ecosystems—ensuring their health and survival—is the essential prerequisite and must receive priority in coastal management at all levels. No other values or uses will be supported with this essential step. To paraphrase Paul Ehrlich, the coastal ecosystem can thrive without economy and development, but the reverse is not possible. We need to exercise new humility and restraint in the use of coastal resources and ensure that, whatever else follows, the essential ecological infrastructure of our coastal and marine environments is protected.

Sustainable development involves concerns not simply about environmental and ecological systems, although they are first-order concerns, but also about social and economic systems. Sustainable coastal development implies an attempt to promote greater livability and an equitable and just distribution of resources and opportunities in the coastal zone.

The feasibility or practicality of achieving coastal sustainability might reasonably be questioned. As population and growth pressures continue to rise in coastal America, isn't sustainability that much harder to achieve? Probably so, yet we believe sustainability remains an important and central goal. What we can aspire to in coastal areas is development and land use patterns that move clearly toward a sustainable coastal zone.

How do we move coastal areas in the direction of greater sustainability, and who (which actors and jurisdictions) should have responsibility for this progress? The existing coastal management framework in the United States has developed and evolved in certain understandable ways. Primary responsibility for regulating and controlling coastal activities and land uses lies with states and, through delegation of authority, local governments. Day-to-day land use management and control reside with the latter. Yet the fundamental national interest in the coastal zone implies a legitimate federal role in encouraging and facilitating sensible state and local management. Coastal management, then, must involve each government level. Each has an important and productive role to play. What follows are some concluding thoughts about the future direction of management activities and strategies at each government level.

An Essential Federal Role

The federal government has a serious and important role to play in the U.S. coastal management framework. We look back to the Stratton Commission's finding that managing the coast is a critical national concern and goal. Despite acceptance of this basic premise, the federal management role has been modest at best: meagerly funded, timid in scope, and conflicted in its goals and objectives. To be sure, the federal Coastal Zone Management Act (CZMA) has served as an important catalyst for the development of state coastal management programs as well as regional and local management efforts. The financial and technical assistance provided by the CZMA, as well as consistency requirements, have served as useful incentives to promote coastal management.

However, many other federal programs and policies influence coastal development patterns, and these generally are not coordinated and often work at cross-purposes. Federal subsidies for coastal development arguably have increased the extent of people and property at risk of coastal hazards and the degradation of sensitive coastal resources, for example. Federal programs and policies should be modified to reduce development subsidies and thereby discourage dangerous and destructive coastal development patterns, to coordinate and integrate federal programs and policies, and to enhance and support state and local coastal management efforts.

We believe federal coastal policy can help bring about more sustainable coastal development patterns. More specifically, future federal coastal zone management efforts aimed at sustainability should include the following action items:

- *Develop and implement a national coastal management policy.* Protection and management of the coastal zone should be a primary national goal. The federal government should prepare a national coastal management policy, which could serve as the basis for and articulation of national coastal management goals and objectives; coordinate the different programs, policies, and actions of many different agencies; and identify a comprehensive management strategy and the necessary steps to ensure that our precious coastal resources and environment are preserved. The policy should take a longer-than-normal timeframe—at least 100 years but perhaps 500 years. The national policy should address the coastal zone in a comprehensive fashion, considering federal actions and policies that occur on land but also near shore and offshore. For instance, the plan should seek to integrate the strategies and objectives of CZMA with those of marine sanctuaries and ocean policy.

- *Work toward integrated national coastal management.* Many coastal commentators have argued for a more integrative framework for coastal management in the United States, and we concur. A national coastal management policy should help, but there are many other steps and strategies that can be undertaken to bring this about. Philosophically, federal agencies should begin to view their missions more broadly. New mechanisms for cooperation and collaboration between agencies are necessary.

- *Make protecting the coastal environment a national priority.* Arguably, as the American population continues to flock to coastal areas, there are no more important environmental tasks than protecting and restoring coastal ecosystems. Protecting the health and integrity of coastal ecosystems should be the first task of coastal planners and planning agencies. Given that by 2025 perhaps three-quarters of the U.S. population will live along the coast, the environmental pressures will be extreme. As growth pressure increases, opportunities for protection and conservation will be lost and restoration will be difficult and costly. Attention to coastal ecosystems should be given priority by federal agencies over other areas and ecosystems less threatened. Indeed, explicitly adopting a *precautionary* policy toward our national coasts is sensible and prudent. Although short-term exploitation, such as expanding offshore drilling to satisfy national energy needs, may represent a quick economic or policy fix, the long-term damage and ecological risks are not acceptable, we believe. Moreover, as we have seen in places such as the Florida Everglades, repairing and restoring damage to coastal ecosys-

tems is a monumental and expensive task. Preventing such degradation and damage in the first instance is the most cost effective and
sensible path.

- *Eliminate or sharply reduce subsidies for dangerous and destructive
  coastal development patterns.* Federal coastal management must
  include a critical assessment and modification of current development
  subsidies and programs that work at cross-purposes to sustainable
  coastal development. The specific program and policy changes that
  should be undertaken include raising National Flood Insurance Program (NFIP) premiums to cover the true market value costs associated
  with coverage, eliminating flood insurance availability in especially
  high-risk coastal locations (e.g., V zones, or within the 60-year erosion zone), eliminating casualty loss deductions under the federal tax
  code, and raising the state and local cost share for disaster assistance
  (e.g., to at least 50% under the Federal Emergency Management
  Agency's public assistance program) unless the jurisdiction is making
  substantial progress to mitigate the impacts of natural hazards. We
  believe coastal property owners should be asked to assume the full
  costs of locating where they choose. The recommendations of the
  recent Heinz Center coastal hazard study to include erosion hazards
  on flood insurance maps and to begin to incorporate the expected
  costs of erosion into the flood insurance rate structure seem a sensible beginning (Heinz Center, 2000a). Moreover, coastal localities that
  choose to encourage or allow risky patterns of development and
  make foolish public investments should be asked to assume the lion's
  share of the costs associated with such decisions. Enactment of the
  Coastal Barrier Resources Act (CBRA), and subsequent expansion,
  represented very positive change at the federal level but could be further expanded. Congress should consider "CBRA-cizing" other sensitive coastal areas (e.g., restricting federal funding for development in
  or near wetlands, estuarine shorelines, sensitive habitat areas) and
  expanding the types of subsidies covered (e.g., bridges and other
  public investments that, though not in a designated unit, induce
  development there).
- *Continue and expand funding and technical assistance for state
  coastal management programs.* The federal government has served
  an important role in facilitating and encouraging state (and local)
  coastal management through financial and technical assistance.
  These funds have been crucial but also meager. Efforts to expand
  funds will further enhance state management capabilities and probably will be repaid many times in reduced property damages, reduced
  environmental destruction, and enhanced public access. In return,

the states should be required to demonstrate progress toward achieving sustainability.

- *Demand performance and accountability.* As observed in Chapter 6, a major criticism of the federal coastal zone management program is that it fails to evaluate coastal states against a clear set of performance standards. Program review is largely procedural and subjective. NOAA must develop clear standards for judging acceptable performance and progress. As a step in this direction, each coastal state should be required to develop and maintain a set of suitable coastal sustainability indicators, which would provide the beginnings of a database for judging progress on a number of key management criteria (e.g., coastal wetlands converted/restored, water quality changes, the amount of property with hurricane hazard zones; see Box 10.1).
- *Expand the focus on mitigation in existing programs; enforce existing*

Box 10.1. A Sample Set of Coastal Sustainability Indicators

LAND AND DEVELOPMENT
- Percentage of coastline urbanized
- Amount of greenfield land developed per year
- Amount or percentage of development occurring on brownfield sites and through coastal infill
- Extent of farmland or rural land lost each year and over time

WATER
- Extent of fishable and swimmable waters; changes in water quality over time
- Extent of pervious and impervious surfaces; changes in pervious and impervious cover

HAZARD EXPOSURE
- Number of structures within 60-year erosion zone
- Number of unelevated structures in floodplain
- Number of older structures built to lower (older) building standards
- Number of hurricane shelters in relation to population

AIR
- Number of days in violation of the federal Clean Air Act

WETLANDS
- Acreage of coastal wetlands converted, each year and over time
- Acreage of existing and protected wetlands

continues

Box 10.1. *Continued*

FOREST AND HABITAT
• Changes in forest cover
• Acreage in forest
• Extent and status of endangered species
• Extent and status of biodiversity hotspots in coastal zone

FISHERIES AND MARINE RESOURCES
• Health of coral reefs, sea grasses, and other marine habitats
• Status and condition of local and regional fisheries
• Number of oil spills

EQUITY AND AFFORDABILITY
• Housing affordability measure
• Unemployment rates in coastal zone

RECREATION AND COASTAL ACCESS
• Number of beach access points (per shoreline mile and/or per capita)
• Acreage of public beach

ENERGY AND RESOURCE USE
• Water consumption (per capita)
• Energy consumption (per capita)
• Recycling rate
• Solid waste generated per year
• Number of treatment plants with tertiary and advanced treatment

TRANSPORTATION AND MOBILITY
• Modal share for walking, bicycling, and transit
• Percentage of built environment bicycle- or pedestrian-friendly

protective programs more stringently. There are a number of existing federal programs, policies, and regulations that have substantial potential for promoting long-term coastal sustainability. Major mitigation requirements exist, for instance, in the Disaster Assistance Act (e.g., state and local mitigation plans) and, if creatively implemented, could do much to promote safer development patterns. A number of existing federal mitigation programs could be expanded and used more effectively. An emphasis on predisaster resilience and hazard avoidance remains the most effective and efficient way to reduce coastal hazards. Moreover, the federal government exercises direct control over certain coastal resources, such as wetlands under Section 404 of the Clean Water Act. Such provisions could be enforced and applied more stringently (e.g., prohibiting all wetlands loss or prohibiting development in buffer zones). There are a number of other mitigation and management provisions of existing federal laws that, consistent with a national coastal management policy, could promote greater coastal sustainability.

- *Expand federal acquisition of sensitive coastal areas.* Although the federal government is not in the best position to exercise direct regulatory control over coastal development, one of its most successful roles has been to preserve coastal lands through acquisition. For example, the establishment of national seashores and wildlife refuges has resulted in the protection of large amounts of coastal land, setting important areas off limits to future growth and development. Federal expenditures for acquisition (direct expenditures or grants to states) are a very efficient use of funds. Some expenditures, though initially costly, can prevent significant federal costs later (e.g., funds that would be spent on disaster assistance) and ensure that limited coastal lands are available to satisfy future environmental and recreational demands of all Americans, not just those who can afford hotels and resorts.

The Leadership Role of States

In the U.S. policy framework, states have taken the lead in coastal management. We expect this pattern to continue because states have both an appropriate geographic scale to consider many coastal problems and the powers necessary to address them. Each coastal state has a somewhat different set of management issues and programs and a somewhat different political and institutional structure, and the U.S. approach has given states flexibility in developing their own appropriate management strategies.

State coastal management programs taken as a whole have accomplished much in the last three decades to encourage more sensitive development patterns. However, there is wide variation in state responses, with some states aggressively managing coastal growth and development and others adopting only minimal management provisions. We believe that each coastal state must establish a minimum set of management requirements, within which local coastal governments might adopt more stringent or innovative requirements if they so choose. We believe states are an important jurisdictional level for establishing and enforcing such standards and for undertaking certain management functions. Specifically, states can help to promote sustainable coastal development patterns in the following ways:

- *Establish minimum coastal development and planning standards.* Many states already impose minimum development standards. We believe these standards should include prohibition of permanent shore-hardening structures (e.g., seawalls, revetments, groins), erosion-based setbacks along ocean fronts, restrictions on building on or near dunes and dune fields, prohibition of development in coastal wetlands and wetland buffer zones, setbacks and other restrictions on development along estuarine shorelines, stormwater management requirements, and beach access requirements. We believe that coastal states should implement these standards more consistently and more aggressively and should consider ways in which existing standards may need to be tightened or expanded. For instance, even the impressive programs of states such as North Carolina could be improved. This state imposes a 60-year setback standard for large buildings, but we believe a minimum 100-year setback is appropriate for all coastal states. Coastal states should also establish minimum substantive and procedural local planning requirements, as many already do. Minimum state regulations are no substitute for detailed local comprehensive planning, and states should ensure that such local plans incorporate certain minimum components (e.g., planning for certain facilities and services, for certain hazardous areas, for hurricane evacuation and postdisaster reconstruction) and are faithfully implemented once adopted and approved.
- *Develop coastal and sustainability indicators.* As mentioned earlier, each state should begin to monitor and carefully analyze over time its progress on a number of key coastal sustainability criteria or measures. Therefore, every state should develop and publicize a comprehensive set of sustainability indicators. Although the choice of specific indicators depends on data cost and availability, we believe a set of such indicators should include the measures suggested in Box 10.1. Several states are now publishing *state of the coast* reports, and new sustainability indicators could be effectively integrated with these ongoing efforts. Such a system of indicators could also be a useful tool in educating the public and guiding state coastal funding decisions.
- *Promote and facilitate strategic retreat.* States are perhaps in the best position to establish and implement a long-term shoreline retreat policy. In light of shoreline erosion, actual and predicted sea level rise,

and the growing recreational and ecological importance of coastal areas, strategic retreat seems the most sensible and cost-effective strategy. Policies that armor the coastline and resist the forces of nature are largely futile and financially and ecologically costly. Where extensive development already exists (e.g., places such as Myrtle Beach, South Carolina; Virginia Beach, Virginia; Ocean City, Maryland) the "softer" approach of beach renourishment may be justified, although it is extremely costly and short-lived. These communities and their residents should be asked to assume the costs associated with not retreating. States can promote strategic retreat in numerous ways. These include many of the policies already mentioned, such as mandatory development setbacks, restrictions on shore-hardening structures, and prohibitions on building immovable structures. Some states, notably Michigan, have developed financial incentives to facilitate relocation of private structures. States should consider a range of programs to assist in relocation (e.g., a state relocation revolving fund, technical assistance).

- *Acquire more coastal land.* The aggressive coastal acquisition programs of a handful of states such as Florida and California suggest the extremely positive role such a strategy can play. Such programs can accomplish a number of objectives, including preservation of important coastal ecological functions, protection of important coastal biodiversity and critical habitat, reservation of lands for future public access and recreation, and prevention of exposure of additional people and property to coastal storms and flooding. States should consider establishing coastal landbanks, which could prioritize and acquire land well in advance and develop steady (and equitable) sources of long-term funding. (A number of sources should be considered, including land transfer taxes, hotel and motel taxes, and sales tax.)
- *Reduce state subsidies and development-inducing investments.* States should curtail subsidies and investments in the coastal zone, adopting their own state versions of CBRA and ensuring that public expenditures in the coastal zone (e.g., highway and road construction, beach renourishment) do not exacerbate hazardous and wasteful development patterns. Other states should follow Florida's lead in adopting a set of infrastructure policies (under the 1985 Omnibus Growth Management Act) designed to reduce development pressures on barrier islands and high-risk coastal hazard areas.
- *Undertake mapping and database assistance.* States are in an excellent position to develop the databases and resource mapping essential for managing coastal development in a sustainable fashion. States

often are in the best position to collect and analyze data on water quality, wildlife habitat, fisheries, and high-hazard risk zones. Such efforts should focus on enhancing understanding of trends and of relationships between degradation and land use patterns and on providing local governments and relevant state agencies with usable and accurate maps by which to make land use and management decisions. The federal government has also assisted in this regard and will continue to play an important role (e.g., producing flood hazard maps under NFIP and funding research under the National Estuary Program [NEP]), as will local governments. Especially important is the development of a statewide geographic information system, which could assist greatly in comparing multiple resource values and integrating transportation, housing, land use, and other decisions affecting the coastal environment.

Managing the Coast at the Local and Regional Level

Local government, perhaps more than any other jurisdictional level, has the potential to change conventional development patterns in coastal America and move human settlement patterns in the direction of sustainability. This is so for several reasons. Historically, land use decisions have been viewed largely as a matter of local prerogative. It is at this level that officials have the management tools, and indeed the opportunity, to influence actual development projects and community-level land use patterns. Although states can and should establish minimum development standards, it is neither technically nor politically feasible for them to address detailed land use matters. Therefore, much responsibility for detailed coastal management in the United States lies, and probably must lie, at the local government level. We believe that coastal localities have tremendous potential for reorienting coastal development and growth.

Specifically, we believe that coastal localities must embrace long-term sustainability as the overarching and unifying theme for all future planning and management. We believe there is much to recommend the vision of sustainable coastal communities, and in Chapter 8 we outlined and discussed in detail what we believe a sustainable coastal community is or could be. To summarize, we believe that sustainable coastal communities should do the following:

• *Develop a sustainable community plan.* Although many coastal localities have already developed land use or comprehensive plans, most have not adopted sustainability as a central goal, nor have they sought to manage or plan in a way that promotes sustainability. Very often such plans represent the most rudimentary classification of land uses and seem designed to facilitate or accommodate conventional destructive and wasteful growth patterns. Coastal sustainability plans would advance a different philosophy, one that seeks fundamentally to reduce the extent and amount of land development, to reduce the resulting human footprint, to reduce the extent of people and property at risk, and to minimize pollution and destruction of the natural environment.

- *Include a sustainability audit as an initial step in each local plan.* Such an audit could include an analysis of the extent to which the community uses resources (water, energy, land), generates waste (water and air pollution and solid waste), places people and property at risk for natural disasters (e.g., amount of development in floodplains), and so on. Future land use and development decisions should then be judged and evaluated according to these important sustainability indices. Each plan should state the strategies and actions to be taken to enhance sustainability as gauged by these measures.
- *Move beyond conventional zoning and land use controls.* Development in coastal regions is not unlike development in many other areas of the country. It is characterized by low-density, wasteful urban sprawl, highly consumptive use of open space and resource lands, and heavy dependence on the automobile. As well as being environmentally destructive, such patterns generally do not result in the creation of "communities" or built environments that are highly livable and exude a sense of place. We believe that future coastal land use patterns should reflect a different vision, one that seeks to limit low-density development. Such a vision should seek to reduce the amount of land consumed in development, guide development and growth into or around existing towns and, where possible, promote infill and adaptive reuse. Such patterns should emphasize mixed-use towns and cities that reduce use of the automobile, incorporate public spaces, and create a sense of place and community. Where possible, we believe, future coastal development should build on the existing network of coastal cities and towns before allowing development of outlying and undeveloped areas. Coastal localities must critically assess the existing policy that determines the characteristics of future development (e.g., quantity, quality, location, design) to see how such patterns could be encouraged. Localities should explore a variety of land use and development measures, including traditional neighborhood ordinances, urban growth

boundaries, clustering standards, transfer of development rights, and land banks.

- *Develop integrative and holistic strategies.* The principle of sustainable coastal communities clearly implies strategies and approaches that are integrative and holistic and look for ways to combine policies, programs, and design solutions to accomplish multiple objectives. Coastal localities can no longer look at transportation decisions apart from land use decisions or affordable housing apart from environmental protection. For instance, growth containment in coastal towns and cities can reduce public facility costs, promote more affordable housing, create vibrant communities, and reduce risk. Such patterns can be furthered by integrating and coordinating decisions about transportation, land use, and a variety of other decisions. The idea of sustainable coastal communities also implies the need to view the community in terms of the resources consumed and waste streams generated by it. A sustainable coastal community is one that aggressively looks for ways to reduce water and energy consumption (resources generally in short supply), reduce waste (air and water pollution, solid waste), promote use of renewables (e.g., solar), and promote recycling and reuse where possible.

- *Focus on coastal restoration as well as preservation.* An important new element of the coastal management at all levels is the emphasis on restoration of coastal habitats and environments. As there are fewer opportunities to protect and preserve coastal resources, there will be greater opportunities to restore damaged and degraded coastal ecosystems. Opportunities will exist on both small and large scales. Plans under way to restore the natural function of the Florida Everglades are an example of the latter, and the restoration of Crissy Field (described in Chapter 9) is an example of the former. Coastal localities, especially, will have many opportunities to engage in restoration, and it should become a more central element in local coastal planning.

- *Reduce the community's overall ecological footprint.* Although more effectively managing land use and growth is an important strategy, coastal communities should recognize that there are a host of other ways in which, through their operation and governance, they can reduce their overall ecological footprints. As we saw in Chapter 8, these actions can include such things as ecological procurement policies, integrated pest management, and policies for promoting more environmentally friendly mobility by city employees, among many others. Communities such as Arcata, California, illustrate that applying a sustainability lens to a variety of local activities can result in significant ecological achievements, including a sustainably managed community forest and use of natural marshlands to treat wastewater. Coastal communities should look critically at the entire spectrum of policies, actions, and decisions that can affect the environment and think more broadly and boldly about what a commitment to sustainable development entails.

- *Expect more from private developers.* As the many examples of positive coastal development presented in Chapter 9 demonstrate, it is possible (and economically practical) for coastal communities to expect and demand a higher standard from private coastal development. Private buildings and developments can be expected to use dramatically less energy, water, and other resources, to use local materials, and to impose much less damage on the coastal environment. Coastal localities committed to sustainable development should set high standards for new growth, and a mix of mandates and incentives can prod private builders and developers to do much better than conventional development. Localities might specify a minimal level of Leadership in Energy and Environmental Design (LEED) certification and provide a density bonus for buildings and projects that go beyond the minimum standards, for example.
- *Recognize the increasing importance of regional institutions and strategies for sustainability.* As discussed in Chapter 7, many coastal resources and problems extend beyond local government boundaries and necessitate regional solutions. We believe that mechanisms for regional cooperation, planning, and management in the coastal zone will become increasingly important in the future. Use of mechanisms such as Special Area Management Plans, estuarine management conferences (under the NEP), and regional planning councils will become increasingly important, and local governments must increasingly be willing to assume a regional perspective where appropriate.
- *Promote public education.* Achieving more sustainable patterns of development and consumption in coastal communities will take a new commitment to educating and engaging the public. Reducing nonpoint agricultural pollutants, for instance, takes commitment and buy-in from farmers. Reducing energy consumption in buildings takes education of developers, builders, and homebuyers. Commitment to protecting and preserving coastal marshes requires a citizenry that understands their ecological and economic value and cares about their condition. Many exemplary models of coastal environmental education now exist, such as Puget Sound's Public

Involvement and Education initiative (PIE) and the Center for Sustainable Living in Charleston, and educating the coastal public must be given a high priority at the local level (as well as at state and national levels).

A Final Note: Defending a Collaborative Framework for Sustainable Coastal Development

In conclusion, it is clear that progress toward sustainable coastal development depends on the concerted efforts of each jurisdictional level: federal, state, regional, and local. There is a natural tendency for some to call for a unified approach, one in which coastal management responsibilities are vested primarily in one agency or jurisdiction. In the U.S. system of government this is unfeasible politically and legally and probably is undesirable. Each jurisdictional level has a special interest and contribution to make to coastal management, and much can be accomplished at each level. Moreover, the coastal management collaboration must extend to the private sector, recognizing the important role played by such groups as the Nature Conservancy and the important influence and power exerted by banks and other financial institutions, developers, and private landowners. Although the collaborative framework is not without its limitations, it holds great promise to move coastal areas toward sustainability.

Bibliography

Adair, Dorothy. 1995. "Humane Habitats." *In Context*. Found at: http://www.context.org/ICLIB/IC42/Adair.htm.

Alexander, C. E., M. A. Broutman, and D. W. Field. 1986. *An Inventory of Coastal Wetlands of the U.S.* Washington, DC: NOAA.

Aquatic Resources Conservation Group. 2000. "Socioeconomic Impacts of Growth Pressure in Selected Seasonal/Resort Communities: Document Analysis and Interview Summaries, Aspen, Colorado and Nantucket, Massachusetts." Final report, May 22, Seattle, Washington.

Armingeon, Neil. 1991. "An Analysis of the National Estuarine Reserve Research System," in *Evaluation of the National Coastal Zone Management Program*. Chapel Hill: Center for Urban and Regional Studies and the Department of City and Regional Planning, University of North Carolina at Chapel Hill.

Arnold, Chester L., Jr., and James Gibbons. 1996. "Impervious Surface Coverage: The Ekegence of a Key Environmental Indicator." *Journal of the American Planning Association* 62(2), 243–258.

Audubon International. 2001. "Audubon Signature Program." Found at: http://www.audubonintl.org/programs/signature/index.htm.

Ballenger, Laurie. 1993. "In the Wake of *Lucas vs. South Carolina Coastal Council:* North Carolina's Oceanfront Setback Regulations." Ocean and Coastal Law Seminar, University of North Carolina at Chapel Hill Law School.

Barnes, R. S. K., ed. 1977. *The Coastline*. London: Wiley.

Beatley, Timothy. 1992. *Hurricane Hugo and Shoreline Retreat: Evaluating the Effectiveness of the South Carolina Beachfront Management Act*. Final report to the National Science Foundation, September.

Beatley, Timothy. 1994. *Habitat Conservation Planning: Urban Growth and Endangered Species*. Austin: University of Texas Press.

Beatley, Timothy. 2000. *Green Urbanism: Learning from European Cities*. Washington, DC: Island Press.

Beatley, Timothy, and David J. Brower. 1993. "Sustainability Meets Mainstreet: Principles to Live—and Plan—By." *Planning*, May, 16–19.

Beatley, Timothy, David J. Brower, and Lou Ann Brower. 1988. *Managing Growth: Small Communities and Rural Areas*. Chapel Hill: Center for Urban and Regional Studies, University of North Carolina at Chapel Hill.

Beller, W., P. d'Ayala, and P. Hein. 1990. *Sustainable Development and Environmental Management of Small Islands*. Park Ridge, NJ: Parthenon Publishing Group.

Berke, Philip. 1989. "Hurricane Vertical Shelter Policy: The Experience of Two States." *Coastal Management* 17, 193–218.

Bernd-Cohen, Tina, and Melissa Gordon. 1998. "State Coastal Management Effectiveness in Protecting Beaches, Dunes, Bluffs, Rocky Shores: A National Overview." [Online] Available: http://www.ocrm.nos.noaa.gov/czm/resource.html.

Bookman, Charles A., Thomas J. Culliton, and Maureen A. Warren. 1999. "Trends in U.S. Coastal Regions, 1970–1998." Addendum to the Proceedings, "Trends and Future Challenges for U.S. National Ocean and Coastal Policy." U.S. Department of Commerce, National Ocean Service, Washington, DC.

Brooke, Steven. 1995. *Seaside*. Gretna, LA: Pelican Publishing Company.

Brower, David J., and Daniel S. Carol. 1984. *Coastal Zone Management as Land Planning*. Washington, DC: National Planning Association.

Bunce, Leah, Jessica Cogan, Kim Davis, and Laura Taylor. 1993. "National Marine Sanctuaries: Critique in Light of the 1992 Amendments." April 15. (Unpublished classroom paper.)

Burby, Raymond J. 1990. "Reforming Relief: An Invited Comment." *Natural Hazards Observer* 15(1), 1–2.

Bush, David M., Orrin H. Pilkey, Jr., and William J. Neal. 1996. *Living by the Rules of the Sea*. Durham, NC: Duke University Press.

Caldwell, Lynton K., ed. 1985. *Perspectives on Ecosystem Management for the Great Lakes*. New York: State University of New York Press.

Caldwell, Lynton K. 1998. *The National Environmental Policy Act: An Agenda for the Future*. Bloomington: Indiana University Press.

California Coastal Commission. 1987. *The California Coastal Resource Guide*. Berkeley, CA: University of California Press.

Calkins, Meg. 2001. "LEEDing the Way: A Look at the Way Landscape Architects Are Using the LEED Green Building Rating System." *Landscape Architecture,* May 2001, 36–43, 90–92.

Carmichael, O. M. 1974. "Transferable Development Rights as a Basis for Land Use Control." *Florida State Law Review* 2, 35.

Carter, R. W. G. 1990. *Coastal Environments*. London: Academic Press.

Center for Marine Conservation. 2001. "Conserving America's Oceans: A Blueprint." Found at: http://www.cmc-ocean.org/bp2001.pdf.

Center for Sustainable Living. 2000. Web site: http://www.113Calhoun.org.

Center for Urban and Regional Studies. 1991. *Evaluation of the National Coastal Zone Management Program*. Newport, OR: National Coastal Resources Research and Development Institute.

Center for Urban Policy Research. 1998. *Eastward Ho! Development Futures: Paths to Growth,* New Brunswick, NJ: Rutgers University.

Center of Excellence for Sustainable Development. Undated. "Jordan Commons, Dade County, Florida." Found at: http://www.sustainable.doe.gov/success/jordan.shtml.

CEQ (Council on Environmental Quality, Executive Office of the President). 1997. "NEPA: A Study of Effectiveness After 25 Years." [Online] Available: ceq.eh.doe.gov/nepa/nepanet.htm.

Chabreck, Robert A. 1988. *Coastal Marshes: Ecology and Wildlife Management.* Minneapolis: University of Minnesota Press.

Chesapeake Bay Foundation (CBF). 2000a. "Philip Merrill Environmental Center," report on the new headquarters building, Annapolis, MD.

Chesapeake Bay Foundation (CBF). 2000b. "CBF's Headquarters Recognized as One of Nation's Greenest Buildings." CBF news brief, November 15.

Christie, Donna, and Paul Johnson. 1990. "State Ocean Policy Initiatives in Florida." *Coastal Development* 18, 283–296.

City of Santa Monica. 2000. "Staff memo: Recommendation to Authorize Staff to Issue a Request for Proposals for the Rehabilitation, Renovation or Development of Affordable Lodging in or Adjacent to the Coastal Zone within the City of Santa Monica," Memo to Mayor at City Council, January 11. Found at: http://pen.ci.santa-monica.ca.us/cityclerk/council/agendas/2000.

City of Virginia Beach, Va. 1997. *Comprehensive Plan* adopted November 4.

Clark, John R. 1977. *Coastal Ecosystem Management: A Technical Manual for the Conservation of Coastal Zone Resources.* New York: Wiley.

Clark, John R. 1996. *Coastal Zone Management Handbook.* Boca Raton, FL: Lewis Publishers.

Clayton, K. M. 1995. "Predicting Sea Level Rise and Managing the Consequences," in *Environmental Science for Environmental Management* (T. O'Riordan, ed.). London: Prentice-Hall.

Cleary, William J., and Tara P. Marden. 1999. *Shifting Shorelines: A Pictorial Atlas of North Carolina Inlets.* Raleigh: UNC Sea Grant, North Carolina State University.

Congressional Research Service (CRS). 1997. *Wetland Mitigation Banking: Status and Prospects.* Washington, DC: CRS.

Conservation Foundation. 1976. *The Sanibel Plan.* Washington, DC: Conservation Foundation.

Costonis, John. 1973. "Development Rights Transfer: An Exploratory Essay." *Yale Law Journal* 83, 75–128.

Coughlin, Robert, and John Keene, eds. 1981. *The Protection of Farmland: A Reference Guidebook for State and Local Governments.* Washington, DC: U.S. Government Printing Office.

Culliton, Thomas J. 1998. "Population: Distribution, Density and Growth," NOAA, found online at: http://state_of_coast.noaa.gov/bulletins/html/pop_01/pop.html.

Culliton, Thomas J., et al. 1990. *Fifty Years of Population Growth along the Nation's Coast, 1960–2010*. Rockville, MD: NOAA.

Cuyvers, Luc. 1984. *Ocean Uses and Their Regulation,* New York: Wiley.

Davies, J. L. 1973. *Geographical Variation in Coastal Development.* New York: Hafner Publishing Company.

Dean, Cornelea. 1999. *Against the Tide: The Battle for America's Beaches*. New York: Columbia University Press.

Dolan, Robert, and Harry Lins. 1987. "Beaches and Barrier Islands." *Scientific American* 257, July, 68–77.

Dowling, Timothy J. 2001. "U.S. Supreme Court Further Muddles Takings Clause: Press Statement of Timothy J. Dowling." Community Rights Council [Online] Available: http://www.communityrights.org/palazzolostatement. html.

Dressler, J. H. 1979. "Agricultural Land Preservation in California: Time for a New View." *Ecology Law Quarterly* 8.

Edgerton, Lynne T. 1991. *The Rising Tide: Global Warming and World Sea Levels*. Washington, DC: Island Press.

Environmental News Network. 2001. "South Carolina Developers See Green in Green." Environmental News Network, April 29.

EPA (Environmental Protection Agency). 2001. "Brownfields Definition." [Online] Available: http://www.epa.gov/swerosps/bf.

Etchart, Gabriela. 1995. "Mitigation Banks: A Strategy for Sustainable Development." *Coastal Management* 23(3), 223–237.

FEMA (Federal Emergency Management Agency). 1986. *Coastal Construction Manual*. February. Washington, DC: FEMA.

FEMA (Federal Emergency Management Agency). 1992a. "Coastal Communities with V-Zones, Cumulative Total from 1978." Special computer run performed by FEMA for the authors, November. Washington, DC: FEMA.

FEMA (Federal Emergency Management Agency). 1992b. "Estimating Probabilities of Exceeding Given Levels of Flood Insurance Losses in a One Year Period." August 4. Washington, DC: FEMA.

FEMA (Federal Emergency Management Agency). 1992c. *National Flood Insurance Program Community Rating System Coordinators Manual*. July. Washington, DC: FEMA.

FEMA (Federal Emergency Management Agency.) 1992d. "NFIP Financial Data and Related Information." Memorandum and information packet, September 2. Washington, DC: FEMA.

FEMA (Federal Emergency Management Agency). 1998. "National Mitigation Strategy." [Online] Available: www.fema.gov/mit/intro.htm.

FEMA (Federal Emergency Management Agency). 2000a. "1999 NFIP Stakeholder's Report." [Online] Available: http://www.fema.gov/nfip/sreport. htm.

FEMA (Federal Emergency Management Agency). 2000b. *Coastal Construction Manual,* FEMA-55. Washington, DC: FEMA.

FEMA (Federal Emergency Management Agency). 2000c. "Evaluation of CRS-Credited Activities During Hurricane Floyd." [Online] Available: www.fema.gov/nfip/crs.htm.

Finnell, Gilbert L., Jr. 1985. "Intergovernmental Relationships in Coastal Land Management." *Natural Resources Journal* 25.

Florida Department of Natural Resources. Undated. *Inside the Florida Keys National Marine Sanctuary.* Tallahassee: Florida Department of Natural Resources.

Florida Power and Light Company. 2000. "Habitat for Humanity, Florida Power and Light Team Up to Build Energy-Efficient Houses for South Dade Families," press release, March 14, found at: www.fpl.com/news/2000/contents/00024.shtml.

Fox, G. M., and B. R. Davis. 1978. "Density Bonus Zoning to Provide Low and Moderate Cost Housing." *Hastings Constitutional Law Quarterly* 3.

French, Peter W. 1997. *Coastal and Estuarine Management.* New York: Routledge.

GAO (General Accounting Office). 1992. "Coastal Barriers: Development Occurring Despite Prohibition against Federal Assistance." Report GAO/RCED-92-115, July. Washington, DC: GAO.

Gaul, Gilbert M., and Anthony R. Wood. 2000. "Along the Water, Disaster Waiting for Their Moment." *Philadelphia Inquirer,* March 5.

Gibson, Tom. 2001. "Seeking an Ideal Environment." *Progressive Engineer.* Web site: www.progressiveengineer.com.

Godschalk, David R. 1979. *Constitutional Issues in Growth Management.* Chicago: APA Planners Press.

Godschalk, David R. 1984. *Impacts of the Coastal Barrier Resources Act: A Pilot Study.* Washington, DC: Office of Ocean and Coastal Resource Management, NOAA.

Godschalk, David R. 1987. "The 1982 Coastal Barrier Resources Act: A New Federal Policy Tact," in *Cities on the Beach* (Rutherford Platt, ed.). Chicago: University of Chicago Press.

Godschalk, David R. 1992. "Implementing Coastal Zone Management: 1972–1990." *Coastal Management* 20, 93–116.

Godschalk, David R. 1998. *Coastal Hazards Mitigation: Public Notification, Expenditure Limitations, and Hazard Areas Acquisition.* Chapel Hill: Center for Urban and Regional Studies, University of North Carolina at Chapel Hill.

Godschalk, David R., and Kathryn Cousins. 1985. "Coastal Management: Planning on the Edge." *Journal of the American Planning Association* 51, 263–265.

Godschalk, David R., Timothy Beatley, Phillip R. Berke, David J. Brower, and Edward J. Kaiser. 1999. *Natural Hazard Mitigation: Recasting Disaster Policy and Planning.* Washington, DC: Island Press.

Godschalk, David R., David J. Brower, and Timothy Beatley. 1989. *Catastrophic Coastal Storms: Hazard Mitigation and Development Management.* Durham, NC: Duke University Press.

Good, James W., John W. Weber, James W. Charland, John V. Olson, and Kelly A. Chapin. 1998. *National Coastal Zone Management Effectiveness Study: Protecting Estuaries and Coastal Wetlands.* Final Report to the Office of Ocean and Coastal Resources Management, NOAA. Oregon Sea Grant Special Report PI-98-001, Corvallis, OR.

Goodwin, Robert F. 1997. "The Effectiveness of Coastal Zone Management Programs in Redeveloping Deteriorating Urban Ports and Waterfronts." [Online] Available: http://www.ocrm.nos.noaa.gov/czm/resource.html.

Gordon, David L. A. 1997. "Financing Urban Waterfront Redevelopment." *Journal of the American Planning Association* 63(2), 244–265.

Gray, William M. 1999. "Climate Influences on U.S. Landfalling Hurricanes Frequency and Destruction," Summary Report to the U.S. House of Representatives Sub-committee on Housing and Community Opportunity (given April 28, 1999). Found at: http://www.house.gov/banking/42899gra.html.

Green Building News. 2000. "Chesapeake Bay Building First to Achieve Top Rating." December 6.

Grenell, Peter. 1988. "The Once and Future Experience of the California Coastal Conservancy." *Coastal Management* 16, 13–20.

Griggs, Gary B., James E. Pepper, and Martha E. Jordan. 1992. *California's Coastal Hazards: A Critical Assessment of Existing Land Use Policies and Practices.* Berkeley: California Policy Seminar, University of California.

Gustafson, Gregory C., and L. T. Wallace. 1975. "Differential Assessment as Land Use Policy: The California Case." *Journal of the American Institute of Planners* 41(6), 379–389.

Hagman, Donald, and Dean Misczynski. 1979. *Windfalls for Wipeouts.* Chicago: American Society of Planning Officials.

Hammatt, Heather. 2001. "Avoiding Suburbia: Developing a New "Small Town" in the South Carolina Cow Country." *Landscape Architecture,* May, 50–55, 97–98.

Hansom, J. D. 1988. *Coasts.* New York: Cambridge University Press.

Heath, Milton S. 1974. "A Legislative History of the Coastal Area Management Act." *North Carolina Law Review* 53, 345.

Heinricht, Mary M. 1996. "Forming a Partnership to Preserve Resources: The Virginia Beach Agricultural Reserve Program." Paper presented to Watershed 96. Found at: http://www.epa.gov.

Heinz Center for Science, Economics, and the Environment. 2000a. *Evaluation of Erosion Hazards in the United States.* Washington, DC: H. John Heinz III Center for Science, Economics, and the Environment.

Heinz Center for Science, Economics, and the Environment. 2000b. *The Hidden Cost of Coastal Hazards: Implications for Risk Assessment and Mitigation.*

Washington, DC: H. John Heinz III Center for Science, Economics, and the Environment.

Henrichsen, Don. 1999. "The Coastal Population Explosion," in *Trends and Future Challenges for U.S. National Ocean and Coastal Policy* (Biliana Cicin-Sain, Robert W. Knecht, and Nancy Foster, eds.). Washington, DC: National Ocean Service, NOAA.

Hobbie, John E. 2000. *Estuarine Science: A Synthetic Approach to Research and Practice.* Washington, DC: Island Press.

Horton, Tom. 1991. *Turning the Tide: Saving the Chesapeake Bay.* Washington, DC: Island Press.

Houghton, J. T., G. J. Jenkins, and J. J. Ephraums, eds. 1990. *Climate Change: The IPCC Scientific Assessment.* Cambridge, Mass.: Cambridge University Press.

Houlahan, John. 1989. "Comparison of State Coastal Setback to Manage Development in Coastal Hazard Areas." *Coastal Management* 17.

Hout, Eldon. 1990. "Ocean Policy Development in the State of Oregon." *Coastal Management* 18, 255–266.

Hudgens, Daniel. 1999. "Adapting the National Flood Insurance Program to Relative Sea Level Rise." *Coastal Management* 27(4), 367–375.

IBHS (Institute for Business and Home Safety). 1999. "Summary of State-Mandated Building Codes." [Online] Available: http://www.ibhs.org/ibhs2/html/publications/Default.htm.

Imperial, Mark T., and Timothy M. Hennessey. 1996. "An Ecosystem-Based Approach to Managing Estuaries: An Assessment of the National Estuary Program." *Coastal Management* 24(2), 115–135.

Imperial, Mark T., Tim Hennessey, and Donald Robadue, Jr. 1993. "The Evolution of Adaptive Management for Estuarine Ecosystems: The National Estuary Program and Its Precursors." *Ocean and Coastal Management* 20, 147–180.

Inman, D. L., and C. E. Nordstrom. 1971. "On the Tectonic and Morphologic Classification of Coasts." *Journal of Geology* 79, 1–21.

Institute for Environmental Negotiation. 1991. *Management of Cumulative Impacts in Virginia: Identifying the Issues and Assessing the Opportunities.* Charlottesville, VA: IEN.

IPCC (Intergovernmental Panel on Climate Change). 2001. "Summary for Policymakers," A Report of Working Group I of the Intergovernmental Panel on Climate Change. New York: UNEP.

Joint Task Force on the Hazard Mitigation Grant Program. 1992. *The Hazard Mitigation Grant Program: An Evaluation Report.* Prepared by NEMA, ASFM, and FEMA. September.

Jones, E., and W. Stolzenberg. 1990. *Building in Coastal Barrier Resource Systems.* Washington, DC: National Wildlife Federation.

Kaiser, Edward J. 2001. *Steering Barrier Island Communities Toward a More Sustainable Future.* Raleigh, NC: North Carolina Division of Emergency Management.

Kalo, Joseph. 1990. *Coastal and Ocean Law*. Houston, TX: John Marshall Publishing Company.

Kalo, Joseph J. 2000. "The Changing Face of the Shoreline: Public and Private Rights to the Natural and Nourished Dry Sand Beaches of North Carolina." *North Carolina Law Review* 78, 1869.

Kaufman, Wallace, and Orrin Pilkey. 1979. *The Beaches Are Moving: The Drowning of America's Shoreline*. Garden City, NJ: Doubleday.

Keene, John, David Berry, Robert Coughlin, James Farnam, Eric Kelly, Thomas Plaut, and Ann Louise Strong. 1976.*Untaxing open space: An evaluation of the effectiveness of differential assessment of farms and open space,* Washington, DC: Council on Environmental Quality.

Klarin, Paul, and Marc Hershman. 1990. "Response of Coastal Zone Management Programs to Sea Level Rise in the United States." *Coastal Management* 18, 143–165.

Klee, Gary A. 1999. *The Coastal Environment: Toward Integrated Coastal and Marine Sanctuary Management*. Upper Saddle River, NJ: Prentice-Hall.

Knott, John L., Jr. 2001. "Transition of Dewees Island to Property Owners." *Dewees Island Chronicles* 9(5), October 27, p. 2.

Knox, George A. 1986. *Estuarine Ecosystems: A System Approach,* Vol. I. Boca Raton, FL: CRC Press.

Krasner, Jeffrey. 2001. "Offshore Wind Farm Blows into Cape View." *Boston Globe,* July 28, p. A1.

Kusler, Jon, et al. 1982. *Innovative Local Floodplain Management: A Summary of Local Experience*. Boulder: Institute of Behavioral Science, University of Colorado.

Leatherman, Stephen P. 1989. "Impact of Accelerated Sea Level Rise on Beaches and Coastal Wetlands," in *Global Climate Change Linkages* (James C. White, ed.). New York: Elsevier Science Publishing.

Lehner, Peter H., George P. Aponte Clark, Diane M. Cameron, and Andrew G. Frank. 1999. *Stormwater Strategies: Community Responses to Runoff Pollution*. New York: NRDC.

Lippson, Alice Jane, and Robert L. Lippson. 1984. *Life in the Chesapeake Bay*. Baltimore, MD: Johns Hopkins University Press.

Lowry, Kem. 1990. "Ocean Management in Hawaii." *Coastal Management* 18, 233–254.

Maine SPO (State Planning Office). 2000. "The Maine Coastal Program: Sustaining Maine's Coastal Resources and Economy." [Online] Available: http://www.state.me.us/spo/mcp/aboutcoast.htm.

Manning, Billy R. 1988. "Building Codes and Enforcement by Coastal States and Territories of the US." National Committee on Property Insurance.

Marlowe, Howard. 1999. "Assessing the Economic Benefits of America's Coastal Regions," in *Trends and Future Challenges for U.S. National Ocean and*

Coastal Policy (Biliana Cicin-Sain, Robert W. Knecht, and Nancy Foster, eds.). Washington, DC: National Ocean Service, NOAA.

McElyea, William D., David R. Godschalk, and David J. Brower. 1982. *Before the Storm: Managing Development to Reduce Hurricane Damages*. Chapel Hill: Center for Urban and Regional Studies, University of North Carolina at Chapel Hill.

Merchant, Mark. 1998. "Land Bank Failure Surprises Islands." *Cape Cod Times,* January 29. Found at: http://www.capeonline.com.

Merriam, Dwight. 1978. "Making TDR Work." *North Carolina Law Review* 56.

Michaels, Sarah. 2001. "Making Collaborative Watershed Management Work: The Confluence of State and Regional Initiatives." *Environmental Management* 27(1), 27–35.

Millsap, B. A., J. A. Gore, D. E. Runde, and S. I. Cerulean, 1990. "Setting Priorities for the Conservation of Fish and Wildlife Species in Florida." *Wildlife Monographs* No. 111, July.

Mohney, David, and Keller Easterling, eds. 1991. *Seaside: Making a Town in America*. Princeton, NJ: Princeton University Press.

National Commission on the Environment. 1993. *Choosing a Sustainable Future*. Washington, DC: Island Press.

National Committee on Property Insurance. 1988. *America's Vanishing Coastlines,* October. Boston: National Committee on Property Insurance.

National Research Council of the U.S. 1990. *Managing Coastal Erosion*. Washington, DC: National Academy Press.

National Research Council of the U.S. 1995. *Beach Renourishment and Protection*. Washington, DC: National Academy Press.

National Research Council of the U.S. 1999. *New Strategies for America's Watersheds*. Washington, DC: National Academy Press.

National Research Council of the U.S. 2001. *Marine Protected Areas: Tools for Sustaining Ocean Ecosystems*. Washington, DC: National Academy Press.

National Research Council of the U.S. and the Royal Society of Canada. 1985. *The Great Lakes Water Quality Agreement: An Evolving Instrument for Ecosystem Management*. Washington, DC: National Academy Press.

National Safety Council. 2000. *Coastal Challenges: A Guide to Coastal and Marine Issues*. Washington, DC: National Safety Council's Environmental Health Center.

Natural Resources Defense Council (NRDC). 1999. *Stormwater Strategies: Community Responses to Runoff Pollution*. New York, NY: NRDC.

Natural Resources Defense Council (NRDC). 2001. *Stormwater Strategies: Community Responses to Runoff Pollution,* New York: NRDC.

The Natural Step. 2001. "The Natural Step's Four System Conditions." [Online] Available: http://www.naturalstep.org.

The Nature Conservancy (TNC). Undated. *The Nature Conservancy's Conservation Business Alliance*. Nassawadox: Virginia Coast Reserve.

NCSU (North Carolina State University) Water Quality Group. "Wetlands Loss and Degradation." *WaterSHEDSS*. [Online] Available: http://h2osparc.wq. ncsu.edu/info/wetlands/wetloss.html.

Neal, William J. 1984. *Living with the South Carolina Shore*. Durham, NC: Duke University Press.

Newman, Morris. 2000. "Gold in the Water: Waterfront Brownfields Along the Eastern Seaboard." *Brownfield News* 4(6).

Nichols, Robert. 1995. "Coastal Megacities and Climate Change." *Geojournal* 37(3), 369–379.

NOAA (Coastal Services Center). 1997. "Alabama Coastal Hazards Assessment," CD-ROM, Charleston, SC.

NOAA (National Oceanic and Atmospheric Administration). 1990. *Biennial Report to Congress on Coastal Zone Management*. Washington, DC: Office of Ocean and Coastal Resource Management, April.

NOAA (National Oceanic and Atmospheric Administration). 1998. "Federal Program Pumps Funds into Wetland Restoration." *Coastal Services* 1(2).

NOAA (National Oceanic and Atmospheric Administration). 1999a. "Rhode Island Designates All Coastal Waters as 'No Discharge Areas.'" *Coastal Services* 2(3).

NOAA (National Oceanic and Atmospheric Administration). 1999b. "State Enhancement Grant Assessments and Strategies: Energy/Government Facility Siting." [Online] Available: http://www.ocrm.nos.noaa.gov/czm/resource.html.

NOAA (National Oceanic and Atmospheric Administration). 1999c. "State Enhancement Grant Assessments and Strategies: Ocean Governance." [Online] Available: http://www.ocrm.nos.noaa.gov/czm/resource.html.

NOAA (National Oceanic and Atmospheric Administration). 1999d. "State Enhancement Grant Assessments and Strategies: Public Access." [Online] Available: http://www.ocrm.nos.noaa.gov/czm/resource.html.

NOAA (National Oceanic and Atmospheric Administration). 1999e. "State Enhancement Grant Assessments and Strategies: Special Area Management Plans." [Online] Available: http://www.ocrm.nos.noaa.gov/czm/resource.html.

NOAA (National Oceanic and Atmospheric Administration). 1999f. "Sustaining America's Coastal Communities and Resources: A Strategic Framework for the Coastal Zone Management Program." [Online] Available: http://www. ocrm.nos.noaa.gov/czm/national.html.

NOAA (National Oceanic and Atmospheric Administration). 2000. *State, Territory, and Commonwealth Beach Nourishment Programs: A National Overview*. Office of Ocean and Coastal Resource Management Program Policy Series Technical Document 00-01, April.

NOAA (National Oceanic and Atmospheric Administration). 2001. "Are We Paving Over Paradise? Maine's Efforts at Directing Development." *Coastal Services,* May/April. [Online] Available: http://www.csc.noaa.gov/magazine/2001/02/maine.html.

North Carolina Administrative Code. 2002. Coastal Management, State Guidelines for Areas of Environmental Concern, General Use Standards for Ocean Hazard Areas. T15A: 07H. 0306 (j).

North Carolina Division of Coastal Management (NCDCM). 1988. *A Guide to Protecting Coastal Resources through the CAMA Permit Program.* Raleigh, NC: NCDCM.

North Carolina Division of Emergency Management (NCDCM). 1998. *Tools and Techniques: Putting a Hazard Mitigation Plan to Work.* Raleigh, NC: NCDEM.

Nummedal, D. 1983. "Barrier Islands," in *CRC Handbook of Coastal Processes and Erosion* (P. D. Komar, ed.). Boca Raton, FL: CRC Press.

OCRM (Office of Ocean and Coastal Resource Management). (undated) CZM Approval Date, Shoreline Miles, Coastal County Populations. [Online] Available: http://www.ocrm.nos.noaa.gov/pdf/statestats.pdf.

Oregon Division of State Lands. 2000. "Wetland Mitigation Banking Guidebook for Oregon." [Online] Available: http://statelands.dsl.state.or.us/.

Oregon DLCD (Department of Land Conservation and Development). 1997. *A Citizen's Guide to the Oregon Coastal Management Program.* Salem: Oregon Department of Land Conservation and Development.

Overholser, Geneva. 2001. "Green Light for Gas Guzzlers." *Washington Post,* August 7, p. A15.

Owens, David W. 1985. "Coastal Management in North Carolina: Building a Regional Consensus." *Journal of the American Planning Association* 51(3), 322–329.

Palm, Risa. 1981. *Real Estate Agents and Special Studies Zones Disclosure: The Response of California Homebuyers to Earthquake Hazards Information.* Boulder: Institute of Behavioral Science, University of Colorado.

Palm Beach County, FL. 1999. *Managed Growth Program: Tier System Overview, Planning, Zoning and Building Department.* Palm Beach: Palm Beach County, FL.

Park, Richard A., Marrit S. Trehan, Paul W. Mausel, and Robert Howe. 1989. "The Effects of Sea Level Rise on U.S. Coastal Wetlands and Lowlands." Report No. 164, Holcomb Research Lab, Indianapolis, Indiana.

Parsons, George R., and Michael Powell. 2001. "Measuring the Cost of Beach Retreat." *Coastal Management* 29(2), 91–103.

Peninsula Township. 2001. "PDR Facts." Information brochure, February 2.

Petrick, John. 1984. *An Introduction to Coastal Geomorphology.* London: Edward Arnold.

Phillips, Claudia G., and John Randolph. 2000. "The Relationship of Ecosystem Management to NEPA and Its Goals." *Environmental Management* 26(1), 1–12.

Pielke, Roger A., Jr., and Christopher W. Landsea. 1998. "Normalized Hurricane Damages in the United States: 1925–1995." *Weather and Forecasting* 13, 621–631.

Pilkey, Orrin H. 1989. "The Engineering of Sand." *Journal of Geological Education* 37, 308–311.

Pilkey, Orrin H., and Tonya Clayton. 1987. "Beach Replenishment: The National Solution?" in *Coastal Zone '87*. New York: American Society of Civil Engineers.

Pilkey, Orrin, William Neal, and Stanley Riggs. 1998. *The North Carolina Shore and Its Barrier Islands: Restless Ribbons of Sand*. Durham, NC: Duke University Press.

Pilkey, Orrin H., and Katherine L. Dixon. 1996. *The Corps and the Shore*. Washington, DC: Island Press.

Pilkey, Orrin, Jr., William Neal, Orrin Pilkey, Sr., and Stanley Riggs. 1980. *From Currituck to Calabash: Living with North Carolina's Barrier Islands*. Durham, NC: Duke University Press.

Pito, Vincent, Jr. 1992. *Accelerated Sea Level Rise and Maryland's Coast: Addressing the Coastal Hazards Issue*. Paper presented to annual meeting of the Coastal Society, Washington, DC. April.

Platt, Rutherford. 1991. "Coastal Erosion: Retreat Is Often the Best Course." *Cosmos* 1, 38–43.

Platt, Rutherford H. 1999. *Disasters and Democracy: The Politics of Extreme Natural Events*. Washington, DC: Island Press.

Platt, Rutherford, Timothy Beatley, and H. Crane Miller. 1992a. "The Folly at Folly Beach and Other Failings of U.S. Coastal Erosion Policy." *Environment*, November, 6–9, 25–32.

Platt, Rutherford, H. Crane Miller, Timothy Beatley, Jennifer Melville, and Brenda G. Mathenia. 1992b. *Coastal Erosion: Has Retreat Sounded?* Boulder: Institute for Behavioral Science, University of Colorado.

Pogue, Pamela, and Virginia Lee. 1999. "Providing Public Access to the Shore: The Role of Coastal Zone Management Programs." *Coastal Management* 27(2/3), 219–237.

Prichard, D. W. 1967. "What Is an Estuary, Physical Viewpoint?" in *Estuaries* (G. Lauff, ed.). Washington, DC: American Association for the Advancement of Science.

Prince, Harold H., and Frank M. D'Intri. 1985. *Coastal Wetlands*. Chelsea, MI: Lewis Publishers.

Pruetz, Rick. 1997. *Saved by Development: Preserving Environmental Areas, Farmland and Historic Landmarks with Transfer of Development Rights*. Burbank, CA: Arje Press.

Puget Sound Water Quality Action Team. 1996. *Promoting Stewardship of Puget Sound: More PIE Success Stories*. Olympia, WA, April.

Puget Sound Water Quality Action Team. 2001. "PIE Projects: Putting Good Ideas to Work," Soundwaves, Winter, 16 (1).

RBGC Associates. Undated. *Bayview, Eastern Shore*. Charlottesville, VA: RBGC.

Regional Science Research Institute, 1976. *Untaxing Open Space*. Washington, DC: Council on Environmental Quality.

Reid, Walter, and Kenton Miller. 1989. *Keeping Options Alive: The Scientific Basis for Conserving Biodiversity*. Washington, DC: World Resources Institute.

Reid, Walter V., and Mark C. Trexler. 1991. *Drowning the National Heritage: Climate Change and U.S. Coastal Biodiversity*. Washington, DC: World Resources Institute.

Riggs, Stanley. 2000. "Did We Create Our Own Flood Crisis in Eastern North Carolina?" in *Eye of the Storm: Essays in the Aftermath* (E. W. Rickert, ed.). Wilmington, NC: Coastal Carolina Press, pp. 94–97.

Rivers West. 2000. *Greenway on the Red,* Forum Proceedings, June. Winnipeg, Canada.

Rose, Jerome G. 1975. "Transfer of Development Rights: A Preview of an Evolving Concept." *Real Estate Law Journal* 3.

Salmon, Jack. 1984. "Evacuation in Hurricanes: An Urgent Policy Problem for Coastal Managers." *Coastal Zone Management Journal* 12 (2–3).

Salvesen, David. 1990. *Wetlands: Mitigating and Regulating Development Impacts*. Washington, DC: Urban Land Institute.

Salvesen, David, and David R. Godschalk. 1999. "Development on Coastal Barriers: Does the Coastal Barrier Resources Act Make a Difference?" Report prepared for the Coast Alliance, Washington, DC.

San Francisco Department of the Environment. 2000. *2000 Annual Report,* City and County of San Francisco.

Sax, Joseph I. 1971. "Takings, Private Property and Public Rights." *Yale Law Review* 81, 149.

Schillinger, Karla L. 1997. "'Playing' Wetland Board Is Excellent Learning Tool for Virginia Beach Students." *Virginia Wetlands Report,* 12(1), 1–2.

Schueler, Thomas R. 1992. "Mitigating the Adverse Impacts of Urbanization on Streams: A Comprehensive Strategy for Local Government," in *Watershed Restoration Sourcebook* (P. Kumble and T. R. Schueler, eds.). Washington, DC: Metropolitan Washington Council of Governments.

Snodgrass, D., G. W. Groves, K. F. Hasslemann, G. R. Miller, W. H. Munk, and W. H. Powers. 1966. "Propagation of Ocean Swell Across the Pacific." *Philosophical Transactions. Royal Society of London* 259A, 431–497.

So, Frank S., Irving Hand, and Bruce D. McDowell (eds.). 1986. *The Practice of State and Regional Planning*. Chicago: American Planning Association.

Spring Island Trust. Undated. "What Is the Spring Island Trust." Unpublished information brochure. Spring Island, SC.

St. Amand, Lisa A. 1991. "Sea Level Rise and Coastal Wetlands: Opportunities for a Peaceful Migration." *Environmental Affairs* 19, 1–29.

Stickney, Wallace E. 1991. "Highlights of FEMA's Hazard Management Programs." Remarks made to Natural Hazards Workshop, July 15, 1991.

Stienstra, Tom. 2001. "Anglers Oppose 'Aquarium' Ocean." *San Francisco Chronicle,* August 8, p. E2.

Stolz, James. 1990. "Preserving Open Land, Nantucket Style." *Country Journal,* November–December, 24–27.

Stratton Commission. 1969. *Our Nation and the Sea: A Plan for National Action*.

Report of the Commission on Marine Science, Engineering & Resources. Washington, DC: U.S. Government Printing Office.

Sullivan, Edward. J. 1994. "The Legal Evolution of the Oregon Planning System," in *Planning the Oregon Way: A Twenty-Year Evaluation* (C. I. Abbott, D. A. Howe, and S. Adler, eds.). Corvallis: Oregon State University Press.

Tampa Tribune. 1995. "Seaside's Lessons in Coastal Living." *Tampa Tribune,* October 25, p. 10.

Thacker, Paul. "South Carolina Developers See Green in Green." Environmental News Network, July 23, 2000.

Thiesing Mary Anne, and Robert W. Hargrove. 1996. *The Hackensack Meadowlands Special Area Management Plan (SAMP): Using a Watershed Approach to Achieve Integrated Environmental Protection.* Environmental Protection Agency, Office of Wetlands, Oceans, and Watersheds. Proceedings from Watershed '96 Conference. [Online] Available: http://www.epa.gov/OWOW/watershed/Proceed/thiesing.htm.

Thorne-Miller, Boyce, and John G. Catena. 1991. *The Living Ocean: Understanding and Protecting Marine Biodiversity.* Washington, DC: Island Press.

Thurow, Charles, William Toner, and Duncan Erley. 1975. *Performance Controls for Sensitive Lands.* Chicago: ASPO Planning Advisory Service, Report Nos. 307 and 308.

Thurow, Charles, William Toner, and Duncan Erley, 1984. *Performance Controls for Sensitive Lands.* Chicago: APA Planners Press.

Tiner, Ralph. 1984. *Wetlands of the United States: Current Status and Recent Trends.* Washington, DC: U.S. Fish and Wildlife Service.

Titus, James G. 1986. "Greenhouse Effect, Sea Level Rise, and Coastal Zone Management." *Coastal Zone Management Journal* 14, 147–171.

Titus, James G. 1990. "Greenhouse Effect, Sea Level Rise, and Barrier Islands: Case Study of Long Beach Island, New Jersey." *Coastal Management* 18, 65–90.

Titus, James. 1991. "Greenhouse Effect and Coastal Wetland Policy: How Americans Could Abandon an Area the Size of Massachusetts." *Environmental Management* 15(1) November/December, 39–58.

Titus, James G. 1998. "Rising Seas, Coastal Erosion, and the Takings Clause: How to Save Wetlands and Beaches without Hurting Property Owners." *Maryland Law Review* 57(4), 1279–1341.

Titus, James, Richard Park, Stephen Leatherman, J. Richard Weggel, Michael S. Greene, Paul Mausel, Scott Brown, Gary Gaunt, Manjit Trehan, and Gary Yohe. 1991. "Greenhouse Effect and Sea Level Rise: The Cost of Holding Back the Sea." *Coastal Management* 19, 171–204.

Town of Arcata. 2001. *Arcata Community Forest Newsletter,* February, Volume 1.

Town of Nantucket, Massachusetts. 1990. *Goals and Objectives for Balanced Growth,* November.

Trembanis, A. C., O. H. Pilkey, and H. R. Valverde. 1999. "Comparison of Beach

Nourishment Along the US Atlantic, Great Lakes, Gulf of Mexico, and New England Shorelines." *Coastal Management* 27(4), 329–340.

Turnbill, William, Jr. 1970. "The Sea Ranch," in *Global Architecture* (Yukio Futagawa, ed.). Tokyo: ADA Edita.

ULI (Urban Land Institute). 1994. "Magdalene Reserve." *Project Reference File* 24(20), October–December.

ULI (Urban Land Institute). 1995. "Maho Bay." *Project Reference File* 25(19), October–December.

ULI (Urban Land Institute). 1996. "Truman Annex." *Project Reference File* 26(14), July–September.

ULI (Urban Land Institute). 1999. "Bonita Bay." *Project Reference File* 29(20), October–December.

University of North Carolina. 1984. *Review of State Programs and Policies to Reduce Coastal Storm Hazards.* Chapel Hill: Center for Urban and Regional Studies, University of North Carolina at Chapel Hill.

U.S. Bureau of Census. 2001. 1990 Census Data. [Online] Available: http://www.census.gov.

U.S. Bureau of Census. 2001. 2000 Census Data [Online] Available: http://www.census.gov.

U.S. Department of Commerce. 1992. *Targeting National Coastal Priorities: Coastal Resource Enhancement Program.* National Oceanic and Atmospheric Administration, National Ocean Service, Office of Ocean and Coastal Resource Management, Coastal Programs Division, Technical Bulletin No. 105. July.Viles, Heather, and Tom Spencer. 1995. *Coastal Problems: Geomorphology, Ecology, and Society at the Coast.* New York: Oxford University Press.

U.S. Environmental Protection Agency (EPA). 1991. *The Watershed Protection Approach: An Overview.* Washington, DC: EPA, Office of Water, December 1991.

Walker, Kenneth. 1997. "Waterfront Revitalization: Reusing Brownfields." *Coastlines.* Boston: Urban Harbors Institute, University of Massachusetts. 7(4). Fall.

Wells, John T., and Charles H. Peterson. Undated. *Ribbons of Sand: Atlantic and Gulf Coasts Barriers.* Washington, DC: U.S. Department of the Interior.

Wilder, Robert J., Mia J. Tegner, and Paul K. Dayton. 1999. "Saving Marine Biodiversity." *Issues in Science and Technology,* Spring 1999.

World Commission on Environment and Development. 1987. *Our Common Future.* Oxford: Oxford University Press.

World Resources Institute (WRI). 2000. *World Resources 2000–2001: People and Ecosystems: The Fraying Web of Life,* Washington, DC: WRI.

Zedler, Joy. 1991. "The Challenge of Protecting Endangered Species Habitat along the Southern California Coast." *Coastal Management* 19, 35–54.

About the Authors

Timothy Beatley is associate professor in the Department of Urban and Environmental Planning at the University of Virginia. His teaching and research interests include environmental policy and planning, conservation of biodiversity, natural hazards mitigation, and environmental ethics. He is author of several recent books, including _Green Urbanism_ and _The Ecology of Place_ (with Kristy Manning). He holds a Ph.D. in city and regional planning from the University of North Carolina at Chapel Hill.

David J. Brower is research professor in the Department of City and Regional Planning at the University of North Carolina at Chapel Hill. His teaching and research interests include coastal zone management, planning law, land use and environmental policy, growth management, mitigating the impacts of natural hazards, and sustainable development. He has undergraduate and law degrees from the University of Michigan.

Anna K. Schwab graduated from the University of North Carolina at Chapel Hill with a law degree and a master's degree in city and regional planning in 1989. Since that time, she has worked full-time raising her four sons and part-time as a research associate at the Center for Urban and Regional Studies at the University of North Carolina at Chapel Hill. Research projects with which she has been involved include coastal zone management, natural hazard mitigation planning, wetlands conservation, local land use planning, special area management planning, beach and shoreline access, sustainable development, the public trust doctrine, development on coastal barrier islands, wastewater treatment in coastal areas, wellhead protection, land banking submerged lands, and planning and the law.

Index